CRITICAL L.

The Life and Work of

Che Guevara

Eric Luther with Ted Henken, M.A.

ALPHA

A Pearson Education Company

International Standard Book Number: 0-02-864199-X
Library of Congress Catalog Card Number: 2001090165

03 02 01   8 7 6 5 4 3 2 1

Interpretation of the printing code: The rightmost number of the first series of numbers is the year of the book's printing; the rightmost number of the second series of numbers is the number of the book's printing. For example, a printing code of 01-1 shows that the first printing occurred in 2001.

Printed in the United States of America

Publisher:
Marie Butler-Knight
Product Manager:
Phil Kitchel
Managing Editor:
Jennifer Chisholm
Senior Acquisitions Editor:
Randy Ladenheim-Gil
Development Editor:
Tom Stevens
Senior Production Editor:
Christy Wagner

Copy Editor:
Cari Luna
Book Designer:
Sandra Schroeder
Cover Designer:
Ann Jones
Production:
Angie Bess,
Svetlana Dominguez,
Ayanna Lacey

CRITICAL LIVES

Che Guevara

Foreword

In February 1957, just three months after landing in Cuba with Fidel Castro to begin the Cuban Revolution, Ernesto "Che" Guevara was asked by an Argentine journalist whether he feared being accused of interfering in the internal affairs of a foreign country. Invoking the name of José Martí, Cuba's nineteenth-century independence leader, Guevara declared, "I consider my country to be not only Argentina, but all of 'América.'" The conviction that he was a citizen not simply of his native Argentina, but of the entire continent that we now call "Latin America" would only grow within Guevara during the ten years that remained of his short, extraordinary, revolutionary life.

In fact, after the triumph of the Cuban Revolution on January 1, 1959, Guevara consciously followed the continental vision and revolutionary example set by both José Martí and Simón Bolívar, the Venezuelan-born "liberator" of much of South America. Ultimately, Guevara was not satisfied with a revolution limited to the confines of Cuba. After spending a few years earnestly building socialism and molding "new men and women" in Cuba, Guevara was eager to apply the lessons of the Cuban Revolution to the rest of what Martí had called "Nuestra América" (our America, as opposed to the "other America" or the United States). In his many writings, Guevara constantly repeats the same message: What has been done in Cuba can be done elsewhere, whatever the odds, in Latin America, Africa, and Asia.

Specifically, Guevara was convinced that the violent path of guerrilla warfare and direct confrontation of U.S. imperialism was both more honest and more effective than the nonviolent political compromise then supported by the Soviet Union and loyally followed by Latin America's communist parties. Not one to mince words, in his final public declaration on April 1967 from the jungles of Bolivia, Guevara openly rejected the Soviet policy of "peaceful coexistence," called for third-world solidarity, and boldly advocated the creation of "two, three ... many Vietnams." Guevara lived and died putting into practice his conviction that "the duty of every revolutionary is to make revolution." It was this conviction that led him to finally abandon the new Cuba he had been so instrumental in creating and dedicate the rest of his life to bringing armed revolution to the rest of the continent—to transforming the Andes into the Sierra Maestra of Latin America.

Eric Luther's concise yet surprisingly comprehensive biography of Guevara clearly benefits from the wealth of new information that has come to light about Guevara's life and death over the past decade. The recovery of Guevara's body in 1997, hidden for 30 years in a shallow Bolivian grave, symbolically coincided with a renewed international interest in Guevara—the man behind the face. To our benefit, Luther makes sense of the many complex and often convoluted political intrigues that surround Guevara's life and times, including Castro's "shadow" government, the causes and consequences of the Bay of Pigs invasion of April 1961, and the dramatic outcome of the Cuban Missile Crisis of October 1962. Furthermore, Luther provides the necessary historical background about the people, places, and world events that influenced the success of the Cuban Revolution and impacted the development of Guevara's revolutionary philosophy. Included here are historical events such the Spanish–Cuban–American War of 1898, the dictatorship of Fulgencio Batista, and the all-important personality of Fidel Castro.

Luther's book takes us with Guevara on his hemispheric journey from Perón's Argentina, through post-revolutionary Bolivia, on board a United Fruit freighter from Ecuador to Central America, through President Arbenz's doomed nationalist economic reforms in Guatemala of 1954, and finally deposits us with Guevara in Mexico. Thanks to Luther's able description and analysis of Latin America in the 1950s, with all its frustrated hopes and unimaginable miseries, we are better able to understand Guevara's increasingly revolutionary consciousness and sympathize with his historic decision to join Castro and his band of young Cuban revolutionaries. In the Cuban Revolution, Guevara had finally found the cause that he had been searching for and to which he would dedicate the rest of his life, becoming "*El Che*" in the process.

By the time Guevara met Castro in the summer of 1955, he had witnessed what he considered three failed revolutions: Bolivia, Guatemala, and Mexico. Joining Castro's revolutionary group, Che was determined to avoid the many political and military pitfalls that had befallen these prior revolutions. In describing Guevara's role in the Cuban Revolution, Luther recognizes Che's major contribution to the successful construction of socialism and the "new socialist man" in Cuba. However, Luther does not ignore the chaos, unnecessary bloodshed, and ultimate failure that many of Guevara's ideas, both on the domestic-economic and international-political planes, often resulted in.

In the end, Guevara's biggest strengths—contagious idealism, limitless passion, principled honesty and rejection of opportunism, acute intelligence, and ultimate self-sacrifice—also turned out to be his Achilles' heel. He blazed an extraordinary, revolutionary path through the second half of the twentieth century, daring others to follow. To his eternal credit, he never demanded more of others than he himself was willing to give. However, in the thirty-four years since his death, few, if any, have been able to live up to his example. Perhaps this is why he is still with us today, a brave, sincere man, challenging us, in the words of Martí, "to cast our fate with the poor of the earth."

Ted Henken, M.A.
April 2001
Havana, Cuba

Introduction

Che Guevara. We know his face but little else. The darkly intense man with the black beret and steely gaze is, for many, an icon without a history, a face without a past, and an idea without substance. Most people know that he was a rebel and a revolutionary, but how many know with certainty for whom or where he fought? Che made a lasting impression on the world—an impression that had to be more than his photogenic face.

We can understand why Che captured the hearts and imaginations of so many people as we follow the path of his adventurous life. From all accounts, Che was about as dedicated and passionate about his beliefs as one could be. His steadfast refusal to compromise or capitulate in the face of adversity is rare indeed. The manner in which he threw himself into his causes reveals a man driven not by selfishness but selflessness.

This is not to say that Che was the perfect martyr or without fault. In the end, he was fatally human and fell prey to the same weaknesses we are all vulnerable to: pride, stubbornness, and denial. He had a thirst for adventure and battle that found a perfect outlet in revolution. He could push others to the breaking point with his expectations and demands, yet he never asked more than what he was willing to give himself. The question is whether or not all his sacrifice was worth it. His kind of dedication and revolutionary zeal is admirable in a fighter but took a major toll on him personally. Besides leading to decisions that ultimately brought him to his death, Che's overwhelming commitment to the

Everyman seemed to leave little else for the people in his life. Underneath the tale of a man instrumental in the Cuban Revolution lies the story of a man who sacrificed everything for his beliefs. Che advocated the breaking down of the individual for the common good, and his own life is an example of this type of deconstruction.

Che's ferocity could be frightening. His distrust and vitriolic hatred for the United States often sounded as if we were the sum total of what he railed against. Che's principled stand against capitalism permeated his life and shaped almost everything he did. He detested what capitalism does to people and believed it placed material concerns above moral ones. Che's bottom line was based on moral, not monetary, grounds, a concept he found sorely lacking in the United States and other capitalist nations.

If one keeps an open mind to Che's arguments and ideals, it is clear to see that he wanted people to take a good, hard look at the world around them and ask themselves, "Is this the way it should be?" Unlike so many of us, Che did not filter out the injustices around him. He was not able to compartmentalize or justify the pain and suffering of others. Instead, he internalized the inequality he found and fought for those who could not fight for themselves.

Whether or not one agrees with his causes is almost beside the point, for the true story of Che Guevara is one of passion, not politics. It was passion that brought him to Cuba, and passion that led him out. It was passion that changed his life during a formative trip through South America, and passion that sustains his image and memory to this day. One does not have to be a socialist to relate to the story of Che; one only has to appreciate his tenacity of spirit.

Although the following pages are an attempt to provide a thorough account of the life and work of Che Guevara, they are far from complete. The more one learns about Che, the more there is to know, appreciate, and study. In many ways, the best thing about Che is the way his story becomes a touchstone for the twentieth century. His iconic importance has proved to be a doorway to larger issues of world history, revolutionary practices, cultural studies, and political theory. The face on the T-shirt is just the beginning.

Part One

From Childhood to Castro

Chapter 1

Childhood: Roots of a Revolutionary

Let me say, with the risk of appearing ridiculous, that the true revolutionary is guided by strong feelings of love. It is impossible to think of an authentic revolutionary without this quality.

—Che Guevara

The end of Che Guevara's life came as he lay, feet and hands bound, on the dusty floor of an old schoolhouse in Bolivia. He had spent the better part of his adult life affecting social change and exporting revolution, but, in the end, he was trussed up like an animal. The man who forever altered the future of Cuba was now staring in to the face of death. As the gun was raised, Che told his executioner, "Shoot, coward, you are only going to kill a man." How right he was. A hail of bullets killed the man but not the myth. Che Guevara would live on, his life and example defying his enemies even in death. What could this one man, this doctor and rebel, have possibly done in his thirty-nine years that would have such an impact on the world that, by the end, even the CIA was instrumental in his demise? What kind of route does a life like Che Guevara's take that finds him transformed into an icon of rebellion and social justice?

Perhaps surprisingly, the boy who would become known as Che, a name synonymous with the plight of the poor and underprivileged, did not come from modest roots. His parents, Ernesto Guevara Lynch and Celia de la Serna, who met in Buenos Aires in 1927, were decidedly upper-middle class. Celia's family bore a long line of pure Spanish noble heritage and owned extensive property. Ernesto, an Argentine blue blood with a fair amount of Irish ancestry and roots stretching back twelve generations, was the great-grandson of one of South America's richest men. The two families already had a slight connection. In the roots of Celia's family tree was Juan Martín de la Serna, a youth leader in the Argentine Radical Party. Juan Martín and Guillermo Lynch apparently shared a political view and took part in the failed 1890 revolution.

Unfortunately this family wealth did not come to Che's father Ernesto. Much of the family fortune had been lost by the time Ernesto was a young man, but he made due with a small inheritance from his father who died when Ernesto was nineteen. At twenty-seven, after attending (but not finishing) college where he studied architecture and engineering, Ernesto invested most of the money he did have in a yacht-building company with a wealthy relative.

Celia was only twenty years old and fresh out of an exclusive Catholic girls' school in Buenos Aires when she met the handsome Ernesto. Celia's parents died when she was a girl and a sizable inheritance awaited her, which would provide for her future husband and family more often than Ernesto's many failed business ventures.

Despite moderate success, yacht-building did not leave Ernesto fulfilled. He yearned for adventure and desired to make his own way, traits later echoed in his son. The outgoing and hot-tempered Ernesto wanted to be his own man, and he wanted to do it through farming. Yerba mate—a native tea drunk throughout South America—became his crop of choice. A friend had convinced Ernesto that growing the tea could make him a fortune of his own, and although he did not have enough funds to both build yachts and cultivate tea, Ernesto knew that he could with Celia's inheritance.

With visions of this "green gold" as motivation, Ernesto set his sights on Misiones, a prime site for growing yerba. Misiones was twelve hundred miles and a world away from Buenos Aires. On the northern border with Paraguay and Brazil, the area was just the kind of place in which a young man could imagine making his own fortune, and Misiones was just then opening up to settlement. Ernesto was feverish with enthusiasm, but Celia's six brothers and sisters were not impressed. Not yet twenty-one, Celia needed her family's permission not only to marry but to receive the inheritance Ernesto so hoped for.

Undaunted by their refusal, Celia and Ernesto threatened to elope, running off to the home of Celia's older sister. Swayed by their determination, her family consented to their marriage, but the inheritance remained off limits. Unwilling to wait for Celia's twenty-first birthday, the two pressed ahead. An order by the court procured Celia a portion of her inheritance—enough to enable the couple to secure a plantation in Ernesto's own promised land, Misiones.

They were married on November 10, 1927, and left almost immediately after for Misiones. With five hundred acres now their own, the couple built a house and turned to exploring and settling their land as well as to boating and fishing. Of their time there, Ernesto would one day write, "There, nothing was familiar, not its soil, its climate, its vegetation, nor its jungle full of wild animals, and even less its inhabitants." He had finally found the adventure he had longed for.

Circumstances, however, soon drew Ernesto and Celia back to more developed territory. Celia was pregnant and needed greater comfort and security in which to give birth, and the jungle they called home provided little of either. Heading down the Río Paraná, the Guevaras landed in Rosario, the third-largest city in Argentina. (For a map of Argentina, see Appendix C, "Maps: Che on the Trail.") Here Celia gave birth to her first child, a month premature.

The premature birth of Ernesto "Che" Guevara de la Serna further complicated an already complicated situation. Most accounts reflect that Che was born on June 14, 1928—which is close, but not exact. As Jon Lee Anderson wrote in his exhaustive 1997 biography, *Che Guevara: A Revolutionary Life*, Che was actually born a month earlier: May 14, 1928. His parents, fearful of family disapproval and scandal, concealed the child's true birth date and, by extension, his true date of conception. The young man who would come to be an international symbol of rebellion had already been conceived when his parents were married. Thus their time in Misiones did more than provide Ernesto and Celia an opportunity to make their own way; it allowed Celia privacy as her body revealed its true condition.

When Ernestito (as his family called him) was a month old, Ernesto and Celia told their families that he had just been born. They claimed they were returning to Buenos Aires for the birth, and that his birth was premature. A delivery at seven months was not unheard of, and a doctor friend falsified the birth certificate to lend credence to their claims.

Unfortunately, while the couple stayed in Rosario and Celia recovered, the baby contracted bronchial pneumonia—a harbinger of the respiratory problems that would plague Che the rest of his life. Once mother and son were well enough and their families had all met Ernestito, the Guevaras returned to Misiones, where the elder Ernesto began the daunting task of clearing the land and preparing his first crop of yerba mate.

Formative Political Leanings

During their time on the Misiones plantation, landowners employed laborers under binding contracts and paid them with private bonds—good only for overpriced items sold by the plantation—rather than cash. The bonds would never cover cash advances, which virtually ensured that the workers would remain in debt. Guevara, disturbed by tales of violence and intimidation used to keep these workers from escaping, went against the prevailing practices of the other plantation owners and paid his men in cash. His good will made him well-liked by his workers and set him apart as a landowner. Although Ernestito was obviously too young to view his father's actions firsthand, they undoubtedly reflected an attitude and outlook that shaped his environment—an attitude of fairness and justice that Che would live and, eventually, die for.

Soon Celia was pregnant again and, in late 1929, the family headed back to Buenos Aires for another birth, a little girl named Celia. Upon returning, Ernesto was desperately needed at his yacht-building business. Things had gone badly and one of the investors had dropped out. Although they had planned to return to their Misiones plantation, it was never to happen. The Guevaras were back to urban life for good.

In another turn of bad luck, the shipyard Ernesto had been trying to save burned to the ground. The insurance had lapsed, and Ernesto's inheritance went up in smoke along with his business. Now Celia's returns from family estates became the main source of the Guevara's income.

Nonetheless, Ernesto lived as if he had not lost a thing. Cracks in the marriage began to surface; Ernesto's playboy ways and financial troubles created an ever-growing distance between his wife and him.

The Asthmatic Child

Another turn of events threw the family further into turmoil. In May 1930 Celia took two-year-old Ernestito for a swim. The water was cold and the wind chilly, and that night Ernestito was besieged by a coughing fit. He was diagnosed with asthmatic bronchitis and given the normal treatments, but the attacks only worsened, lasting for several days. It was soon obvious that he suffered from chronic asthma. Nothing seemed to help, and the young boy's wheezing was matched only by his parents' desperation for a cure. Ernesto bitterly chastised Celia, blaming the chilly day at the beach as the cause of Ernestito's condition. Asthma would plague little Ernestito for the rest of his life. In fact, one of his first words was said to have been "injection"—a call for medicine when he felt an attack coming on.

Celia may have been to blame, but only genetically. She had many allergies and suffered from asthma herself. In the later years, some of Ernestito's younger siblings were afflicted with asthma attacks as well, but none as severely as Ernestito's. The exposure to cold air and water may have exacerbated his condition but most likely did not cause it.

The dampness of Misiones ruled out a return to the plantation where Ernesto had planted both yerba mate and his hopes for fortune, so remaining in the drier climate of Buenos Aires was the only option. Ernesto's mother, Ana Isabel, and unmarried sister, Beatriz, were called upon to help with the care of young Ernestito. It was a task they performed with great love and affection, showering the little boy with attention.

Still, Ernestito suffered from attacks, sometimes as many as three a day. His illness was at the center of every family decision, guiding where they would go next. On the advice of doctors, the family trekked to the Córdoba providence, moving back and forth from its drier climate to Buenos Aires. Ernestito's attacks continued erratically, never seeming to fully recede. Soon, the visits to Córdoba became permanent. The family moved to Alta Gracia, a small town near Córdoba (the second largest city in Argentina). The region was famous for its fine, dry climate, and many people suffering from various respiratory conditions took solace there.

The move may have been favorable for his son (his asthma attacks lessened), but Ernesto did not share in the benefits. When the rest of the family would take long hikes and swimming trips, he would stay home. Money was running low, and Ernesto's long period without meaningful employment was wearing him down, leaving him depressed and frustrated. Feeling trapped by his son's affliction, Ernesto only grew more distant and disagreeable with his wife. Still, whatever problems the couple might have had, Ernesto's devotion to his son was not in question. He often sat through the night with his young son, fearful that he would suffer an attack in the night. In a particularly touching memory, Celia remembers Ernesto's compassion for his suffering son: "[He] became accustomed to sleeping seated on [Ernestito's] bed, so that the latter, reclining on his chest, could better beat the asthma." As the years went on, Ernesto would also bond with his son during the long hours of bed-rest his asthma demanded. He taught Ernestito how to play chess, a skill that he would enjoy the rest of his life.

Another boy, Roberto, had been born to the family in May 1932 while they were still living in Buenos Aires, and another baby, Ana María, was born in January 1934. The mounting responsibility continued to wear on Guevara Lynch. Unable to return to Buenos Aires because of his son's health, Ernesto could not find any work locally. To make matters worse, his only hope for income, the yerba mate plantation, faltered. Market prices for the tea had dropped at a steep rate, and even Celia's estate earnings had decreased. Doctors for young Ernestito were not getting any less expensive, and the couple still lived beyond their means, taking summer holidays and employing servants. Ernesto finally gained employment in 1941, improving a golf course, but even then only for a relatively short period of time.

Kept home by his asthma attacks, Ernestito did not attend school with any regularity until he was nine years old. The severity of his disease simply made it impossible for him to leave home. His father later remembered, "As the doctors advised, I had a large balloon of oxygen at hand so that I could give the boy a blast of gas when the worst moment [of the attack] came." But young Ernestito was already displaying the tenacity and stubbornness he would become famous for as an adult. Already he was determined not to take the easy way out. "He did not want to depend on this treatment, and he tried to bear the attack as long as he could, but when he could no longer stand it and his face was turning purple from the choking, he would wriggle and point to his mouth to indicate that it was time. The oxygen relieved him immediately." How telling it is that, even though immediate and assured relief was but a whisper away, Ernestito insisted on waiting until the last possible moment before giving in to his disease.

Because school was not an option, Ernestito was home-schooled by his mother Celia, learning how to read and write under her tutelage. It was at her knee that he first learned to share her love of fiction, philosophy, and poetry. This intense period with his mother foreshadowed the bond they would share for decades to come. With his grandmother and aunt still often caring for him as well, Ernestito rarely, if ever, lacked maternal attention.

Asthma often kept Ernestito bedridden for days at a time, and he spent the hours playing chess and especially reading books, seeking solace in words and ideas. As he grew older, Che often remarked how these periods of confinement only deepened his love of reading, a love he never outgrew. Pictures of Che as a child seem to capture the effect that these hours of quiet quarantine had on him. His pale skin and haunted dark eyes gave him an intensity rarely seen in children. He often seemed to glare through the camera, rather than at it. It was as if he were looking into the photographer, not the lens. He often had somewhat of a sickly look about him, as if he had either just gotten over a bout of asthma or one was coming on. He tended to alternate between stocky and slight, once again a result of intermittent asthma attacks.

He was not always so complacent, however. When asthma-free, Ernestito would attack outdoor activities with competitive gusto, as if to make up for lost time. Some of his favorite sports included soccer, table tennis, golf, and horseback riding. He would also go shooting at a local range, swimming in streams, and hiking in nearby hills. While Ernesto opposed such strenuous activities for his son, Celia encouraged them. She wanted him to grow up as normally as possible, perhaps overcompensating for the perception that she had caused his asthma in the first place. Plus, Celia herself had a taste for danger. Although she was an experienced swimmer and knew the risks, she nonetheless would often brave the dangerous currents of the Paraná River, tempting the rushing water to carry her away. Ernesto later remarked that his son had inherited his "tendency to face danger" from his mother.

Their different approaches only underscored the tension between Celia and Ernesto. They both reportedly had hot tempers, engaging in shouting matches that became legendary with the neighbors. Economic problems were sometimes the cause, but it was Ernesto's philandering with other women that would often drive their tempestuous feuds.

As all children do, Ernestito would overexert himself and often come home wheezing to the point of exhaustion, sometimes even carried in by others. He would not be deterred, however, throwing himself back into sporting activity as soon as physically possible. Ernesto eventually gave up trying to control his eldest son, realizing it was a battle he would never win. How bittersweet it must have been for Ernestito to run and play, all the time knowing it would end much too soon and he would find himself, once again, alone with his books.

Eventually, the school authorities came calling and nine-year-old Ernestito was required to attend classes. His mother reluctantly let him go, undoubtedly enjoying their time together as much as he. It was March 1937, and Ernestito was almost a year older than most of his classmates when he entered the second grade. His asthma had hardly subsided, however, and later that year he was to miss twenty-one school days, presumably due to attacks. Or perhaps, used to long days at home with his mother reading and playing with his siblings, he was just as happy to remain home with them. Although he was not always physically in school, he still seemed to take it somewhat seriously. On days he didn't attend class, his siblings would copy his assignments and bring his schoolwork home to him.

As Anderson writes, schoolteachers remembered him as a "mischievous, bright boy, undistinguished in class, but who exhibited leadership qualities on the playground." He was also described as a "show-off," always competitive and prone to childish pranks such as drinking ink out of a bottle, shooting fireworks into a neighbor's dining room, and eating chalk in class. He was often the ringleader of a rambunctious group of children who met and played in his backyard, even setting an accidental fire or two.

Ernestito also showed an interest in theater, often dressing up in various guises such as an ancient Greek or Indian. He also appeared as a boxer in a school play. His love of reading must have contributed greatly to his ability to imagine himself as someone else.

Che's early schooling was very unique in a continent where elites rarely mixed with people from different social strata. Public education in Argentina differed from the rest of Latin America in that it was universal and equalizing. The schools Ernestito attended in Alta Gracia took in all students, poor and better-off alike. Ernestito suddenly found himself among children poorer than those he'd known before. One might imagine that the timing of this exposure contributed to its impact. Unlike his classmates and siblings, he had not grown up with the experience of constantly being around others less fortunate than he was. Now nine years old, this sudden shift in atmosphere must have been a shock. This early experience of academic and backyard equality would come into play as the adult Che interacted with the Cubans he fought so hard to help.

The Shape of Things to Come

Years later, people of Alta Gracia remarked on Che's tendency to hang out with the poorer children rather than those more like him. As Ernestito's household became the gathering place for many of the neighborhood children, there were more of them at the dinner table than just those named Guevara. Among them were many from the poorer sections of town. Discrimination never seemed to be a family trait. When faced with more mouths, the family would simply divide what they had into smaller portions. It is impossible to imagine that these simple acts of sharing by his mother would not have affected Ernestito. He saw firsthand that it was not only fair and right to love your neighbor, it was natural. The image of a dinner table with room for all was never far from his mind in later years as he struggled to eradicate social inequalities.

The Guevaras also stood out for their religious views, or more pointedly, their lack of religious views. Ernestito's beloved caretaker and paternal grandmother, Ana Isabel, was an atheist, raising her children in secular ways, and former Catholic schoolgirl Celia had stopped attending Mass altogether. By the time Ernestito attended school, Ernesto and Celia even requested that their children be excused from religious classes. Religion was not entirely discarded, however—all the Guevara children had been baptized in the Catholic fashion.

In their overwhelmingly Catholic surroundings, the Guevaras' overt anticlerical views only underscored their already-bohemian reputation, but Celia's compassion and commitment made it hard to dislike her, even if she did not espouse to believe in God. Celia was the first woman in her area to wear trousers and drive a car. Still she was able to get along quite well in the community. She used her car to drive neighborhood children to and from school, endearing her to other parents. Additionally she started the school's cup-a-day-of-milk program by paying for it herself. The local school board later made the program official, ensuring every child, no matter how poor, received some basic nourishment every day. Celia also was active in feminist causes. She held many meetings in her home as Argentine women fought for civil rights.

During these formative years, Ernestito watched his father become politically active, at least in theory. During what was known as the Chaco War (1932–35), when Paraguay and Bolivia fought over Chaco Boreal, a wilderness shared by the two countries, Ernesto followed the conflict carefully. Decidedly in favor of Paraguay, Ernesto shared his interest with his children. They would weave the details of the Chaco War into their playtime, dividing their teams during war games into Paraguayans and Bolivians.

The Chaco War (1932–35)

The Chaco War was a conflict between Bolivia and Paraguay over the Chaco Boreal, a sparsely populated region to which both countries laid claim. In 1906 Bolivia began constructing small forts in the Chaco Boreal, inching progressively farther into what Paraguay considered its territory. Paraguay then countered with its own forts and settlements to bolster its claims. Full-scale warfare broke out in 1932. A truce was agreed upon and a final treaty was signed in 1938, giving Paraguay three fourths of the region and Bolivia the rest. About fifty thousand Bolivians and thirty-five thousand Paraguayans died in the war.

But it was with the Spanish Civil War (1936–39) that Ernestito first began to understand the gravity of battle. When General Francisco Franco and his fascists took the upper hand, Spanish Republican refugees began to arrive in Alta Gracia. The Guevara children became close friends with some of these children, and the war took on a personal tone. In addition, Celia's sister Carmen moved in with them. Carmen's husband had gone to Spain to cover the war for a Buenos Aires newspaper. His accounts of the struggle, read by his wife to the family, clearly impacted the Guevaras. Ernesto formed a group that supported Republican

Spain and continued to befriend exiles fleeing the war. Ernestito spent many nights listening to stories of military exploits, soaking in the violent tales. Soon he was plotting the battle's developments, marking a map with flags, and learning how fights were won and lost by the Republican and Fascist armies. The children continued to work war games into their playtime, staging fights with slings and stones. These backyard battles could get heated, with Ernestito and his brothers suffering leg injuries that left them limping for days.

Spanish Civil War (1936–39)

The Spanish Civil War was a conflict in Spain following the failure of a military rebellion to overthrow Spain's democratically elected government. The war divided Spain both geographically and ideologically. It brought to power General Francisco Franco, who ruled Spain from the end of the war until his death almost forty years later. By the time the war was over, an estimated five hundred thousand people had been killed in combat or by execution or had died as a result of hunger or wounds. An additional two hundred fifty thousand to five hundred thousand supporters of the losing side left Spain to avoid persecution.

Once Franco had triumphed, Adolph Hitler and his Nazi government began to make a mark as World War II commenced. Ernesto threw his political efforts into supporting the Allies, and his young son, undoubtedly mimicking his father, joined a youth organization dedicated to the same cause. Fearing a Nazi invasion of Argentina, Ernesto gave public speeches warning his fellow citizens of such dangers. He kept a watchful eye on a German settlement near Alta Gracia, spying on them and claiming to have seen military training exercises carried out with wooden rifles. Argentina's position throughout the war was less fervent—the country remained officially neutral until the defeat of Germany was in sight.

As World War II ended, Ernestito had become a teenager. Starting high school at fourteen, he was short for his age and still an avid reader, continuing to immerse himself in the adventure stories of Jules Verne and Emilio Salgari. He and his sister both attended classes in Córdoba, and the family soon made the obvious choice to move there.

Things were looking up, at least financially: Ernesto had found a partner in the city to start a building company. However, Ernesto and Celia's marriage was falling apart. A fifth child was born, Juan Martín, but Ernesto's constant dalliances with other women made their union unmanageable. To add insult to injury, Ernesto often spent much of the money he did make, not on his family, but on the young women he spent time with. Despite the strains, the couple did not part, perhaps because divorce was not yet legal in Argentina or maybe for the sake of the children.

Ernestito became considerably more handsome each year of high school. His intensity made him all the more attractive, and his tousled hair, solid build, and piercing eyes only magnified his appeal.

Ernestito demonstrated a passion for sports. Trying out for and making the rugby team, he came to be known as a fearless player, exhibiting his trademark ferocity on the field. He would run madly toward the other players shouting, "Out of the way, here's El Furibundo [furious] Serna!" Much of the time, however, he played goalie. His asthma made it too difficult for him to run for extended periods of time. Table tennis also became a favorite pastime for Ernestito; he even built himself his own makeshift table so he could improve his game. And target practice with his father was a frequent Sunday activity (Ernestito had learned to handle a pistol when he five), with the two taking turns shattering bricks with their displays of accuracy. All the while, however, his passion for sports was matched by his love of reading. While waiting to practice rugby, Ernestito could be found reading Freud, Dumas, and Steinbeck.

Asthma continued to plague him, however, and his family grew increasingly concerned. They often tried unorthodox approaches to relieve him of his suffering. Sleeping with sandbags, drinking bizarre mixtures of tea, and even attempts at faith healing were all employed in an effort to rid him of his ailment. Perhaps the most bizarre stab at a remedy came when Ernesto was told that sleeping with a live cat could help his son: "I fetched a stray cat and put it in bed with him. The outcome was that the cat was smothered and Ernesto was still laid low with asthma." Mattress and pillow stuffing was changed, cotton sheets were exchanged for linen and nylon ones, draperies were stripped, and carpeting was replaced, but still his symptoms persisted. Cold water seemed to bring on an attack, a fact that may have contributed to his infamous aversion to bathing later in life. In 1943 the president of Argentina, Ramón Castillo, was overthrown by a group of military officers. Castillo was seen as pro-German: In January 1942, shortly after the Japanese attack on Pearl Harbor, Argentina and Chile were the only American nations to refuse to sever relations with the Axis powers. Both liberal and nationalist Argentines (wary of foreign economic interests) were hopeful about the change. The new regime, headed by the radically nationalistic war minister General Pedro Ramírez, clamped down: Elections were postponed indefinitely, congress was disbanded, the press was silenced, and faculty members of the country's universities who protested were fired. Political parties were discarded and religious teachings were made mandatory as well. In Córdoba, teachers and students alike rose up in protests, and many of them were arrested. Among them was Alberto Granado, an older friend of Ernestito. As weeks dragged on without the release of Granado and the others, Córdoba's secondary-school students marched in the streets calling for their release.

Surprisingly, fifteen-year-old Ernesto was not among them. He thought the march was a futile gesture that would accomplish nothing, and displaying an outlook that would prove prophetic, he declared he would not take to the streets without a pistol. It would be some time before Ernesto would become politically active in a significant way. In fact, most of his classmates remembered him as uninterested in politics. The interest he showed as a young boy, marking battles with tiny flags, had yet to grow into activism. As he would one day write, "I had no social preoccupations in my adolescence and had no participation in the political or student struggles in Argentina." (For an understanding of the Argentine political climate of Che's youth, see "Argentine Shifts in Power," in Appendix B, "Relevant Struggles and Histories.")

El Loco

His teenage years brought Ernesto a new nickname: "*el loco.*" A propensity for pranks and recklessness took hold as he approached adulthood. Shocking teachers and fellow students continued to be his trademark. His daredevil exploits included tightrope walking over deep ravines on a metal pipe, jumping from high rocks into rivers, and riding his bicycle along dangerous railroad tracks. He now looked the part as well. With his dark-brown hair, intense gaze, and intoxicating confidence, Ernesto had become undeniably handsome. His asthma may have still been a problem, but his exterior was anything but sickly.

In 1945, however, Ernesto began to grow more introspective, developing a great interest in philosophy. He was no longer just a reader but a writer as well. It was at this time that he wrote the first of many philosophical dictionaries: handwritten notebooks that documented the thoughts of noted thinkers. Love, immortality, death, and morality were just a few of the subjects covered within its pages. He would eventually compile seven such notebooks over the next ten years, drawing on an ever-deepening lexicon of authors. Aristotle, Freud, Hitler, Marx, Nietzsche, and H. G. Wells—his capacity for knowledge and depth of interest was as varied as it was limitless.

Ernesto's readings also reflected his growing interest in Latin American literature, especially the disparities that existed with the lives of the Latin American people. He had begun to look at the reality of the world around him—and not just the world he found in books. Opening his mind came easily to him. He had grown up in a home that welcomed all types of people, and his mother proved to be his greatest inspiration. Celia was forever assembling a wide variety of people, regardless of social standing. While growing up he had come in contact with painters, poets, and professors, a creative bunch that seemed to embody the egalitarian ideal. He would come to remember his childhood home as "a fascinating human zoo."

By 1946 Juan Perón had attained the presidency in Argentina. (For an understanding of Juan Perón, see "Perónism," in Appendix B.) Employing a populist rhetoric that appealed to disenfranchised workers, Perón had nonetheless broken up organized labor parties on his way to the top. Many in Argentina deeply distrusted Perón and his charismatic wife Evita. They were viewed as barely disguised fascists who threatened the upper and middle classes alike. However, their popularity proved unstoppable. Ernesto's eighteenth birthday came ten days after Perón took office. More than thirty years later, both he and the Peróns would be displayed as singing and dancing characters in the Broadway musical *Evita*.

The road waiting for Ernesto was a wild one indeed, and it was just around the corner.

Chapter 2

A Change of Direction

I dreamed of becoming a famous investigator ... of working indefatigably to find something that could be definitively placed at the disposition of humanity.
—Che Guevara

Undeniably intelligent and on the brink of manhood, Ernesto, now a high school graduate, secured a job at a public works office in Córdoba. It was his first real paying job, and he received an assignment to inspect road materials in Villa María, a town to the north. Young Ernesto was planning on studying engineering at university the coming year, but events would alter his plans.

While he was working in Córdoba, his family moved back to Buenos Aires. His parents' marriage was worse than ever, and his father's financial woes were ever increasing. Behind in taxes and faced with declining profits from his crops of yerba mate, Guevara Lynch had no choice but to sell the plantation in Misiones, the site of his early dreams of fortune. He also let go, in a way, of his marriage. Ernesto would now live primarily in his office, only visiting the family home.

Ana Lynch, the beloved grandmother who had been so influential in Ernesto's life, suffered a stroke in 1947 at age ninety-six. The family had moved in with her upon their return to Buenos Aires and sent word to Ernesto that her condition was not good. Ernesto abandoned his job and returned to Buenos Aires to be by her side. For seventeen days he kept watch over her and her ailing health. It must have been especially meaningful for him as he tended to the woman who had nursed him through so many sickly nights. Plagued by complications and heart problems (cancer has also been reported as a factor), Ana Lynch drew her last breath.

Her death put Ernesto on a new course—that of medicine. Although the death of his grandmother was an obvious turning point, other factors undoubtedly contributed to Ernesto's change of plans. First of all, there was the persistence of his own ailment. Still suffering from asthma with regularity, the weakness inside Ernesto's own lungs must have provided a burning inspiration to find a cure. Considering his ambition and intensity, it would have been fitting that he be driven to cure himself of what had caused him so much pain and discomfort. And although his interest in the field would wane, at the start of his studies Ernesto was dedicated to medicine, spending up to twelve hours a day in the library.

Moreover, in 1946 his mother Celia was diagnosed with breast cancer and in 1947 underwent a mastectomy. While initial reports were favorable, another operation in 1950 would remove what little was left of her breast, as well as her reproductive organs. The threat of losing his mother, coupled with the thought of perhaps being the one to save her, must have been powerful motivation.

After the death of Ana Lynch, the family moved out of her apartment and used the money from the sale of the Misiones plantation to buy a house in Buenos Aires. By now Guevara Lynch, ejected from his wife's bed, found a permanent home on the couch.

After applying to the Faculty of Medicine at the University of Buenos Aires, Ernesto found employment at an allergy-treatment center. He worked for a doctor named Salvador Pisani, first coming to his attention as a patient. Admiring Ernesto's intelligence and enthusiasm, Pisani brought the young medical student on as a research assistant. Ernesto was surer than ever of his decision to specialize in allergy treatment and research.

Although his grades during his university training were acceptable, they never set him apart. But to understand how impressive he could be, one had to look at his interests and pursuits beyond his classes, not just the evidence recorded in grade books. (On the side, Ernesto and a friend also developed an insecticide they hoped to market, but the venture never really took off.)

While in his first year of medical school, Ernesto was called upon to register for Argentina's military draft. Not surprisingly, his asthma was detected and he was not accepted. Not yet exhibiting the aptitude to be a soldier, Guevara would later find humor in his rejection, saying his "shitty" lungs finally brought something good his way.

His asthma may have kept Guevara from the military, but it did not keep him from adventure. Wanderlust had always held sway over him, and his desire for adventure continued to push him along. He began taking hitchhiking trips, each time roaming far-ther and farther from Buenos Aires. He most often returned to Córdoba to visit friends, but his jaunts became more expansive with time.

Even with his studies, allergy research, and hitchhiking excur-sions, Guevara somehow made time to keep up with the personal pleasures of his childhood. He found time to start a magazine, *Tackle*, devoted to rugby and lasting eleven issues, and he was still an active player who loved to take the field when given the chance. Chess continued to be a part of his life as well. In 1949 he was a participant in the university "Olympics" as both a rugby and chess player. He seemed to thrive on the diversity of his interests: The physicality of rugby and the mental challenges of chess gave him a chance to both outthink and outrun his opponents. The rugby player in him gave his family pause for concern, however. Not surprisingly, Ernesto's doctors seriously recommended against him taking part in such strenuous activities. Ernesto would not take heed, however, and the best his father could do was convince one of his son's classmates to shadow him as he ran up and down the field. Armed with an inhaler, he would be there to relieve Ernesto if he was racked with an attack.

Perhaps most important, Ernesto's reading became even more voracious. At one point, he devoured all twenty-five volumes of a series titled *The Contemporary History of the Modern World*. And as if reading nonstop was not enough, Guevara began keeping a detailed index of all his selections. Among the titles he recorded, one finds the beginnings of his interest in socialism and communism. Stalin, Lenin, and Marx were just a few of the philosophers and thinkers he was covering in his studies. Still, the presence of these men most likely was a result of Guevara's interest in philosophy rather than politics. No other events at this time indicate that he was active in a political sense. In fact, Guevara would admit later that his earliest readings of Marx and Lenin made little sense to him.

Socialism and Communism

Socialism, as its very name implies, is a doctrine that demands state ownership and control of the fundamental means of production and distribution of wealth. This is to be achieved by reconstruction of the existing capitalist system of a country through peaceful, democratic, and parliamentary means. Specifically, socialism advocates nationalization of natural resources, basic industries, banking and credit facilities, and public utilities. It places special emphasis on the nationalization of monopolized branches of industry and trade, viewing monopolies as contrary to the public welfare. It also advocates state ownership of corporations in which ownership has passed from stockholders to managerial personnel. Smaller and less-vital enterprises would be left under private ownership, and privately held cooperatives would be encouraged.

Communism has come to signify those theories and movements that, in accordance with the teachings of Karl Marx and Friedrich Engels, advocate the abolition of capitalism and private profit by means of violent revolution, if necessary. Lenin defined a socialist society as one in which the workers, free from capitalist exploitation, receive the full product of their labor. Most socialists deny the claim of communists to have achieved socialism in the USSR, which they regarded as an authoritarian tyranny.

One of the oddest things about Guevara at this time was his lack of political involvement and interest. His family, like virtually all of the Argentine liberals, as well as the wealth oligarchy, was adamantly anti-Perón. Perón marked his reign with an iron-fisted repression of his opponents, and his anti-intellectual and authoritarian stances must have been painful for a family like the

Guevaras to live under. Yet Guevara himself stayed to the side, reading and studying developments but apparently not thrusting himself into the heart of them. He continued to be more involved in medicine and literature than politics.

El Chancho

While studying medicine, Guevara's indifference to style and even hygiene became his trademark. Often bragging about how long it had been since he had washed the clothes he was wearing, he embraced a new nickname, "*el chancho*" (the pig). One of the hallmarks of his wardrobe at the time was a white shirt known as "the weekly," so named because that was how long he would wear it before washing it. Even then "washing" meant wearing it in the bathtub. He never wore a tie, and his footwear was usually a pair of old boots, sometimes not even a matched set. Ernesto clearly enjoyed the notoriety and attention his appearance brought him, even using it to charm young women.

Perhaps this indifference to style and hygiene was the first tangible expression of a blossoming political outlook. While others in his social class were dedicated to looking the part, Guevara reveled in his working-class exterior. With his dirty windbreaker, ill-fitting shoes, and grayed-with-grime shirts, he was definitely making a statement. He did not care what others thought and seemed to want them to think him low class. Perhaps this was his way of separating himself from his social standing and the beginning of a philosophy that would come to guide his life.

As his term in medical school continued, Guevara displayed a dedication that sometimes took unorthodox forms. One memorable example dovetails with his mother's illness: Outfitting a laboratory in the family home, Guevara kept rabbits and guinea pigs in cages, injecting them with cancer-causing agents. He was even known to bring amputated body parts home from school for his own private experiments. The grisliness of his interests aside, Guevara carried with him an insatiable yearning for answers, which took off as Guevara embarked on the most formative trip of his young life.

Hitting the Road

The first day of 1950, Guevara, now twenty-two, set off on one of his frequent road trips. Only this time he was not on foot. Astride a bicycle outfitted with a small Italian motor, Guevara rode off. On many of his earlier treks he had taken a friend, but this time Guevara was solo. Leaving home was yet another extension of childhood habits for Guevara; growing up he would often take off for hours at a time, sometimes motivated by his parents' fighting, sometimes motivated by curiosity alone. He was already displaying the kind of love of the road that inspired him to keep going. He later remembered the trip as almost intoxicating: "As the days went by, my flesh was weak and cried out for a mattress, but my spirit was willing and the ride went on."

Heading off for adventure, he wound his way to his birthplace, Rosario, before reaching Córdoba. After carousing with boyhood pals for several days, he made his way to see his old friend, Alberto Granado, whose imprisonment he had not protested years before. Alberto, six years older than Guevara and working in medicine as well, was employed at a leprosy clinic near San Francisco del Chañar. Naturally, Guevara was interested in his friend's work there and longed to know more. After spending several days together going on rounds and consulting with patients, Guevara was deeply touched by the people he met. He repeated again and again the need to treat the patients more humanely; they were people, after all, just like the doctors and nurses who cared for them. Guevara thought a friendly approach would prove just as beneficial as good medicine.

In one specific instance, Granado and Guevara clashed over the treatment of a pretty young girl who was showing symptoms of leprosy on her back. Upon meeting Guevara, the young girl pleaded to him to be set free. Because her symptoms were so isolated, she made a plausible case that her detainment was cruel and unfair. Guevara was sympathetic. However, Granado tried to convince his less-experienced friend that her condition was serious and contagious. He applied both heat and cold to the large spots of deadened flesh on her back, but the girl felt nothing. Taking the demonstration further, Granado shocked Guevara when he stuck a long hypodermic needle into a patch of dead flesh on her back. Smiling in triumph, Granado's satisfaction over her lack of reaction was greeted with a withering stare from Guevara. After the patient was ordered out of the room, Guevara blasted Granado, appalled by his lack of sympathy and sensitivity.

For Guevara, a man who would dedicate his life to those in need, it not only mattered what was done for people, but also how it was done. True, Granado had helped the girl the best he could, but his callous method greatly upset Guevara, who was beginning to put a human face to suffering. The treatment of this young girl seems to have marked a turning point for him.

Soon Guevara was off again, although this time with company. He had convinced Granado to come with him on the first leg of the trip, and the two headed off to see more of northern and western Argentina, areas Guevara had never seen. Surely Buenos Aires and medical school seemed farther away than ever.

Their time together proved short, however, and Alberto soon turned back. Alberto was pulling Guevara and his bike behind his motorcycle, which proved difficult because the rope kept breaking. The two agreed to travel together another time, and Guevara continued on, crossing uncharted territory. He traveled through scores of small towns, passing through the lives of the people in them. He stopped at hospitals in hopes of lodging and scrounged for meals along the way, all the time charting his progress in a diary. Journaling became a lifelong practice for Guevara, and his thoughts, resonant and romantic, provide a snapshot of what his life on the road was like. Claiming hatred for civilization ("the absurd image of people moving like locos to the rhythm of that tremendous noise"), Guevara's time alone was proving revelatory, and a return to the city must have seemed distasteful. Unable to continue to Bolivia because of road and weather conditions, Guevara began his return home. His fourth term of medical school was coming up quickly. When asked to reflect on what he had seen while away, Guevara waxed philosophical about his journey:

*What do I see? At least I am not nourished in the same
way as the tourists ... no, one doesn't come to know a
country or find an interpretation of life in this way. That
is a luxurious façade, while its soul is reflected in the sick
of the hospitals, the detainees in the police stations or the
anxious passengers one gets to know, as the Rio Grande
shows the turbulence of its swollen level from underneath.*

He had seen his own country from a vantagepoint beyond his
social standing, and he was dismayed by what he saw. The faces of
the leprosy patients, homeless vagabonds, and socially marginal-
ized people he met along the way found a home in his pages and in
his mind. He knew they deserved to be treated better, especially as
others were living so well, often at the expense of the poor. It was
an outlook he would carry with him always. In all, Guevara traveled through twelve different provinces and crossed twelve hundred kilometers, but the distance traversed internally was far
greater.

Upon his return, his lengthy journey gathered immediate attention. The company that made his bicycle engine, Amerimex, convinced Guevara to do an advertisement for them, extolling the
virtues of their product. The photo accompanying the ad, taken
the first day of his trip, is striking. With a spare tire thrown around
his shoulders and his hands firmly gripping the handlebars, the
powerfully handsome Guevara looks like an aviator off to win the
war. His chiseled face and strong chin set steadfast against the wind
give him the look of a matinee idol, his charisma leaping off the
page. This early image of Guevara, inspirational and captivating,
was only the beginning.

Che in Love

Now in his fourth year of medical school, Guevara underwent
another change. He fell in love. He had considerable experience
with women; handsome and brash, his conquests were many. But
for the first time, he felt true emotion, and the relationship was
more than physical. Her name was Maria del Carmen "Chichina"
Ferreyra, a beautiful and wealthy sixteen-year-old girl he met while

attending a wedding in Córdoba. Maria came from a wealthy and established family, and the two were instantly smitten with each other. On the surface, Maria represented everything Guevara had come to distrust in his own society; her wealth and privilege set her apart in the most obvious of ways. But the heart is unpredictable, and Guevara's was no exception.

Soon Guevara was spending his travel time not on solo adventures through the heart and soul of the "real" Argentina, but back to Córdoba and the arms of the girl he loved. And not unlike his father before him, Guevara was soon pressuring the young girl to be with him always. He wanted to marry and travel together throughout South America. Not surprisingly, Maria's family was not in agreement. While his eccentric manner was charming at first, he now appeared dangerous, and they fought the romance. Forbidden to be together, Guevara and Maria continued to meet in secret whenever they could.

On his next break from the university, Guevara took a turn as a nurse on a boat that belonged to a state petroleum company. Having traveled on land so extensively, he undoubtedly thought the sea might have a similar pull. He took several tours on the vessel, going to such places as Brazil, Trinidad, and Venezuela, but Guevara was less than satisfied, complaining that the ship rarely docked long enough to do any substantial exploring.

By June 1951, back on land and back in school, twenty-three-year-old Guevara had two more years of training before receiving his medical degree, but his love for the road and Maria had dampened his enthusiasm. Wanting to combine the two, he even suggested that he and Maria get married, spending their honeymoon touring the continent. Although he would never marry Maria, he soon satisfied his desire to see South America for himself. He continued his studies but with less dedication and verve. Romantically, he suffered a similar fate. Separated by distance and her family's opposition, Guevara nonetheless pined for his young love, hoping that one day he would claim her as his own.

Then, as if an answer to his prayers, Alberto Granado resurfaced. Granado, back in Córdoba, had been planning to take a yearlong trip along the whole of South America and wanted a partner. Tired of his work, Granado longed to roam free again, as he had as a child. Of course he thought of Guevara. Ready once again to taste the open road and tired of his daily life, Guevara accepted his offer, and the two began planning their continental trek. As often happened with them, the friends' plans quickly mushroomed; they soon dreamt of extending the trip all the way to North America. On January 4, 1952, almost two years to the day since Guevara had set off for his first real solo journey, Guevara and Granado took off from Buenos Aires on a motorcycle, christened "*la poderosa II*" (the powerful one, named nostalgically after a bike from Granado's youth), to see Maria. Guevara wanted to see her one more time before he left.

They arrived in Miramar, the beach resort where Maria was staying, and Guevara pleaded with her to wait for him. Initially only going to stay for two days, the Granado and Guevara remained in Miramar for eight. Obviously torn, Guevara eventually left the resort without a firm "yes" from his love, but without a "no" either. Perhaps she had grown tired of the distance or less enamored by the dashing young rebel with dirty clothes and alarming intellect. Or maybe she knew, in her heart, that he belonged elsewhere. Guevara was not a man prone to settling down, despite his declarations of devotion. Still, like most young loves, the pull was infectious, and Maria must have felt a desperate pang of regret as Guevara sped off with Granado, two gypsies bound for the open road without her.

In his book, *Chasing Che: A Motorcycle Journey in Search of the Guevara Legend*, Patrick Symmes recounts meeting up with Maria more than forty years after she and Guevara parted. In re-creating Che's South American motorcycle trip, he had tracked her down in the town of Córdoba. Now a historian, she initially was reluctant to discuss her relationship with the young Ernesto. However, she made a clear delineation between Ernesto, the boy she knew and loved, and "Che," the man and icon he would become: "Che Guevara is now a consumer product; it is incredibly ironic." She could talk about "Che" and his iconic and historical importance, but to speak of "Ernesto" was obviously difficult. First loves are always painful, and the experience of watching the object of your adolescent affection and obsession skyrocket to such meteoric heights of notoriety must have been overwhelming for Maria. Everyone wanted a piece of her past. In the end, after spotting a poster of him plastered upon a wall, all she would really say is, "They don't even know who he was." Clearly the Ernesto she knew was very different than the Che the world came to know.

The Road Through South America

The two were out for eight months, covering an amazing amount of ground: down the Atlantic coast of Argentina, through the Andes and into Chile, angling up to Peru and Colombia, and making their way to Venezuela. Along the way, Guevara continued to keep a journal, and years later his journals were rewritten as a narrative and published as *The Motorcycle Diaries: A Journey Around South America*. Rewriting his diaries was a habit of Guevara's, so when reading them, one must keep in mind that a more mature and focused author may have revised them. As he wrote in the introduction, "The person who wrote these notes died the day he stepped back on Argentine soil. The person who is reorganizing and polishing them, me, is no longer me, at least I'm not the me I was. Wandering around our 'America with a capital A' has changed me more than I thought." Still, enough of the original spirit of Guevara's experiences remains as a testament to his journey. (For a map of Che's South American motorcycle journey, see Appendix C, "Maps: Che on the Trail.")

Although his family often worried after Guevara as he took off on these sojourns of his, they knew it was simply part of who he was—perhaps mostly in retrospect, however. Years later Guevara Lynch wrote of his son's wanderings as a concentrated effort to better understand the poor of the world. While Guevara's journeys were a form of social research, at this point in his life he was most likely motivated by personal, rather than political, factors. But as Guevara followed his own winding road through South America, he soon found a deeper meaning in his wanderings.

It is through *The Motorcycle Diaries: A Journey Around South America* that many people first come to know Guevara, living through his own words the thoughts and emotions he had as he experienced his own continent and its people. The writings also reflect Guevara's strong interest in poetry, as the words, rife with meaning and beauty, display his talent for prose. As the book reveals, the experience proved to be much more than the simple road trip of a restless college student.

The going was rough as they struggled to hold on and keep control of *la poderosa*. On one particularly trying day, the two were thrown off the motorcycle nine times. As they camped out under the stars, their beds beside their tempestuous stead, Guevara reveled in their adventure:

> We seemed to breathe more freely, a lighter air, an air of
> adventure. Faraway countries, heroic deeds, beautiful
> women whirled around in our turbulent imaginations. But
> in tired eyes which nevertheless refused sleep, a pair of
> green dots representing the world I'd left mocked the free-
> dom I sought, hitching their image to my fantasy flight
> across the lands and seas of the world.

Maria's eyes were green. Even here, lying beneath a blanket of stars and at the foot of unimaginable adventure, Guevara was haunted by the woman he had left behind. Little did he know that, decades later, Maria would see his eyes staring back at her as well, only not in the stars, but rather on posters, propaganda, and T-shirts that never seemed to go away.

The pair were barely on their way, making it to Choele Choel, before Guevara's health interfered. It was not asthma that sidelined the young adventurer, but a high fever that landed him in the hospital for a short time. Not to be deterred by something as silly as sickness, the two were back on the road in roughly four days.

La poderosa's health did not last long either. The front of the bike frame broke late one night, forcing the two to camp out in depressing conditions of wind and cold. Using only wire to patch the motorcycle together, the two soldiered on. Having welded the bike back together at a mechanic's shop, travel continued on toward San Martín de los Andes. On the way, another hiccup: a punctured back tire.

Having repaired the tire, Guevara and Granado stopped at the ranch of a Guevara family friend, where they were put up for the night in the kitchen of the farm laborers. For all his delight, seeing his continent and meeting its people, Guevara learned all too quickly that he was still an outsider by virtue of his lighter skin. Of the night Guevara would later write, "They weren't very communicative on the whole, typical of the subjugated Araucanian race, still wary of the white man who in the past brought them so much misfortune and still exploits them." Hungry for insight and connection, Guevara was denied the experience because of history: "When we asked them about the land and their work, they answered by shrugging their shoulders and saying 'don't know' or 'maybe,' which ended the conversation."

Having made it to San Martín, at the foothills on the Andes, Guevara and Granado stayed in the area for more than a week. The Andes are the principal mountains of South America and one of the greatest mountain systems of the world with some of the world's highest peaks—more than fifty of them soaring higher than twenty thousand feet. Only the Himalayas of south central Asia are higher. While there, the two found lodging in a tool shed provided by a National Park superintendent. He also gave them temporary employment, helping to organize a barbeque held at a weekend motor race. Needless to say, they ate well.

The beauty and majesty of the area moved Guevara to briefly contemplate eventually giving up the road and settling down: "Maybe one day when I'm tired of wandering, I'll come back to Argentina and settle in the Andean lakes, if not indefinitely at least in transit to another conception of the world." Even in fantasy, Guevara could not commit to only one place, only one conception of the world.

After an extensive and dangerous hike up the peak facing yet another lake, they headed on to Bariloche. Before departing the region, Guevara wrote a letter to his mother describing his trip and the beauty they had found: "plagued by a thousand problems which we solved with our usual resourcefulness, we reached San Martín de los Andes, a wonderful spot amid virgin forests, with a beautiful lake. You have to see it, it's certainly worthwhile." He also

31

described how the two were making ends meet on the road, relying mostly on the generosity of strangers and distant family friends.

Taking the Seven Lakes route, they enjoyed the ride ("the scents of nature caressing our nostrils"), but *la poderosa* was soon acting up again as a seemingly endless line of punctures appeared in the rear tire. Stifled by their lack of patches, the two found refuge in the shed of a caretaker near Lake Nahuel Huapí. Their hopeful night of rest was disturbed, however, by a nighttime visitor. Warned of wild, vicious pumas before turning in, the sound of claws scratching at the door woke them both up. Guevara sprung into action, firing his revolver into the darkness. As Guevara looked up, a torch lighted the doorway. It was not a puma lying dead at their feet, but Bobby, the "nasty grumpy" dog that belonged to the caretaker's wife.

The next day Alberto took the tire to be fixed while Guevara stayed behind. Sure of refusal, Guevara declined to ask to stay with the caretaker. After all, he had killed their dog. Finding refuge with another nearby resident, Guevara found himself put up in the kitchen with a friend of his new temporary landlord. Ironically, nighttime would once again prove potentially dangerous for him. Around midnight, Guevara reached for his asthma inhaler, sparking a response from his bunkmate. As Che later wrote: "I sensed his body rigid under his blankets, clutching a knife, holding his breath. With the experience of the previous night, I decided to keep still for fear of being knifed, in case mirages were contagious in those parts." Ironically, asthma had again threatened to be the death of Guevara, however indirectly.

Arriving at Bariloche, bad news reached Guevara. Maria had written him a "Dear Ernesto" letter and, perhaps out of pride, Guevara elected not to tell us why in his journal. Reportedly his young love had begun seeing someone else, but family pressures undoubtedly played a hand in her decision to set him free. He attempted to respond with "a weepy letter" but to no avail. "In the half light, magical fingers hovered but 'she' wouldn't appear. I thought I loved her until this moment when I realized I couldn't feel, I had to think her back again. I had to fight for her, she was mine, mine, m ... I fell asleep."

Letting go of Maria may have been harder than he let on, but nonetheless, a melancholy sense of freedom must have come with her decision: "I suddenly caught myself flying off with the sailor to distant lands, well away from what my own current drama should be."

Once again on the road, Guevara was able to put the breakup into perspective. Standing up in the mountains over Chile, the vista was impressive. Staring into the vastness of it all, Guevara seemed content to move on: "It's a sort of a crossroads, at least it was for me at that particular moment. I was looking to the future, up the narrow strip of Chile and what lay beyond."

The path into Chile required the two to load *la poderosa* onto a boat that "oozed water from every pore." Guevara and Granado paid for their passage by pumping water out of the vessel. Along for the ride were several Chilean doctors, and our resourceful travelers embellished a bit, holding themselves out as leprosy doctors. It was not too much of a lie; they both had experience and were medical students. The doctors they held court with were suitably impressed. They were not familiar with the disease and had never even seen a leper. They did know, however, about a leper colony on Easter Island. Before parting with the doctors, the two, scientific curiosities piqued, secured a letter of introduction to the President of the Friends of Easter Island, who lived nearby in Valparaíso.

Heading northward through Chile, they found the people to be exceedingly welcoming. Once again, Guevara found himself the object of media attention. In the port of Valdivia, the travelers stopped by the local newspaper. Continuing their ruse as "leprosy experts," they were written up under the headline "Two Dedicated Argentine Travelers on Motorcycle on Their Way Through Valdivia." Their "media tour" continued in the next town, Temuco, with their "expertise" getting even bigger billing: "Two Argentine Experts in Leprology Travel South America on Motorcycle." Guevara seemed to thrive on the attention and got a real kick out of their ruse: "This was our audacity in a nutshell."

La poderosa was on her last leg and, soon after leaving Temuco, suddenly and inexplicably veered sideways. While Guevara and Granado were unhurt, the bike fared much worse. One of the steering columns was broken and the gearbox was smashed. But it would be another town—Lautaro—another repair, another scrape. Drunk on Chilean wine, Guevara and Granado arrived at a village dance. Hopelessly tone-deaf and an incompetent dancer, Guevara nonetheless invited a married woman to dance. Once he had her out on the floor, he soon tried to coax her outside with him. A bit of a struggle between the two ensued, and the evening came to a crashing close as Guevara and Granado ran into the night, a mass of angry dancers on their heels. While they made their getaway, Granado complained to Guevara about "all the wine her husband might have bought us."

Seeing fit to hightail it out of town, Guevara and Granado left early the next morning. Yet another disastrous turn on the bike found the brakes, both front and back, breaking off as they rounded a tight bend at a high speed. They veered off toward a group of cows, but, amazingly, emerged unhurt from the ordeal, the bike tightly wedged in between two rocks. *La poderosa,* however, never fully recovered, even after some rudimentary repairs. The two men caught a ride into Los Angeles, and *la ponderosa* was left at a volunteer fire station. As Guevara puts it, they were now "nonmotorized bums."

Staying on for a while at the fire station, the two turned their attention to the three daughters of the building's caretaker: "prime examples of the charm of Chilean women who, ugly or pretty, have a certain spontaneity and freshness which is immediately captivating." Apparently the ghost of Maria did not impede Guevara's penchant for flirting and conquest.

While at the firehouse, always open to new experiences, the two did the logical thing and pitched in on the firefighters' exploits. Admonishing the crew for not including them on an earlier run, the last night of their stay brought the freshmen firefighters some action. As a house ferociously burned, Granado heard some desperate meowing from the only section of the home untouched by the blaze. It was the family's cat, too terrified to leap to safety. Granado sprung into action, heroically saving the cat. "As he received effusive congratulations for his peerless courage, his eyes shone with pleasure behind the huge borrowed helmet."

It is not just Guevara we get to know through the diary, but Granado as well; his loyalty, humor, and daring become as real to the reader as they were to Guevara. It is a testament to Guevara's friendship that his private journal affords his companion with such a warm rendering. It is not only his own thoughts and feelings he records, but those of his buddy as well.

Interestingly, Granado also kept a diary of the trip that was eventually published as *Testimony: With El Che Across South America*. Granado's entries are rawer than Guevara's polished and rewritten memories, but they do provide an interesting alternate view of the same trip. Symmes compares the differences in the accounts by writing, "Granado, a devoted supporter of the Cuban regime, was careful to do his part by heightening the noble motives behind Che's motorcycle journey." For example, in Granado's telling, it is Guevara who saves the cat's life during their firefighting adventure. Symmes deduced that Granado, living in Cuba when his diary was published, had everything to gain and nothing to lose by boosting Guevara's image as a hero. In contrast, Symmes writes, "Che's account put the emphasis on something slightly less noble: he wanted to have some fun." While the pursuit of fun was definitely the impetus for the trip, the end result would bring Guevara a deeper understanding of the complexities of South America.

Grabbing a ride, Guevara and Granado (with *la poderosa* strapped on the back of a lorry) made their way toward Santiago. They had been on the road two months and were now on the western side of the continent. Their trip had taken them southward toward the tip of South America, and they were now angling back north. Depositing *la poderosa* at a local garage, they bid farewell to the bike, setting out on foot.

While in Santiago, the two secured visas to Peru and ran into some old friends, a water-polo team from Córdoba also in the city. The team was obviously uncomfortable with the meeting:

> [T]hey didn't know whether to introduce us to these "distinguished Chilean society ladies," as they eventually did, or pretend not to know us (remember our idiosyncratic attire), but they managed the tricky situation with as

> *much aplomb as possible and were very friendly—as*
> *friendly as people could be from worlds as far apart as*
> *theirs and ours were at that particular moments in our*
> *lives.*

Guevara's awareness and understanding of their uncomfortable meeting reflects a subtle change in societal awareness. His time on the road was already beginning to heighten his sensitivity to the divisions between the haves and the have-nots.

Two Tramps on the Road

Stripped of their motorbike and headed toward Valparaíso, Guevara continued to sense a change in how the two were perceived. No longer belonging to "a time-honored aristocracy of wayfarers, bearing our degrees as visiting cards to impress people," now, with just their feet as transportation, they were "two tramps with packs on our backs, and the grime of the road encrusted in our overalls, shadows of our former aristocratic selves." The change was obviously not limited to just their clothes. They were getting down to the bare essence of the land and living a "common" life for the first time.

The trip was obviously harder without motorized transport, but they continued on, eager to taste the next adventure. Hitching rides once more became their pastime. Once in Valparaíso, the "leprosy experts" inquired about making the trip to Easter Island. Disheartened by the news that no boats were going there for the next six months, they investigated the option of flying. Easter Island, with its famous face-shaped stone megaliths, is located in the South Pacific Ocean about 3,700 km (about 2,300 miles) west of the Chilean coast. The appeal of their trek was not entirely altruistic; it was more than leprosy research they were interested in: "Easter Island! Our imaginations soar, then stop and circle around: 'Over there, having a white "boyfriend" is an honor'; you don't have to work, the women do everything—you just eat, sleep and keep them happy."

Amidst these fanciful dreams of paradise, Guevara came face-to-face with a painful reminder of the reality of poverty in South America. The two spent time exploring the city, especially its poor areas. Valparaíso's bands of beggars paralleled the beauty of the view of a large bay and towering hills: "Our dilated nostrils inhale the poverty with sadistic intensity."

Upon hearing Guevara's boasts of medical expertise, a shop owner asked him to visit an old woman suffering from (of all things) severe asthma and desperately in need of attention. The contact with her grounded Guevara in a very genuine and emotional way. Once again, a human face was attached to suffering. Seeing that the woman was in dire straits, her surroundings rank and dirty, Guevara pondered just what being a doctor meant to him:

> It is in cases like this, when a doctor knows he is powerless in such circumstances, that he longs for change; a change which would prevent the injustice of a system in which until a month ago this poor old woman had had to earn her living as a waitress, wheezing and panting but facing life with dignity. ... It is then, at the end, for people whose horizons never reach beyond tomorrow, that we see the profound tragedy which circumscribes the life of the proletariat [working class] the world over.

Suddenly, the voice dreaming about a life of leisure and hedonism was drowned out by a call for a socially responsible government, one that would care more about all its people rather than simply the upper class. He was also disturbed by the way the family's poverty makes the sick member a source of bitterness and resentment. He was seeing firsthand how that, without the means to properly care for their suffering loved ones, the family tends to see them as a drain on already insufficient resources. That the woman was suffering from severe asthma seemed telling as well; it would not have been much of a leap for Guevara to imagine himself lying in such a state.

Easter Island no longer a viable option, the trek continued its original course. Determined not to walk the Northern Chile desert, a voyage up the coast by boat seemed the way to go. Denied permission by maritime authorities to work on a ship, the duo decided to stow away. Slipping aboard the San Antonio, Guevara and Granado hid in a toilet in the officers' quarters. Much to their dismay, the facilities were hopelessly backed up and reeking of waste. Sick to his stomach from the environment, Granado soon could not help contributing to the disgusting mess. After five hours of sickening exposure, they presented themselves to the captain as stowaways. Once again the pair's luck held fast and the captain's reaction to his surprise guests was a positive one. All he asked in return was their work. For Guevara, the price to pay seemed karmic and unfair: His job was to clean the putrid toilet while Granado peeled potatoes in the kitchen: "There's no justice! He adds a fair portion to the accumulated muck and I have to clean it up!"

Heading for Antofagasta, the sea worked its magic on Guevara, reinforcing his decision to make this journey: "There we discovered that our vocation, our true vocation, was to roam the highways and waterways of the world forever. Always curious, investigating everything we set eyes on, sniffing into nooks and crannies ...." (*The Motorcycle Diaries: A Journey Around South America,* replete with this kind of romantic imagery, is not only a journaling of Guevara's ever-growing social awareness, but a tale of his deepening love of the world and the adventures it offered.)

Back on land, Guevara and Granado headed for Chuquicamata, the famous United States–run copper mine, the largest open-pit mine in the world. On the way, they met a communist couple, who, like the old asthmatic woman, impacted Guevara politically and personally. The sight of them, huddled together for warmth without even a blanket for comfort, symbolized "the proletariat the world over." Despite all his reading and intellectual pursuits, Guevara was benefiting from the experience of these "real people" in a way he had never done before. Moved by the couple, Guevara wrote, "It was one of the times when I felt the most cold, but it was also the time when I felt a little more in fraternity with this, for me, strange human species."

The Chilean Communist Party was widely persecuted, and Guevara began to strongly identify, if not with this miner and his wife's cause than with their humanity. His words reflect the bitterness of the region to its "foreign domination" by the United States. While the United States–owned mining companies reaped huge profits, Chile was largely beholden to the revenue the mines produced. When the copper market fluctuated, so did Chile, hence the drive for nationalization of the mines. In response, the United States had pressed for the Chilean government to break up the mining unions and outlaw the Communist Party.

Guevara began to develop a real empathy and understanding of communism not through books or political theory, but rather through the people he met during his travels. As he and Granado shared the cold night together, this "strange human species" was coming into sharper focus for Guevara. Describing the miner as having "nothing more than the natural desire for a better life," Guevara began to see that, even if the man and his wife did not fully grasp the political implications of communism, they clearly understood what it promised. This was the couple's daily life, their reality. They had no home to return to, no place of refuge and warmth. Spending the night with the couple gave Guevara a harrowing glimpse at their world, a world he found upsetting and unfair.

Touring the mine also filled Guevara with distaste for a society that allowed such injustices against its own people. He absorbed not only the machinations of the mine, but also the plight of the people who worked it. A debate was raging in the region over the nationalization of the mines, and Guevara feared that the workers were being discounted in the fracas. The cruel reality of human suffering as an accepted consequence of corporate greed was all too evident.

Guevara's exposure to the people and hardships on this trip grew his political awareness at an alarming rate. He began to fully understand that the exploitation of the worker was a widespread problem. He also noted the poor medical treatment the miners received, which was hardly a proper reward for the sacrifices they had made. Every day, every town, every experience seemed to bring another revelation.

As the trip wore on, the "nonmotorized bums" made their way into Peru. As they left Chile, Guevara synthesized his experience into a political, emotional, and aesthetic assessment of the country. He recorded predictions about Chile's political and economic future, predictions every bit as revealing of their author's intellectual insight as they were accurate forecasts of political and economic events to come. Now able to make all the pieces fit, his views reflected this newfound awareness of social injustice in its many forms.

Once in the Indian town of Tarata, Guevara and Granado saw firsthand the effects of the Spanish conquest, describing a population almost dead inside, as if "they go on living simply because it is a habit they can't give up." It is a sobering portrayal of what Guevara saw as the result of four centuries of white domination. Wandering through the Andes for the next several weeks, the inescapable contact with the indigenous people of these areas made it impossible for him to ignore the weight of the past, a past that he himself, by blood, was born from.

The time spent in Cuzco, built on the ruins of the Incan capital, inspired Guevara to write page after page about the history and architecture he found there: "The only word to sum up Cuzco is evocative." Especially inspiring to Guevara were the temples and palaces of the region, especially Machu Picchu. In describing the ancient structure, he also found North America the target for his frustrations. Bemoaning North American tourists' plundering of the ruins for mementos, Guevara was disgusted by the "moral distance" separating them from the people who built such great monuments. In a particularly bitter passage, Guevara wonders "What use was the patient labour of the Indians who built the palace of Inca Rocha, subtly shaping the edges of the stone, when confronted with the violent energy of the white *conquistador* and his knowledge of bricks, vaulting, and rounded arches?"

Clearly Guevara was feeling a kinship with these indigenous "conquered races," especially the warrior elements of their cultures, the lengths they went to in defense of their place in the world. He knew that, no matter the differences, he was closer to them than the Northern Anglo-Saxons would ever be. Be they *mestizos* (persons of mixed European and Native American ancestry), Indians, or European, the people of Latin America shared a common language, mutual history, and culture—and problems. At the heart of the problem, Guevara saw the awesome economic power of the

United States. As he had written of Chile, they had to "get the tiresome Yankee friend off its back"—not an easy feat. The far-reaching economic power of U.S. investment was awesome and threatening. He began to believe the same sentiment held true for most of the continent.

Moving on through Abancay, Guevara had an intense asthma attack that left him barely able to stand. After his attack abated, the two continued their journey to Huambo, home to a leper colony that they wanted to visit. Once there, Guevara once again complained of the treatment the patients received, reiterating his stance on the need for humane, not simply medical, treatment for patients.

After four months of traveling they arrived undeniably broke, but happy, in Lima, the capital of Peru. They stayed in Lima for a little over two weeks, finding refuge with Dr. Hugo Pesce, director of Peru's leper-treatment program and founder of the clinic in Huambo. Pesce arranged for the two to stay in a leper hospital in Lima.

Guevara and Pesce, a communist, spent many long hours together, forging a bond that would be underscored years later. According to Jon Anderson Lee (*Che Guevara: A Revolutionary Life*), Pesce was the first man of medicine that Guevara had ever met who was dedicated to the "common good"—the kind of life Che wanted for himself. Ten years later, Guevara would send Pesce a copy of his first book, *Guerrilla Warfare*, with an emotional inscription, thanking him for instigating "a great change in my attitude toward life and society."

Upon leaving the hospital, Guevara received a send-off from the patients that touched him greatly. In a letter to his father, he shared how many of them had tears in their eyes, so grateful for the way Guevara and Granado treated them with dignity and respect, willing to touch them without gloves. After so often complaining about the treatment of leprosy patients, it must have been gratifying to see firsthand what his recommended approach, treating patients like people rather than animals, could do for these patients.

More than four decades later Patrick Symmes (*Chasing Che*) visited the same leper colony as he followed Guevara's trail and found that the legend of Che's visit was still oft repeated and the length of his stay exaggerated to several months rather than two weeks. The reason for this, according to Symmes, was simple:

> For millions of the dispossessed all over Latin America, there were no other heroes. Che was a necessity, not a possibility; if he hadn't existed, they would have invented him anyway, and often did. The point of the legend was always the same, and as powerful as it was simple: Che lived and died for us.

No longer striving to reach the United States, the two still had plans to reach Venezuela. First, however, they visited yet another leper colony. The San Pablo leper colony was the largest of Pesce's three treatment facilities and located in Peru's Amazonian region. It took seven days on the *La Cenepa* to reach Iquitos, and during the long boat ride down the Río Ucayali, an asthma-stricken Guevara found himself thinking of his old life and love. The memory of Maria weighed heavy on his mind as he imagined her wooing some new beau. But as he stared up into the star-scattered sky and wondered if it was worth it, the answer came as clear as a bell: yes.

After arriving in Iquitos it was another six days before they could take a boat to the San Pablo leprosy clinic. The delay may have been for the best; Guevara was all but bedridden with his asthma while they waited for transport.

While at the clinic Guevara celebrated his twenty-fourth birthday. The staff threw him a festive party, and when it came time to make a toast, he rose to the occasion with his newfound political awareness. He spoke about the unity of Latin America and how they were all, in reality, one race. After trekking his way through a great deal of South America, Guevara seemed particularly qualified in his judgment.

A raft ride down the mosquito-plagued Amazon brought the duo to Leticia, Colombia, where they would catch a twice-monthly plane to the capital, Bogotá. While in Leticia, they were hired as soccer coaches and took the local team to a respectable second place showing in the playoffs.

In Bogotá, the two were less comfortable. Finally wearing down ("We feel like we've been around the world twice") and citing the repressive local dictatorship, the overbearing police, and an impending uprising, they were more than happy to move on.

A bus ride to Caracas signaled the beginning of the end for Guevara and Granado. Although they talked of continuing on to Central America and Mexico, their completely exhausted funds told them otherwise. Ernesto tried returning to Buenos Aires, while Alberto elected to stay in Venezuela and find work.

After such an intense time together, parting could not have been easy for Guevara and Granado. As they said good-bye, they continued to make plans. Guevara would get his degree in a year and rejoin Granado at the clinic. The two imagined even greater adventures for themselves down the road.

With a letter of recommendation from Dr. Pesce, Alberto took a job at a leprosy clinic near Caracas, and Guevara wrangled a seat on a plane. Guevara's uncle, Marcelo, bred horses, and a flight was taking his cargo of racehorses from Buenos Aires to Miami. When the plane stopped in Caracas to refuel, Guevara boarded, and after unloading the animals in Miami, he was to fly back to Buenos Aires.

Guevara's flight home did not go as planned, however. Once in Miami, the plane's engine was found to be faulty. Repairs dragged on for a month, and Guevara spent the time with Jaime Roca, a cousin of Maria, the girl he had left behind. Roca was in Miami studying architecture, and the two whiled away their time together, going to the beach and exploring the city. Although his diaries are without a single mention of his stay in America, Guevara later told friends that he had witnessed white racism against blacks while in the United States and that the police had continually dogged him about his political affiliations. Apparently, the experience did little to improve his impression of the United States. Still, the absence of entries about Guevara in the United States is surprising. Symmes concluded that, for Guevara, "the

United States did not—could not—exist in any actual state for him. America was a state of mind."

When Guevara finally touched down in Buenos Aires, it was September 1952. For eight months he and Granado had logged thousands of miles on the road and an immeasurable distance within themselves. He had seen much more than just the sights of South America, he had seen the faces of its people. He knew that while he was returning to relative stability, those who had touched him were not. They continued to huddle under blankets on frigid nights as they fled from persecution, work for unfair wages in unsafe conditions, and suffer from poor medical care. The inequity he witnessed bored into his consciousness and his writing, forcing him to draw a moral boundary.

The Motorcycle Diaries ends not on an actual entry, but rather on a surreal note. Titled "As an Afterthought," the few paragraphs tell of a strange meeting between Guevara and a mysterious man who had come, in the dead of night, to share a revelation: "The future belongs to the people and gradually or suddenly they will take power, here and all over the world." He went on to write how the man told of the nature of revolution, that it is "impersonal" and "will take their lives and even use their memory as an example or an instrument to control the young people coming after them." Could this man actually be speaking of the "Che" to come? Of the influence his legend would someday wield? The words continue to be eerily prophetic as the man told Guevara of his inevitable fate:

> *I also know—and this won't change the course of history
> or your personal impression of me—that you will die with
> your fist clenched and your jaw tense, the perfect manifes-
> tation of hatred and struggle, because you aren't a symbol
> (some inanimate example), you are an authentic member
> of the society to be destroyed.*

This dark tale of revolution whispered in the night most likely was not an actual event, but rather a symbolic tale of the awakening Guevara felt out on the road. He had come home "not the same" as he was before, and this account serves as a kind of manifesto of passion and violence:

> *I knew that when the great guiding spirit cleaves humanity*
> *into two antagonistic halves, I will be with the people ...*
> *howling like a man possessed, will assail the barricades*
> *and trenches, will stain my weapon with blood and,*
> *consumed with rage, will slaughter any enemy I lay my*
> *hands on.*

A spirited road trip and spiritual journey had been undertaken.
He was home now, but it would not be long before Guevara was off
again.

Chapter 3

Guatemala, Mexico, and Meeting Castro

I met him during one of those cold Mexican nights, and remember that our first discussion was about world politics. After a few hours—by dawn—I had already embarked on the future expedition. Actually, after the experience I had had walking through all Latin America and the finishing touch in Guatemala, it wasn't hard to talk me into joining any revolution against a tyrant, but Fidel impressed me as an extraordinary man.

—Che Guevara

Back in Argentina Guevara found a country in an orgy of grief. Eva "Evita" Perón had died of cancer just five days before his arrival. For two weeks her body laid in state as thousands of people passed by for one last look at their beloved Evita. Her death may have signaled an end for the Perón regime, but its legacy was only beginning. Evita would become a symbol of both sinner and saint to the world and continues to captivate and perplex people into the twenty-first century. Perhaps it was a time for legends, for Ernesto "Che" Guevara was entering a phase of his life that would bring him similar heights of both adoration and infamy, worship and wariness, love and hate.

Faced again with medical school, Guevara had fourteen exams left to pass. Studying ferociously, up to fourteen hours a day, Guevara applied his patent intensity to the task at hand. In addition to his studies, Guevara worked, once again, for Dr. Pisani. Soon he published a paper about his findings on allergy research. Along with Dr. Pisani and several others, Guevara was listed as co-author for a paper called "Sensibilization of Guinea Pigs to Pollens Through Injections of Orange Extract," which was published in *Alergia*, a scientific quarterly.

The young medical student became more politically vocal, sharing his experiences with friends and speaking out about the imperialism of the Yankee and the continued suppression of Latin America. There is also evidence that he was becoming disgusted with the rule of Juan Perón, openly rejecting the mandate that his university education include the study of Perónist doctrine. Years later, it would be Guevara dictating to Cuban students what they had to study.

His interest in disease (coupled with his recklessness) sometimes brought danger. In November 1952, after failing to use the filter on a machine designed to grind up the entrails of patients who had died from infectious diseases, Ernesto became seriously ill. After a day or two of real concern he pulled himself together enough to take (and pass) a major round of exams at school. He passed the remaining exams over the coming months, and in April 1953 Guevara could officially call himself "doctor."

The Road Calls Again

The accomplishment brought little in the way of complacency, however, and less than a month later he was back on the road. On this journey he was accompanied by Carlos "Calica" Ferrer, a childhood friend from Alta Gracia. As before, he kept a journey of his travels, calling it "Once Again." The work has never been made public, but Che's widow, Aleida March, made it available to Jon Anderson Lee for his book *Che Guevara: A Revolutionary Life*. Excerpts show how eager Guevara was to recreate his earlier experience on the road: "[T]his time the name of the sidekick has changed, now Alberto is called Calica, but the journey is the same:

two disperse wills extending themselves through America without knowing precisely what they seek or which way is north."

The two planned to go to Bolivia; Guevara wanted to visit the Incan sites there before returning to the temple ruins of Machu Picchu in Peru. Eventually the duo planned to reach Venezuela, where Alberto Granado was still employed at the leprosy clinic near Caracas. The promise of a job there was attractive to Guevara, but most likely, he just wanted to move. The previous trip around the continent only whetted his appetite. The burning desire to comprehend the reality and struggles of Latin America, as well as civilizations long gone, had called him out once more.

His parents' marriage had only worsened in his absence, and their bickering proved painful to Guevara. After months in the open countryside, four walls must have proved confining, especially when the space inside those walls was thick with tension and bitterness. His mother, Celia, was especially sad to see him leave this time. His latest undertaking shattered any notion she may have had that his earlier trip was just a phase. Instead of settling down, now that he was done with school he was more inclined to roam than ever. As his train for Bolivia left the station, Celia ran after it, tears running down her face, her handkerchief fluttering in the air, certain she would never see her beloved son again.

On July 11, 1953, the two made it to La Paz. Situated in western Bolivia and located on the La Paz River, La Paz is Bolivia's largest city. The city sits amid the Andes Mountains and is about 11,900 feet above sea level, making it the highest large city in the world. It was a time of tremendous upheaval for the country; the Nationalist Revolutionary Movement (NRM) had assumed power a year earlier after a popular revolt. After disbanding the army and nationalizing the mines, a controversial agrarian reform law was about to be put into effect. The political climate was thick and unsettled, with armed militias roaming the streets and threats of countercoups in the air. The ruling coalition was fractured from within, with the right- and left-wing branches championing opposite agendas.

Guevara shared these feelings of political unrest in a letter to his father, noting that "Human life has little importance here and it is given and taken without any great to-do. All of this makes this a profoundly interesting situation to the neutral observer." Once more, Guevara was acting as political observer, carefully noting the society around him.

In the 1950s Bolivia was one of the poorest of Latin America's countries—and the most Indian. The indigenous people had toiled for centuries at the hand of a few dominant families. Not surprisingly, Guevara found himself in sympathy with the downtrodden masses, condemning the manner in which "the so-called *good* people, the cultured people" refuse to accept the importance now placed on the native people in the region.

Despite an avowed dislike for the "good" people, Guevara spent a fair amount of time with them. Through the influence of an Argentine acquaintance, Guevara and Calica were living a heavily active social life within the expatriate Argentine community. Even though Guevara wanted to know more about the ongoing Bolivian revolution, he found himself hobnobbing with La Paz high society—the very people most threatened by the changes taking place. While Guevara may have had some pangs of remorse about this dichotomy, his companion, Calica, had none. He was quite happy to agree with the racist, elitist attitudes of these new rich white friends.

An example of the differing attitudes of the two can be found in their reactions to the government. When visiting the Ministry of Peasant Affairs (a department whose job it was to implement the agrarian reform bill), Guevara and Calica watched as the chief official held audience with several of the people for whom the bill was designed to help. As the representatives of the various Indian groups were led in, they were dusted with DDT. In a reaction that echoed his response to needles plunged into the backs of leprosy patients, Guevara thought the fumigation of these people to be insulting, no matter how necessary. Calica, on the other hand, found it perfectly natural for the official to protect himself and his office from the lice and bugs these people brought with them.

Wanting to see the mines for himself, Guevara (along with the less-interested Calica) arranged a visit. The visit echoed Guevara's trek to Chilean mines, and he was equally moved. They toured an area where, before the revolution, guards had turned machine guns upon the miners and their families. Now the mines belonged to the state. Once again, Guevara saw evidence that as long as Latin America was dependent upon the United States, independence was but a dream.

But Bolivia was far from completely removed from United States' interest. The Eisenhower administration warned the new government to move slowly. Only the mines of the three largest tin companies were nationalized, and the Untied States still dictated prices. Bolivia was beholden to the United States on two fronts: as a buyer of their materials and, due to a huge U.S. pileup of tin during World War II, as arbitrators of pricing. With all that tin in reserve, the United States could dictate the world price by selling off its stock.

Meanwhile, in Cuba, a daring attack against the military dictator Fulgencio Batista was making news. A group of armed rebels stormed the Moncada army barracks in Santiago. Batista decried the attack, in which nineteen soldiers and eight rebels died, as communist, but the country's Communist Party denied any involvement. Among the remaining rebels taken into custody were the group's twenty-six-year-old leader, Fidel Castro (see Appendix A, "Fidel Castro"), and his brother Raúl. The Batista regime eventually executed sixty-nine of the rebels taken captive, attempting to claim the deaths as a result of the battle (as would happen to Che in Bolivia). When the truth of the rebels' deaths was exposed, Castro grew in his stature as hero.

Guevara and Calica had been in La Paz for nearly a month when, with half their money gone but newly acquired Venezuelan visas in their pockets, they hit the road. It was during his revisit to Cuzco and Machu Picchu that Guevara began to fully realize that Calica was no Alberto. In a letter to his mother, Guevara wrote how Alberto reveled in the Incan culture but that Calica could only complain about the dirty streets. Instead of admiring the architecture, Che was dismayed that Calica only saw his dirty shoes. The culture of Cuzco was not evocative for Calica; he could only see dung and litter. A three-day bus trip later, they were in Lima, where Calica was finally happy, because the city was modern and clean with familiar comforts. Also, Guevara had a chance to catch up with his old friend, Dr. Pesce, the communist doctor from the leper colony whose outlook had so impacted Guevara during his motorcycle trip. The two once again enjoyed hours of discussion "on a wide range of topics."

Batista's Cuba

Having already served as president of Cuba from 1940–44, Fulgencio Batista returned from the United States in 1952 to run for president again. When it became apparent that he did not have strong support among voters, Batista organized a bloodless military takeover and became dictator. Batista, however, underestimated the Cuban citizens' loyalty to their reformed constitution (overhauled in 1939) and anti-Batista movements abounded.

Since Batista's coup, Cuba had become known as "the whorehouse of the Caribbean," catering to Americans who liked to come to Havana to drink, gamble, and frequent brothels. Batista was known to employ extreme tactics to enforce his rule, and government corruption was a mainstay during his tenure. Accordingly, Batista become a symbol to many of Cuba's idealists. They saw him as a pimp who sold the country to degenerate foreigners. For a country recently adoptive of many constitutional reforms—universal suffrage, equal rights, fair elections, free political organization, agrarian reform, labor safety codes, minimum wages and maximum work hours, retirement pensions, national insurance guarantees, and the right to strike—this kind of oppression and exploitation was unacceptable.

After an asthma-riddled bus ride for Guevara, the two arrived in Ecuador at the end of September. A boat ride brought them to the port city of Guayaquil, where they were met by Ricardo Rojo, a young Argentine lawyer and political refugee who befriended Guevara in La Paz. Along with Rojo were three other Argentine law students, who, like Rojo, were heading for Guatemala. Looking for adventure, the four were interested in the political climate—a leftist revolution was underway. Guevara was undoubtedly intrigued by their plans.

Staying for three weeks, the heat and dampness of the tropical area proved debilitating for Guevara's health, and his asthma plagued him frequently. Health issues aside, he enjoyed the time spent with his new friends. Rojo and one of the students, Oscar Valdovinos, had already shipped out to Panama in mid-October, and the other two, Gualo García and Andro Herrero, were going to follow on the next boat. From there, the four were planning to continue on to Guatemala. Guevara enjoyed a kinship with these fellow journeymen (perhaps growing weary of Calica) and was not quite prepared to head on to Venezuela. Confiding in Herrero, Guevara expressed how this camaraderie had been missing from his life, even within his own family. These feelings of companionship conflicted Guevara about his next move. A job was waiting for him with Alberto Granado at the leprosy clinic in Venezuela, but his restless spirit, coupled with this newfound fraternity and a desire for adventure, remained strong. In a letter to his mother, Guevara would soon describe himself as a "100% adventurer." When García invited the two to come along to Guatemala, Guevara's agreement was a forgone conclusion.

Revolution Calling

The road to Guatemala had a roadblock or two. First, they needed Panamanian visas, which required having an onward passage. Flat broke, they were forced to appeal to ship captains. They needed free passage and assurances for the Panamanian authorities that they were just passing through. Neither was easy to come by.

While time wore on without any luck, Calica grew impatient and moved on to Ecuador's capital, Quito. Guevara said if things did not get moving soon, he would abandon his Guatemalan plans and join Calica in the capital and the two would go on to Venezuela. Calica eventually made it to Venezuela and found work, never to see Guevara again.

Finally, a Panamanian ship captain was convinced to give the three men a place on his ship and a false letter vouching for their onward passage. Unfortunately, the group's lodging bill had grown unmanageable and a deal had to be struck: Herrero would stay behind and chip away at the debt (a friend in the area agreed to settle most of it if Herrero stayed and worked for him), while Guevara and García went ahead. Herrero (who never would make it to Guatemala) later told how Guevara cried "like a child," telling him how much his friendship meant to him as he bid his friends good-bye at the dock. Central America was calling, and an emotional Guevara pressed on toward another country, another adventure, and a meeting that would change his life forever.

Upon reaching Panama, Guevara and García found that Rojo and Valdovinos had gone ahead to Guatemala. While trying to find their own passage, Guevara and García quickly made friends and tried to pick up some extra cash. It was in Panama that Guevara had his first nonmedical work published, an article in *Panama-America* about his Amazon raft adventure with Alberto Granado. Another article by Guevara also came to light at this time. "Machu Picchu: enigma de piedra en América" was published in *Siete* after being delayed due to its criticism of U.S. imperialism.

Their boat to Guatemala delayed, the two decided to go by land. At first they ran into problems getting visas to Costa Rica, but soon they were on their way. While in transit, Guevara took note of the United Fruit Company's domination of the area and, again, the medical facilities along the way that doled out varying treatment dependent upon social and economic standing: "As always, the class spirit of the gringos can be seen." After a trying journey, they made it to San José, the capital of Costa Rica.

While in San José, Guevara had his first meeting with Cubans—and not just any Cubans, but rebel Cubans who had taken part in the Moncada attack against the Batista regime. They told him of their leader, Fidel Castro, and how he led the storming of the army barracks earlier that year. He would meet other Moncada fighters in Guatemala, and in less than two years, find himself aligned with their leader and their cause. In addition, Guevara met two vital figures in leftist Latin American politics, Juan Bosch (of the Dominican Republic) and Rómulo Betancourt (of Venezuela).

The Moncadistas

Among the many organizations that demanded the removal of Cuba's leader, Fulgencio Batista, was a group known as the moncadistas, led by Fidel Castro. The group's July 26, 1953, attack on the Moncada military barracks in Santiago made the rebels heroes and martyrs.

In what became known as the "History Will Absolve Me" speech, Castro defended his actions in a court hearing, arguing that the government, not his movement, was in violation of constitutional law because it took power illegally and committed atrocities against defenseless prisoners. Unrepentant, Castro promised to lead a revolution that would oversee land reform, industrialization, housing construction, greater employment opportunities, and expanded health and welfare services. Apparently unmoved, the court sentenced Castro to fifteen years in prison.

In 1954 Batista won the presidential election, running unopposed after other parties refused to participate. The following year he felt confident enough to free all political prisoners, including Castro. Castro soon left for Mexico with a small number of followers to plan a revolutionary movement they would call the 26th of July movement after the date of the Moncada barracks assault.

While in Costa Rica, Guevara again came across the plantations of the United Fruit Company, a group that would soon deeply affect the future of Guatemala, his destination. His response to the massive operation was, by now, typical of his growing hatred for capitalism and foreign domination. His past observations had set him on a path to communism that this experience only solidified. He believed there was no other way to enact substantial change for the workers. In a letter to his Aunt Beatriz, Guevara wrote how, upon seeing the United Fruit complex, he would not rest "until I see these capitalist octopuses annihilated." His rhetoric had become increasingly violent, eschewing the peaceful foundation of socialism in favor of the extreme revolutionary aspects of communism. Continuing to abandon his previous neutral scientific stance, Guevara now invested a personal stake in the continent, and his writings reflected his growing desire for revolution and revenge. After two months of travel, Guevara arrived in Guatemala as 1953 drew to a close.

Guatemala—Deeply Divided

Guatemala's culture is an uneasy mix of Native American ways and a strong Spanish colonial heritage, consisting of more than twenty different ethnic and linguistic groups. About half of Guatemala's population is mestizo (known in Guatemala as ladino*), people of mixed European and indigenous ancestry. Ladino culture is dominant in urban areas and is heavily influenced by European and North American trends. But unlike many Latin American countries, Guatemala still has a large indigenous population, the Maya, who have retained a distinct identity. Deeply rooted in the rural highlands of Guatemala, many indigenous people speak a Mayan language, follow traditional religious and village customs, and continue a rich tradition in textiles and other crafts. The two cultures have made Guatemala a complex society that is deeply divided between rich and poor. This division, rooted in a centuries-old conflict of economic and labor exploitation, has produced much of the tension and violence that have marked Guatemala's history.*

Guevara was not alone on his journey to Central America; hundreds of Latin American leftists had arrived in Guatemala, eager to see a socialist experiment in action. Wondering whether it would be successful, many thought the very future of Latin America would be decided there, and they wanted to be witnesses. Guatemala was Central America's largest and most populous nation, mostly poor, disenfranchised Indians. The plantation economy was typical—coffee, bananas, and cotton—with horrible social conditions. That year Guatemala's unemployment rate was second only to Bolivia in Central and South America.

While in Guatemala, Guevara met several people who shaped his future, not the least of whom was Hilda Gadea (the two were introduced by Richard Rojo). Gadea, a short, plump woman with Chinese-Indian features, was an exiled leader of the youth wing of Peru's PRAA (People's Revolutionary American Alliance). It was Gadea, now working with Arbenz's government, who introduced Guevara to many of the Latin American political exiles gathered in the area. On her first meeting with Guevara, she later wrote that he made "a negative impression on me. He seemed too superficial to be an intelligent man, egotistical and conceited." Her attitude was also representative of a prevailing mindset many in South America held for Argentines, a common perception that Argentines were snobs. She soon changed her mind, though, and the two proved to be an intellectual match, both able to hold their own in discussions of politics and philosophy. She would become his first wife, although apparently one could hardly call the marriage passionate, at least physically.

Arbenz and the United Fruit Company

Guatemalan President Jacobo Arbenz Guzmán's most revolutionary act was the land reform law of June 1952, which attempted to take unused agricultural land from large property owners and give it to landless rural workers. Most upset at this turn of events was the United Fruit Company. In 1953 the law approved the taking of twenty-five thousand acres of United Fruit lands (banana crops mostly) and offered compensation that the company thought inadequate. More than four hundred thousand acres of government-owned land was also distributed to rural residents. In addition, Arbenz permitted the Communist Party to organize and consulted with leftist labor leaders.

While in Guatemala, Guevara found an outlet for his growing political leanings and, for the first time, openly identified with the leftist revolution. Telling his family that the country had the "most democratic air" in Latin America, Guevara spent the next eight-and-a-half months closely following the unfolding Guatemalan political drama. In his letters home there are obvious signs of his growing political assuredness: "This is me, the real me, like it or not; you can't do anything about it, so you'd better get used to the idea."

Through Gadea, Guevara met several high-level members of Arbenz's government through whom he hoped to gain a medical position. Initially he hoped to find work at a leprosy clinic in the remote jungle of Petén, but vexed by roadblocks to his medical certification in the country, he was unsuccessful. Still, the meetings proved fascinating to Guevara, giving him the chance to share an insider's view of the revolution.

Arbenz and the CIA

United Fruit's propaganda campaign against the Guatemalan revolution influenced the U.S. government. The Central Intelligence Agency (CIA) had been involved in an armed uprising organized by United Fruit in March 1953 and was pursing other plans to overthrow Guatemala's government using the code name "Operation Success." The United States launched a plan to overthrow Arbenz with the help of the governments of Nicaragua and Honduras. A group of Guatemalan exiles, commanded by Colonel Carlos Castillo Armas, were armed and trained by the CIA and U.S. Marine Corps officers. The group invaded Guatemala on June 18, supported by the CIA, which used radio broadcasts and leaflets dropped on the capital to create an illusion of a much stronger invasion force. The Guatemalan army refused to resist the invaders, and Arbenz was forced to resign on June 27. A military government replaced him and disbanded the legislature. The new government arrested prominent communist leaders and released some six hundred political prisoners arrested under Arbenz. Castillo Armas became president.

Guevara also began consorting with Cuban exiles, having been intrigued by the rebels he met in San José. The Cubans stood out because they were actual veterans of an armed uprising against a dictatorship—the Castro-led battle against Batista—and not just theorists. These men had the blood of armed battle on their hands, not just an idea of revolution in their minds. They had been granted asylum by the Arbenz government and were awaiting further instructions from their leadership. Full of fiery tales about their fearless leader, the Cubans, especially a rebel named Ñico López, were passionate and confident of their eventual victory and spoke often about their experiences with Guevara. Castro had been sentenced to fifteen years in prison, but his undaunted followers remained certain that he would nonetheless emerge to lead them to victory. But for the time being, Guatemala remained Guevara's focus, not Cuba.

Gadea continued to be the mainstay in Guevara's life. The two discussed politics for hours, with each approaching revolution from different sides. Guevara continued to espouse violent revolution of the Marxist vein while Gadea countered with a more socialist view. Guevara grew more insistent on the need for a direct confrontation with "Yankee imperialism." He was unconvinced that elections alone could affect real revolutionary change—the parties involved invariably being forced by the right to give in to the imperialist influence of the United States.

Different than other women he had known, Gadea's passionate commitment and sharp intellect attracted Guevara, but he never found her especially physically appealing. His journal entries are often cold and callous about her appearance. Still, Gadea was dependable and loyal, often helping him financially and tending to him during his bouts with asthma. Their relationship remained platonic for several months, and Guevara continued to seek physical fulfillment elsewhere.

The political climate in Guatemala continued to fester as the CIA become intimately involved with plans to overthrow Arbenz (see the preceding sidebar), giving Guevara further ammunition for his heated and often bitter arguments in favor of armed revolution. Furthermore, Guevara became frustrated by what he saw as unwillingness in others to fight for Guatemala's revolution, faulting the Arbenz government itself as too complacent to defend itself.

Misgivings aside, Guevara remained steadfast in his rapt attention to the crisis. Finding Guatemala more interesting than Bolivia, Guevara admired the country's struggle against all odds. In light of the impending invasion and eventual removal of Arbenz, many political exiles fled, perhaps proving Guevara's charges of disloyalty. But Guevara claimed he would remain in Guatemala, ready to face whatever the revolution brought.

During this time, Guevara began weaving together his two loves, medicine and politics. He started writing a book he planned to call *The Role of the Doctor in Latin America*. Designed as a manual for the role of the doctor in a revolutionary society, it outlined a social function for the doctor, not just a medicinal one, but a political one as well. He saw the doctor as an agent of social change, coming to know the intimacies of the people he cared for and the plights they suffered as the only way to elevate awareness and consciousness. This brand of social medicine dictated that the physician confront established rules of order before making a difference. His work on the book led him deeper into the writings of Marx, Lenin, and Engels. In the meantime, Guevara continued to search for a job in the medical field and hoped the experience would provide material for his writing. Although the book was never completed, the intention to do so dictated much of Guevara's plans.

In late March of 1954, it seemed he might actually secure a job in the Petén, a humid jungle region that would undoubtedly have enflamed his asthma but, at the same time, his political passion and writing as well. The Guatemalan Doctors' Union was to have the final say about his acceptance, and their approval initially seemed likely. In light of his impending departure, Gadea pressured him for a commitment in a letter. Writing in his journal, he was characteristically cavalier about his response, saying he could only offer her casualness, nothing more.

Much to his frustration, Guevara's job prospect in the Petén continued to dim as the conflict in Guatemala heated up. By late April, another opportunity beckoned—a job in the study of parasitic disease at a banana plantation in the town of Tequisate. Obtaining Guatemalan residency seemed to be the only hurdle Guevara would have to clear for the position. Once again, Gadea pushed for more from the young man she spent so much time with. Still unwilling to commit and forced to leave Guatemala to renew his visa, Guevara made his way to El Salvador. Returning with his credentials in order, the job nonetheless remained elusive.

In May the United States uncovered evidence of a Soviet involvement in Guatemala when a ship, the *Alfhem*, carrying Czechoslovakian arms for the Arbenz forces was detected. This was just the kind of incentive Washington needed to shore up support for the action in Guatemala. The State Department publicly denounced the arms shipment, and President Eisenhower warned that this could mean the creation of a communist dictatorship in Central America. In late May a group of CIA agents set explosives on railroad tracks to stop delivery of the recently delivered weapons into Guatemala City. Although the train was not stopped, gunfire erupted and resulted in the killing of one

Guatemalan soldier and the wounding of several more. U.S. prop-aganda efforts to expose the communist threat in Guatemala were stepped up as brochures, films, and newspaper articles were circu-lated throughout Latin America.

Four days after Guevara celebrated his twenty-sixth birthday, June 18, 1954, the invasion of Guatemala by the U.S.–backed Liberation Army began on the ground as Colonel Armas drove his troops across the Honduran border. In the days that followed, bombs fell on Guatemala City. Guevara was perversely fascinated by the violence and wrote to his mother that it all made him "smack my lips with glee." Watching the people as they ran in ter-ror from the bombs was a "a lot of fun." All the activity provided him relief from the "monotony" he was living in. The comments are disturbing in their gleefulness and betray Guevara's tendency to run hot and cold—one moment passionate and empathetic and the next analytical and clinical.

Soon, "Operation Success" proved just that: a success. Arbenz was forced to resign on June 27. Although he had recently signed up with an armed militia group organized by a communist youth organization, Guevara never made it to the battle. Guevara com-plained bitterly about the turn of events in Guatemala, blaming Arbenz's reluctance to arm the people (coupled with the "reac-tionary" press and the Catholic Church) as a major cause of fail-ure. With the rise of Armas, martial law was declared, the agrarian reform law was overturned, and all political parties, labor unions, and peasant organizations were outlawed. Virtually anyone con-nected to the Arbenz government of communism was arrested, and the embassies filled with asylum-seekers, Guevara included, albeit reluctantly. It was not until after Gadea was arrested, a sure sign that he was next, that Guevara sought refuge at the Argentine embassy.

While in the embassy, Guevara set his sights on another desti-nation: Mexico City. Arbenz, most of his allies who evaded cap-ture, and other Latin American political exiles forced from Guatemala were bound for the city. The Mexican capital was a sanctuary of sorts for left-wing political exiles from around the world, and Guevara thought it the most logical place for him to go.

Deeply bored and plagued by asthma, Guevara's time at the embassy was characterized as full of "meaningless arguments and every other possible way of wasting time." After being so active in Guatemala, confinement for a rambler like Guevara was a special kind of hell.

Despite U.S.–led opposition, Armas began approving safe-conduct visas for many of the exiled refugees in the embassies. Eventually Guevara was offered passage home to Argentina, but adamant about going to Mexico, he refused and left the embassy in late August. Finding Gadea, released from prison and hopefully awaiting a visa to Peru, Guevara set about his plans to make it to Mexico. By now the two had consummated their relationship, but Guevara was far from committed, expressing little dismay over leaving her. Despite his lack of dedication to Gadea, the two made plans to meet up in Mexico City. In two weeks time, Guevara was out of Guatemala and headed for Mexico City.

"Monotony" in Mexico

Upon arriving in Mexico, Guevara had a difficult time. He had no money and struggled by with odd jobs, including those of night watchman and photographer ("I earn my keep taking pictures of brats in the park"). He also took photos and did some reporting for the official Argentine News Agency, *Agency Latina de Noticias*. In March 1955, Guevara covered the fourth Pan-American Games for the agency. Soon after the event, though, the agency was shut down and he found himself again unemployed. He eventually found medical work, but the position, as an allergy researcher at the city's General Hospital, was intermittent and paid poorly.

Always wanting to move, Guevara planned to spend about six months in the region before heading out to see the world he had not seen: the United States, Europe, the socialist countries of east-ern Europe, and the Soviet Union. Guevara had become a staunch supporter of the Soviet Union and planned to officially join the Communist Party. While in Guatemala, he had also developed a similar admiration for the Chinese Revolution and hoped to visit that country as well.

His desire to travel continued to fester in him. According to Paco Ignacio Taibo II (*Guevara, Also Known as Che*), during Guevara's twenty-two-month stay in Mexico, his letters reveal one hundred and sixty-one planned or desired journeys and adventures. He wanted to see the world and never stopped writing or thinking about it.

While in Mexico, Guevara continued to reassess his experience in Guatemala and his belief in communism. Guevara direly predicted that the Guatemalan conflict was but the first in an inevitable global war between the United States and communism. In a letter to his father, Guevara found the activities of Vice President Richard Nixon especially suspicious, accusing Nixon of taking stock of the countries and sizing up what they could contribute to the Guatemalan conflict.

Writing to his mother, Guevara said that during his time there, "I left the path of reason and took on something akin to faith ...." Before long, Guevara's "faith" would find a center in Fidel Castro. A poem written while in Mexico reveals both his yearning to travel and his growing political loyalties:

> *I am alone in the inexorable night ...*
> *Europe calls me with a voice like vintage wine,*
> *A whiff of pale flesh, of art treasures.*
> *On my face I feel the soft impact*
> *Of the song of Marx and Engels.*

In Mexico, he found further proof of his anti–United States position, charging that the country was, in essence, owned by the United States with their labor leaders all bought and paid for by U.S. companies.

Soon, Gadea reappeared in Guevara's life, having paid to be smuggled into Mexico. The two were together again, which pleased her more than him. Their relationship resumed where it had left off, with Gadea clearly wanting more than Guevara was willing to give. Gadea's later accounts of her relationship with Guevara do not portray the ambivalence that his personal writings do—hers insist that Guevara wanted to get married but that *she* refused. A case of "he said, she said," their separate accounts of the relationship rarely agree.

In a twist of fate, Guevara was reunited with Ñico López, the Cuban rebel fighter who had regaled him in Guatemala with tales of Fidel Castro and his rebellion that could not fail. Guevara was on duty as a volunteer at General Hospital when López showed up seeking treatment for a friend stricken with allergies. He told Guevara that Fidel and his brother Raúl were sure to be released from prison soon. As it turned out, Castro's followers had been coming to Mexico City since early 1954, preparing for the day when their revolution in Cuba would begin again. Pressure was mounting on the island for Batista to grant Castro and his men amnesty, and with characteristic optimism, López was sure the day was almost at hand. The plan was for Mexico to serve as a base for training exercises designed to organize forces that would one day return to Cuba and overthrow Batista. Guevara remained in con-tact with López and his fellow exiles during the coming months, eventually coming face-to-face with their leader.

The coming of 1955 found Guevara and Gadea still struggling to find work in Mexico City. Sticking together out of necessity (at least according to Guevara's account), they moved in together to help make ends meet. His life with her took on a "monotonous Sunday-style rhythm." He did find time to pursue his daredevil inclinations though, attempting to scale Mt. Popocatépetl, a 17,800-foot volcano overlooking Mexico City. The expedition with his Cuban friends wreaked havoc on his asthma, but with the determination he had carried since birth, Guevara and the group reached the lower lip of the crater. Later describing the attempt, Guevara wrote, "Mountain climbing is lovely, but one thing both-ers me: An old-timer of fifty-nine came along and climbed better than any of us."

Mountain climbing aside, Guevara's self-described "monotony" was soon disrupted by events taking place in Cuba. In May 1955 Fidel Castro, his brother Raúl, and eighteen others were released from prison. More determined than ever to redeem his country, the charismatic and audacious Castro publicly vowed to continue his fight against Batista. He recruited new members for his forces and officially formed the "July 26 Movement," named for the date of the attack that landed the rebels in jail. Soon violence began anew, and bombs exploded in Havana. Castro blamed the government, which, in turn, blamed Raúl, issuing an arrest warrant for him. Avoiding arrest and sent ahead by his brother, Raúl reached Mexico City by June. With his arrival, Guevara's future was set in motion.

Cuba

After the "Spanish-Cuban-American War" (1898) the United States occupied Cuba, and Cuba established a government that met the approval of the United States. In 1903 the Platt Amendment was concluded which granted the United States three important rights: the right to intervene in order to "protect Cuban independence," the prohibiting of Cuba to contract treaties with countries without the prior approval of the United States, and the ceding of the Guantánamo Bay for use as a U.S. Naval base. Before 1959 elections were often fraudulent, and U.S. interventions, both military and diplomatic, seated presidents and put down civil revolts.

Between 1902–58 Cuba adopted two constitutions. The constitution of 1901 was similar to the United States' Constitution in providing for executive, legislative, and judicial branches. After a popular revolution ousted quasi-dictator Gerardo Machado in 1933, Cubans debated the form of government they most wanted. In 1940 Cubans passed a new constitution that promised expanded civil rights and a generous welfare state. Civil unrest continued as the government failed to meet constitutional promises, and corruption permeated all branches of government. In the 1950s President and Dictator Fulgencio Batista suspended freedom of association and of the press, and he used military force to repress open political opposition.

Che and Castro

On June 24, 1955, Raúl Castro met up with his fellow Cuban rebels in Mexico City and before long was introduced to Guevara and Gadea. Raúl and Guevara were of like minds and immediately connected. They both agreed that the course to gaining power in Latin America required war, not elections. It was only through power that society could be transformed from capitalism to socialism. Raúl's faith in his older brother, Fidel, provided the backbone to his beliefs, and the young man promised to bring his brother to meet them as soon as he arrived in Mexico City. The two men continued their friendship and met almost every day.

It was at this point that Soviet officials apparently had their first contact with the Cuban revolutionaries. According to Jon Anderson Lee (*Che Guevara: A Revolutionary Life*), Raúl Castro met up with a Soviet Foreign Ministry official named Nikolai Leonov. The two had apparently become friends at a European youth festival two years earlier, before Raúl joined his brother's movement. According to Leonov, the two bumped into each other again on the streets of Mexico City, rekindling a relationship that brought Leonov to meet a young doctor, Ernesto Guevara. Guevara was immediately interested in Soviet life, asking Leonov question after question. Leonov offered to share some Soviet literature and Che accepted. Che also joined the Russian-Mexican Cultural Relations Institute in an effort to better understand the USSR. Although their paths would cross again, Leonov says he did not see Guevara in Mexico again. With the simple lending of a few books, the twisted nature of the Cuba–Soviet relationship had begun.

Fidel Castro arrived in Mexico in early July. The twenty-two months spent in prison had done nothing but solidify his resolve. While imprisoned, he and his men had become national celebrities, and Castro intended to use his high-profile status to further his cause. Castro had also learned from the Guatemalan revolution, realizing that he must secure a strong power base in Cuba without drawing the ire of interests of the United States. Learning from Arbenz's mistakes, Castro knew he would have to proceed discretely.

When they met, Castro and Guevara talked for several hours, an all-night meeting of the minds (Castro is famous for his ability to talk passionately for hours) that revealed a mutual sympathy for revolution: "To have met Fidel Castro, the Cuban revolutionary, an intelligent, young, and very self-assured guy, is a political event. I think we hit it off." Many topics were discussed during the long hours between dusk and dawn, including Guevara's take on the Guatemalan conflict and Castro's plans for Cuba. Among the many things Guevara would remember from his first meeting with

Castro was the determination he felt to "stop whining and fight." Castro was certain he was going to win, and Guevara was certain of Castro. In the coming weeks, Gadea would also become convinced of Castro's legitimacy, committing herself to revolution alongside Guevara.

By the end of their marathon discussion, Castro invited Guevara to join his guerilla forces as their doctor. Guevara accepted immediately. After the meeting, Guevara told Gadea that Castro had really reached him, providing him with a leader he could fight for. Guevara, now known to his Cuban friends as "Che" (Argentine for "buddy"), had found the cause he had been searching for.

Not surprisingly, the two shared animosity toward the United States. Castro deeply resented the U.S. presence in Cuba. The United Fruit Company had deep roots in Cuba, and the wealthy class of landowners grew richer while the workers lived in poverty, all facilitated by Cuba's plantation economy, dependent on exportation. The acceptance of Batista's regime by Washington only deepened his resolve to bring American interests in Cuba to an end. The U.S. Naval base, Guantánamo Bay, situated even today in a sheltered inlet of southeastern Cuba, was also a point of contention for Cuban nationalists. Castro's love of Cuba and Che's theories of social change and fairness would prove complementary as they pursued their most common trait: a desire for revolution.

Of course, there were differences between the men. While Castro was seemingly focused on the attainment of power, Che primarily saw power as a road to achieve social change. It would be up to men like Guevara to steer Castro's revolution toward socialist ends, even if they were achieved by communist means. Moreover, Che came from a society family, well-acquainted with the confidence and standing such a heritage brought. Castro's father was from peasant stock; a destitute immigrant who had nonetheless achieved more than a modest amount of wealth in land, sugar, lumber, and cattle. Although born into more wealth than Guevara, Castro's roots were quite different from his new comrade's. (For more on Fidel Castro see Appendix A.)

Meeting Fidel Castro was not the only turning point in Che's life at this time. Soon after his decision to join the rebel forces, Gadea told Che she was pregnant. He married her in August, and the two spent their honeymoon in southeastern Mexico. Che suffered from severe asthma attacks while on the trip but still managed to enjoy the ruins of the region, climbing up and down them while taking photos and spouting poems.

As to be expected, the union and impending birth did not elate Che. He mentioned his marriage rather dismissively to his own family in a letter home: "I don't know if you've received the … news of my marriage and of the coming of the heir …." And in his journal, Che clearly states that this marriage, despite Gadea's hope otherwise, would not be a long one.

Che also found yet another human face (once again that of a woman) that symbolized the suffering of the poor. He called her "Old María." She was a patient in the hospital he worked in and suffered from acute asthma. His empathy with her is evident in a poem he wrote, "Old María, You're Going to Die," the night she passed away:

> [Y]our life was horribly dressed with hunger,
> and ends dressed by asthma,
> the most red and virile of vengeances
> I want to swear it on the exact dimension of my ideals.

He closed the poem with a promise he spent the rest of his life trying to fulfil:

> Rest in peace, old María,
> rest in peace, old fighter,
> your grandchildren will alive to see the dawn.

Armed with a cause, saddled with a bride, and with a baby on the way, the man now known as "Che" was standing on the threshold of a new adventure, an adventure that would bring him glory, adoration, condemnation, and, ultimately, death.

Part Two

Che the Revolutionary

Chapter 4

The Making of a Soldier

*I see myself being sacrificed to the authentic revolution,
the great leveler of individual will, pronouncing the exemplary* mea culpa. *I feel my nostrils dilate, savoring the
acrid smell of gunpowder and blood, of the enemy's death;
I brace my body, ready for combat, and prepare myself to
be a sacred precinct within which the bestial howl of the
victorious proletariat can resound with new vigor and new
hope.*

—Che Guevara

Che now had a mission to go with his ideology. Although
Castro and his rebel forces were not directly aligned with
socialism and communism (Castro's espoused plans were rooted in
a much more constitutional vein), they were all focused on rebellion and the overthrow of Batista. Castro had outlined his plans
earlier that year in an essay titled "Manifesto No. 1 to the Cuban
People." Two thousand copies had been smuggled into Cuba and
distributed among the citizens. Some of the reforms in the manifesto included ...

- The restoration of the 1940 constitution.
- Elimination of the feudal landowning system by the country's oligarchy.
- An agrarian plan to distribute the land to peasants.

- A profit-sharing system in the sugar mills.
- The nationalization of public services.
- A mandatory rent decrease.
- An ambitious housing and education program to benefit all Cubans.

In short, the rebels planned to revitalize and revolutionize virtually every aspect of Cuban society through radical measures to achieve a more humane environment. Che shared the ideas of Castro, if not the details. If he had engaged the Cubans in a detailed examination of their reformist platform, he may very well not have agreed. Che had ideals of his own, but the struggle had to be won, first and foremost, before anyone's plans would be realized.

Castro was in covert contact with members of his army still in Cuba and laying the groundwork for the invasion. The revolution was slowly coming together, but it was not only men making it work. Many of the members were women (including Castro's sisters), who set up financial networks and secured "safe houses" for the rebels. Their contributions were many and crucial to Castro's eventual success. Women were also invaluable in Mexico, often offering their homes as meeting places while Castro planned his revolution.

The point of entry was decided: a lonely stretch of land along southeastern Cuba, near the Sierra Maestra mountain range. The mountains of Oriente would serve as ground zero for Castro's revolution. The area was symbolic for several reasons, not the least of which was that the Oriente Province was Castro's birthplace. Second, the region also served as the beginning of several other important battles led by Cuba's nineteenth-century patriots against the Spanish. These Cuban legends included José Martí, Castro's boyhood hero.

Castro had always aspired to follow in Martí's footsteps and now he would—literally. Che himself drew a comparison between the two: "Fidel is the best thing to come out of Cuba since Martí. He is going to make the revolution happen." Earlier revolts for Cuba's independence ultimately led to the Spanish-American War (see the following sidebar). Martí eventually died in the struggle for

Cuba's independence; Castro and his men vowed they would, if need be, do the same.

José Julian Martí

Born in Havana in 1853, José Martí was a Cuban writer and patriot whose poetry, politics, and death in battle positioned him as a martyred symbol of Cuban aspirations to independence. At the age of 16 he was imprisoned in Cuba as a revolutionary after having founded a small newspaper called La patria libre *(The Free Fatherland). Banished to Spain, Martí published* El presidio Político en Cuba *(1871), the first of many pamphlets advocating Cuban independence from Spain. He earned his law degree from the University of Zaragoza in 1874. He then traveled and worked variously as a journalist and a professor in France, Mexico, and Guatemala. Returning to Cuba in 1878, he was exiled again in 1879 for his continued revolutionary activities.*

While living in New York City from 1881 to 1895, Martí was active in the Cuban Revolutionary Party and founded its journal, Patria *(1892). He and a group of armed revolutionaries set sail for Cuba in 1894 to stage an invasion of the island. The group was intercepted in Florida and sent back. The following year, however, he reached Cuba, along with the independence hero General Máximo Gómez y Báez. Martí was killed a month later during a skirmish with Spanish troops at Dos Ríos.*

Martí's poetry was a precursor of the modernismo *movement in Spanish and Latino literature, and Martí was lauded for his simple, fluent style and his personal, vivid imagery. His writings include numerous poems, essays, and a novel.*

It was not only symbolism and sentiment that drew Castro to the area; there was a pragmatic reason for the choosing of Oriente as well. Cuba's second largest city, Santiago, was close by. Castro's underground leader, Frank País, was stationed in Santiago and prepared to supply the group with resources for the coming attack.

The commander of Castro's rebels was Colonel Alberto Bayo, a Cuban-born Spanish Civil War veteran and military man. Retired from the Spanish army, Bayo (who only had one eye, the other lost in combat) was managing a furniture factory in Mexico and serving as a university lecturer while Castro prepared his plans. Eventually he would abandon his other pursuits and dedicate himself to Castro full-time. He would not, however, make the journey to Cuba. Limited space and his age would keep him in Mexico.

The Spanish-American War

The Spanish-American War was the brief war—lasting less than four months (April–August 1898)—in which the United States battled Spain. Most of the fighting occurred in or near the Spanish colonial possessions of Cuba and the Philippines, nearly halfway around the world from each other. The defeat of the Spanish marked the end of the republic's colonial empire and the rise of the United States as a global military.

The war grew out of the Cuban struggle for independence. Throughout the early 1800s, a series of revolutions ended Spanish authority throughout South America, Central America, and Mexico. The harshness that Spain employed in squelching Cuban demands for a degree of local autonomy and personal liberty roused support for the cause of Cuban independence in the United States. Cuban independence became the stated objective of the war.

Castro's net spread wide; he traveled to the United States, touring the Cuban communities of Florida, New York, Philadelphia, and New Jersey to shore up support. All the while, he continued contact with his cohorts in Cuba, imploring them to raise money and setting up guidelines and responsibilities for members.

Training for Battle

Meanwhile, Che and the others began a strict regimen of physical training. Although physical activity was nothing new for Che, he must have felt enormous pressure to perform well. He had battled asthma all his life and succeeded despite the odds, but now the stakes were higher. Che's determination to do as well, if not better than, the others drove him to new heights of self-discipline. He limited his diet and continued his mountain climbing, reaching the top of Popocatépetl and planting an Argentine flag.

For the men, long walks around the city were Bayo's orders of the day, as were challenging hikes through the hills of the capital's outlying areas. It was during their training missions that Che's infamous disdain for personal hygiene, while unusual socially, played in his favor. While the others were disturbed by the prospect of days on end without bathing, Che had grown accustomed to it long ago.

A Mexican wrestler, Arzacio Vanegas, joined to help train the men, instructing them to climb backward and sideways on their trips to strengthen every part of their legs. Vanegas, using his wrestling knowledge, also taught them the finer points of physical combat, giving the men training in personal defense.

During his training, Che also severely limited his diet, hoping to trim down and fight off his ever-present asthma attacks (he believed they were sometimes brought on by his choice in foods). While he did lose weight, his asthma attacks continued. Vanegas happened to see Che struggling with his inhaler during one strenuous climbing session. Later Che asked for his confidence in not telling anyone, even Castro, about his condition. Although he was probably mistaken, Che thought the others were unaware of his affliction.

Bayo covered guerrilla warfare and took a few of the men, including Che, to a firing range where they could shoot in privacy, sometimes practicing on live turkeys. The use of the birds enabled them to simulate firing upon live moving targets. Bagging a turkey was not just a show of artillery prowess; the successful turkey shooter got to eat the bird as well.

Initially Antonio del Conde, the owner of a small gun shop in Mexico City, was supplying the group with weapons. He, like so many others, became enamored with Castro and his enormous appeal and magnetism. Castro was a master of recruitment, and del Conde would continue to help his rebels, offering up both arms and storage for their use.

Halfway through his military training, Che became a father. In the middle of February 1956, Gadea gave birth to a little girl, named Hilda (Hildita) Beatriz. Delighted at her arrival ("she makes me happy twice over"), Che nevertheless held serious misgivings about his marriage, and relations between Gadea and him grew more and more distressed. Any hopes that a baby would bring them closer together seemed ill-placed and fruitless. In a letter to a friend in Buenos Aires, Che wrote that the arrival of Hildita, while giving him great joy, only reinforced his inability to live with her mother. He would not be swayed by this family life; in fact, he was more dedicated to the revolution than ever. With Che's encroaching departure, Gadea undoubtedly knew his absence would be permanent—one way or the other. When Che finally left Mexico for Cuba, Gadea and the baby returned to her family in Peru.

The heavy training continued and Che's ability to keep up with the others proved exemplary. Rated excellent in discipline, shooting, and physical endurance, Che was quickly rising in esteem, both within himself and among his fellow fighters. So much so that Che was soon appointed a leader of one of the Mexico City "safe houses." These refuges were set up around the city in the beginning of 1956 as more and more of Castro's faithful came to join the crusade. Initially, only Castro and Bayo knew the location of these houses. Strict codes of secrecy and discipline were enforced on the men living in them, with death the threatened punishment for betrayal. The men were now living as if the war had already begun.

As it turned out, Castro was well-founded in his adherence to tight security. In early 1956 Batista condemned Castro's plans, and the police arrested many Castro-sympathizers in Cuba. Soon a plan to assassinate Castro was hatched. When Castro announced he was well aware of the plot and who was behind it, the push for his death slackened. Still, Cuban agents and the Mexicans they employed did their best to keep an eye on Castro and reported his activities to Batista the best they could.

Che was not only training his body, but his mind as well. He knew the fighting would not last forever (at least he hoped it would not), and Che wanted to be intellectually prepared for the day when real change could be implemented. Che was not in this just for the battle, but for what the battle could bring. Studying economics, Marxism, and political theory, Che was cramming for the most important exam of his life.

Initially Che's Argentine heritage posed a problem for some of the others. Tellingly, not everyone called him "Che." Some addressed him as "El Argentino," perhaps to play up his difference. Che had a history of feeling out of place in Mexico. In a letter to his mother written months earlier, he told her, "I feel like something out of a tango, a bit Argentine, I mean, a feature I've nearly always disowned." Castro later remembered the friction between his rebels and Guevara as hurtful—to both him and Che. To Castro, Che's dedication to Cuba far outweighed the fact that he was not born there. To him, Che was one a unique and special find: "someone who was not born in our land but willing to shed his blood for it." Che more than matched the admiration, writing a passionate poem called "Canto a Fidel" and dedicated to Castro:

> Let's go, ardent prophet of the dawn,
> along remote and unmarked paths
> to liberate the green alligator [a metaphor for Cuba
> because of its shape] you so love ...
> When the first shot sounds
> and in virginal surprise the entire jungle awakens,
> there, at your side, serene combatants
> you'll have us.
> When your voice pours out to the four winds
> agrarian reform, justice, bread and liberty,
> there, at your side, with identical accent,
> you'll have us.
> And when the end of the battle for
> the cleansing operation against the tyrant comes,
> there, at your side, ready for the last battle,
> you'll have us ...
> And if our path is blocked by iron,
> we ask for a shroud of Cuban tears
> to cover the guerilla bones
> in transit to American history.
> Nothing more.

While it is not exactly worthy of Homer, the ode to Castro does offer a glimpse into Che's dedication and mindset at the time. The recurring refrain of "at your side ... you'll have us" reveals that, at last, amongst this ragtag group of rebels, Che hoped he had found a group he could truly feel a part of, even if he was Argentine.

Fulgencio Batista y Zaldivar (1955).

Castro's crew was overwhelmingly Cuban, of course, but Che was not the only non-Cuban in the mix. A Mexican, a Dominican, and an Italian merchant marine were also on board. Che was himself well aware of his lack of Cuban experience and was cautious about seeming as if he were teaching them about their own country. He did not want his own healthy ego to taint the men's feelings toward him. He may have been one of their political leaders and ideological instructors, but he was well aware that he was not the only one and that he was, if nothing else, *not* Cuban.

The reservations of the others and this self-awareness about his own heritage must have preyed on Che's confidence to some degree. Although he showed every outward sign of complete confidence (for instance, in his poetry), he would remark later that he was privately doubtful about the rebels' chances for success. Even so, he said he had been willing to fight even if it meant dying for the ideal behind the campaign. Apparently, ultimate success in Cuba did not mean as much to Che as the revolution itself. This mindset would eventually led Che to his demise—but not in Cuba.

Che's letters home also supported the idea that he might not have been entirely committed just yet. He talked about the Cuban plans but continued to downplay them, relating his full intention to further his education and follow his famous wanderlust to other far-off destinations. Was Che expressing real doubts or merely being "Che"? Did he think this ragtag bunch of rebels would eventually fall apart, like so many other similar groups? Or it is very possible that he was just protecting his family, not wanting to alarm them until the game was truly in motion? Whatever the reason, it was only a matter of time before Che had shed all reservations about his participation in the revolution.

Soon the men set up camp outside Mexico City, where their training could continue in greater concealment. Castro had begun to receive funding from supporters in the United States and Cuba, and arms were beginning to be stockpiled. At a ranch in Chalco named the *Santa Rosa,* about thirty-five miles east of the city, the group continued their guerilla education. With its high stone walls and isolated location, the Rancho San Miguel was an ideal place for their training. The ranch, for sale at almost a quarter of a million dollars, was secured through a ruse. Che, pretending to be a wealthy Salvadoran colonel (he always had expressed an interest in theater), expressed his desire to buy the ranch, but only if certain repairs were made. The "colonel" offered to rent the ranch, while several of his laborers brought it up to his specifications, and only then he would buy it. The owner agreed and the group had its compound. The training continued in Chalco and Che moved there, as the chief of personnel, full-time.

Castro, always the showman, desperately wanted the invasion of the July 26 Movement to launch, appropriately, on July 26, the third anniversary of his daring raid on Moncada. Although that date proved impossible, he was steadfast in his insistence that they would begin before the year's end. He had made a public declaration that the revolution would start in 1956 ("I can tell you with absolute certainty that in 1956 we shall be free or we shall be martyrs!") and was determined to fulfill his own prophecy. In addition, other factions were rising to take on Batista, and Castro would not be outdone. A general sense of rebellion was on the upswing in Cuba but none proved to be as organized and focused as Castro's team. Castro had already formally broken with the Ortodoxo Party and was a political free agent, beholden only to his own reformist social agenda.

A Stay in a Mexican Jail

Six days after Che celebrated his twenty-eighth birthday, June 20, 1956, things took a turn for the worse. Mexican police arrested Fidel and two others in Mexico City. Apparently Cuban embassy officials' attempts to bribe Mexican police officials into keeping an eye on Castro had paid off. In a matter of days, almost all of Castro's forces had been arrested as well. The safe houses proved to be anything but, as armed officers seized documents and stockpiled arms. Bayo and Raúl went into seclusion and Che stayed at the ranch. Gadea, alerted to the raids, had hidden Fidel's letters and Che's political writings but was arrested anyway. She and Hildita spent a night in custody before being released.

Those arrested were accused of conspiracy with Cuban and Mexican communists to assassinate Batista, and Havana officials had ordered their deportation. Even though they were kept in a facility that was more a detention center than a jail, many of the men were tortured, their hands and feet bound while being dunked into freezing cold water. Castro (apparently not tortured himself) denied any communist connection while those remaining free planned his legal defense. Despite the suspicions of conspiracy, the official charge against the men was violation of Mexican immigration laws.

On June 24 they came for Che at the ranch. Of course, aware of their plans, he had moved most of the weapons to safety. He and twelve others were waiting for the police when they arrived. Fidel was with the officers and urged the group to surrender peacefully.

He knew that a shootout would only end in tragedy for the rebels. As the Cuban Revolution took shape, Castro's natural pragmatism would prove to be one of his greatest strengths. After a peaceful surrender, the men were all remanded back to prison.

Under police questioning, Che eventually admitted not only to his connection to Castro and the desire to overthrow Batista, but his communist loyalty and his belief in armed revolution throughout Latin America as well. Che had not been "broken"; it was his complete and utter conviction of beliefs that motivated him to be so forthcoming. As Gutiérrez Barrios, the young official who would later come to aid Castro, remembers: "The only one who confessed to his ideology was Che. When he was questioned by the public prosecutor he stated that his ideology was Marxist-Leninist, quite clearly. The others didn't, because none of them had those characteristics." Never one to pass up a spirited contest of intellects, Che, even in jail, refused to hide his most powerful weapon: his mind. Even if it was counter-intuitive and foolhardy, he was going to defend his beliefs.

The last thing Castro needed, however, was for the U.S. government to suspect communist involvement. He knew that, as in Guatemala, any U.S. involvement would end his revolution before it began, and Castro continued to deny any affiliation with the Communist Party; however, although Che's statements were not given publicity, a connection Che had with the Soviets was. Some of the conservative newspapers pointed out Che's membership in the Russian-Mexican Cultural Relations Institute. Also found among Che's belongings was the card of Nikolai Leonov, the Soviet agent who had met Che briefly and loaned him some books on the Soviet way of life. In light of this discovery, Leonov was soon called back to the USSR, his apparent involvement in the scandal an embarrassment for the government there.

On the outside, Castro's defense was toiling to gain his release and made intermittent headway. A judge managed to delay the deportation order and bribery was reportedly attempted among some Mexican government officials. Even though the bribe failed, twenty-one of the men were released after a hunger strike, but Castro, Che, and a man named Calixto García remained in jail.

While in prison, Che wrote his family and admitted the extent of his involvement: "Some time ago, quite a while now, a young Cuban leader invited me to join his movement, a movement for the armed liberation of his country, and I, of course, accepted." His future now lay with the Cuban Revolution, a future uncertain at best: "I either triumph with it or die there … throughout life I have looked for my truth by trial and error, and now, on the right road, and with a daughter who will survive me, I have closed the cycle." When faced with the threat of death, Che again turns poetic, closing the letter by quoting the work of a Turkish poet: "I will take to the grave only the sorrow of an unfinished song."

Later, after his mother expressed dismay at his decision, Che passionately declared his solidarity with his fellow prisoners to her in a letter: "In these days of prison and the previous ones of training I identified totally with my comrades of the cause … the concept of 'I' disappeared totally to give place to the concept of 'us' … really it was (and is) beautiful to be able to feel that removal of I."

Celia, long familiar with Che's intensity, must have been surer than ever that her dire prediction of never seeing her son alive again was bound to come true. His commitment to radical politics and revolution ("Not only am I not a moderate but I will never try to be one") only reinforced her sense of impending doom for her son.

It was while they were in prison that one of the first known pictures of Che and Castro together was taken. The photograph is remarkable, if for nothing else, because of their youthful appearance. In time, they both would grow their trademark beards and adopt a constant uniform of fatigues (with Che known for his all-around sloppy appearance). But this photo captures a moment before all that. In it, Castro, round and thick, looks decidedly natty with his dark jacket and tie, neatly combed hair, and trimmed moustache. He is balanced by the nearly opposite image of Che. Standing next to a mess that can only be assumed is his bed and desk, Che is shirtless with his pants undone and belt hanging loose, his handsome face gazing from underneath a tousled head of thick black hair, and his torso lean and strong. He looks like a schoolboy, late for class while his older brother waits patiently by. It is almost impossible to believe what these two young men were about to attempt, let alone accomplish.

It was a Mexican police official, Captain Fernando Barrios, who eventually came to Castro's aid. Barrios would go on to be Mexico's secret police chief for thirty years, and his actions proved a long-standing sympathy for Latin American revolutionary exiles. Castro publicly named Barrios as someone who could clear Castro of any communist connections, and his testament carried considerable weight. Fidel was released on July 24 and ordered to leave the country within two weeks. Che and García remained, the only two of Castro's men left behind bars. Officially they were most guilty of immigration violations, but Che's avowed dedication to communism could have only lengthened his stay.

Now out of jail, Castro moved quickly. The others had been dispersed to outlying areas of Mexico, and the attention generated by their jail time had obviously heightened scrutiny of their actions by Batista's agents. Castro returned Che's loyalty, vowing to not desert him, even as the revolution pressed on.

In the middle of August, Che and García were freed. Their fifty-seven-day stretch had been truncated by a bribe from Castro, making good on his word. Years later, Che would write about the release, commenting that Castro "compromised his revolutionary attitude" for the release of his friends. Che insisted that Castro should not delay the revolution for his sake and that he understood if he had to be left behind. Instead, Castro was steadfast in his dedication to Che, promising to not "abandon him." Che found that "Those personal attitudes of Fidel, with the people he appreciates, are the key to that fanaticism he awakens in others."

It was about liberation and revolution, yes, but it was also about the cult of personality as found in the undeniably powerful charisma and pull of Fidel Castro. He was a man capable of weaving a spell that left virtually no one unaffected. Che was no exception.

Gathering Steam

"Free" men once again, Che and García quickly followed the others underground. They were told to get out of Mexico within a matter of days, but first Che revisited his role as father. For three days he stayed with Gadea and little "Hildita," undoubtedly a visit permeated with the anticipation of his coming departure. After retreating from Mexico City to a town not far away, Che would still see Hildita whenever Gadea could steal away for furtive visits. Che's sadness was tempered with the faith that he doing the right thing for his daughter. Gadea would later tell how Che would cradle the little girl in his arms, telling her why he had to leave her to continue the struggle "against the great enemy, Yankee imperialism." Che's dedication to the cause had overcome all other emotions, even those of paternal love. It may seem unfathomable, this unbreakable devotion to liberating a country he had never even visited, but that is exactly what made Che the unique person he was and the person he would become: "I live with an anarchic spirit that makes me dream of new horizons."

After waiting months, Guevara and García were only too aware that the time for action was drawing near. It is yet another testament to Che's unflagging devotion that he never wavered, he never even considered abandoning his mission. As Castro frantically pulled together all the strings of his plan, the reality of the situation finally hit home, and the men were asked to provide the names of whom should be notified in the event of their deaths. There it was, pure and simple, the specter of death was now a constant, nearly tangible, companion to them all.

Fidel was able to cobble together a partnership of sorts with the Directorio Revolucionario, a radical revolutionary movement stationed in Cuba. The two groups issued a joint statement expressing their common goal of ousting Batista but did not join forces, per se. They did, however, agree to keep one another informed of their plans and to cooperate once Castro's crew landed in Cuba.

Soon forty new recruits were on hand. Fresh from Cuba, the men were sent to remote bases that had been established after the loss of the ranch in Chalco. Most of Castro's officers had joined him in Mexico City, with a few stationed in Cuba. One major hurdle remained: passage to the island. Despite some attempts, Castro had yet to secure the boat that would land his men on the shores of Cuba. Castro was low on funds and desperate. Relief came in the form of former Cuban President Carlos Prío Socarrás. Castro and Prío had a rocky past, and the two were currently competing to oust Batista. An uneasy alliance was formed and Prío funded Castro's search for a boat. It is likely that Prío had ulterior motives for his generosity. He could have conceivably foreseen Castro doing the revolution's groundwork while he came in from above, reinstating himself as leader. Or maybe he thought Castro was a convenient scapegoat, attracting Batista's attention so Prío could make his own move. The bottom line? Castro left the meeting with fifty thousand dollars, whatever Prío's motivations may have been.

By the end of September Castro (again with the help of Antonio del Conde) had found his ship. Called the *Granma*, the thirty-eight-foot yacht was neither seaworthy nor big enough, but it was his. Along with the boat came a house situated on the Pánuco River in a Gulf town called Tuxpan in Veracruz. Castro immediately sent several men to the house where they could concentrate on getting the *Granma* up to snuff.

A Rat

While the Granma *was being upgraded, a traitor was uncovered. The Mexican police, acting on information provided by the Cuban secret service, raided a safe house where one of the men, Pedro Miret, was staying. Miret was arrested and his weapons and documents taken. Castro knew he'd been ratted out and suspicions quickly mounted as to the identity of the weak link in their chain. Rafael Del Pino, a close friend of Castro's, was a prime suspect. He'd recently disappeared and was one of the few people aware of Miret's whereabouts. In later years evidence would suggest that Del Pino had been an FBI informant. Even so, those in the revolution, if they knew, never identified the traitor. Despite this setback, Castro continued on—but with a new sense of urgency.*

Castro received advice from all sides that the time was not right for the invasion. His Oriente commander, Frank País, told him that his people in Cuba were not prepared. Their job was to instigate armed uprisings in eastern Cuba when the forces landed. The Cuban Communist Party let Castro know that it, too, thought it was too soon. Castro refused to relent and asked that all parties support the revolution once it began. Although he had never aligned himself with the Communist Party, Castro was enough of a pragmatist (and opportunist) to not spite it. Che's growing Marxist influence may have also been of importance in these matters.

The political situation in Cuba had grown increasingly murky. The chief of Batista's Military Intelligence had been assassinated and it appeared that someone somewhere was going to take a stab at real revolution. Castro knew that someone had to be him. To make matters worse, two men soon deserted the rebel ranks, only increasing Castro's fear of detection.

Preparing to Sail

On November 23 Castro was as ready as he was ever going to be. The rebels were summoned to Pozo Rico, a town south of Tuxpan, and told they would load up *Granma* and depart on the twenty-fourth. Batista knew they were coming, he just did not know when or where. Publicly, Batista's regime discounted any threat of success by Castro, but military and sea patrols were nonetheless ratcheted up.

After sending a secret message to País, Castro and his men began their final hours in Mexico. With an estimated five days of travel time, the invasion was slated to land at Playa las Coloradas, a deserted beach in Oriente, on November 30. The rebels were assembled after quickly leaving their homes, taking virtually no personal possessions with them. Left behind in Che's quarters were books that he may have been reading at the time of his departure: *The State and Revolution* by Lenin, as well as Marx's *Das Kapital*. Also left behind was his inhaler, a regretful move, as his asthma gave him great difficulty during the coming days at sea.

As final preparations were made and the boat loaded up with arms and equipment, a thousand uncertainties must have been pressing down on them all: What if there's another traitor? What if Batista knows exactly when we're coming, or worse yet, where we're landing? What if the choppy waters prove too much and we're snatched into the murky depths, denied even the sight of our destination? What if I never again see my wife, children, family, friends? What if we're simply not ready? What if …

Although the revolutionaries faced seemingly infinite possible outcomes, the possibility of liberation proved too strong, their hard work and training too important, and their dedication and certainty too resolute to become mired in doubts raised by questions of "what if." But in facing such an unknowable future, even the strongest man would have felt compelled to look into himself and ponder his own death.

In the tension-filled hours before departure, even Che was not immune. In a letter to his mother intended for her if he should die, Che expressed his own fears, noting that although "the signs are good," he may very well indeed be heading toward his grave. In what may be his final words to his beloved mother, Che is full of emotion: "I kiss you again, with all the love a good-bye that resists being total. Your son." In truth, his trip to the grave was just beginning.

In the early morning hours of November 25, 1956, eighty-two men in a boat meant for twenty sailed out into the Gulf of Mexico and, from there, into history.

Chapter 5

The Cuban Revolution

*... [T]he guerrilla has come to put his life on the line,
to trust it to the luck of a tossed coin. And in general,
whether or not the individual guerrilla lives or dies weighs
little in the final outcome of the battle.*
—Che Guevara

As the *Granma* sailed out toward Cuba, the eighty-two men aboard were soon racked with difficulties. The choppy waters rendered almost all of them violently seasick, and Che himself suffered an asthma attack. Despite his own ailment, Che did what he could to live up to his position as group doctor, attempting to help the sickest on board. As for himself, he had no medicine to alleviate his asthma. In writing about the trip in his journal, Che painted a scene of nightmarish sickness: "Men with anxious faces were grabbing their stomachs. Some stuck their heads in buckets and others flopped down in the strangest positions, immovable and with their clothes vomit-stained."

After three days, the boat started taking on water and a faulty clutch forced them to go at half speed so as not to ruin the engine. Those not rendered helpless by illness found themselves bailing water out of the boat in around-the-clock shifts. The situation was seemingly desperate. Years later Castro would describe the boat as "a nutshell bouncing around the Gulf of Mexico."

A lack of food only added to the misery onboard, much of their food supply had been left behind in their haste to leave Mexico. In what was a harbinger of hard times to come after the Cuban Revolution, Castro was forced to ration out the little food they did have. Of course the food situation was tempered a bit by the over-whelming seasickness that gripped many of the men: They couldn't have kept anything down even if they had had an appetite.

On November 30 the rebels began to hear (via the ship's radio) of uprisings in Cuba, especially in Santiago. Fighting in the streets was occurring and acts of sabotage being carried out. The crew felt helpless, unable to take part in the action. As the reports continued, it appeared as though the rebels (whichever group they belonged to) were being beaten down.

To make matters worse, the trip took seven days, not five. In addition to the engine problems, the weight of the men and the weapons slowed their expected speed considerably. When the boat did land, it was far from its planned spot. "Landed" is not exactly correct, for the boat more or less shipwrecked in a very swampy area southeast of their scheduled destination. That may have been just as well as Batista, aware of their planned landing in the Oriente Province, had mobilized ground forces in the area, hoping to squash the invasion before it even began. In addition, the Cuban air force was under orders to search for suspicious boats off the coast. There is evidence another traitor working against the rebels was in their midst: The day they left a message had been sent to Batista's forces that warned, "Boat sailed today with plenty staff and arms from Mexican port." In total, more than thirty thousand men were waiting for this tiny boat filled more with revolutionary dreams than realities.

On December 2, 1956, despite detection efforts by Cuban armed forces in the air and at sea, the *Granma* and its cargo of eighty-two hungry, shaky revolutionaries made it into an area called Belic, a swamp about a mile and a half southeast of Las Coloradas, the planned landing sight. (For a map of Cuba, see Appendix C, "Maps: Che on the Trail.") After more than one hundred seventy-two hours at sea, they found themselves stuck on a mud flat two thousand yards from shore, most of the men, on orders from Castro, disembarked and made their way toward land. Visibility was low, only about fifty yards, and land was but a shadow in the distance. The others, including Fidel's brother, Raúl, soon followed after overseeing the removal of their meager supply of arms and equipment. The group had about ninety rifles, forty pistols, three machine guns, and two anti-tank guns, and not all of the equipment even made it to dry land.

After two hours of difficult travel through swamp ("surrounded by clouds of gall midges and mosquitoes," Che would later write), the first of the revolutionaries reached dry Cuban soil, a strip of beach facing a row of coconut trees. Their fellow revolutionaries, after having waited two days for the *Granma* to appear, had left the area the night before, leaving no friendly faces to greet them. As they lumbered out of the water some of the exhausted rebels had to be carried by others—hardly an auspicious start to a revolution.

They were fired upon almost immediately. Bombs and gunshots reined down from the sea and air as the rebels scrambled into the surrounding brush. At least there were no ground troops to contend with yet. Disoriented and scared, they split into two smaller groups and made a desperate attempt just to stay alive as the assault from government planes continued from above. Che was finally in Cuba, for better or worse, wandering in circles with his fellow rebels and hoping his two years of training would pay off. After two days, the groups were reunited and moved inland and eastward, heading for the Sierra Maestra, Cuba's highest mountain range. They were a motley crew, described by Guevara later as "an army of shadows."

Che's Choice

In what would be the first of many betrayals, the guide that led the group to an area called Alegría de Pío informed the army where they were, and in the afternoon of December 5, the rebels found themselves in combat for the first time. Chaos reigned as bullets flew fast and furious. Many of the men simply fled, while others, frozen in fear, were killed in the attack. In the midst of the onslaught came a moment often repeated as a defining one for Che. He had a choice to make: a box of bullets or a backpack full of medicine. He chose the bullets. Although in the coming months he would continue to serve as doctor to the rebels, civilians, and even captured Cuban soldiers, many see Che's choice of ammunition over medicine at this juncture as his ultimate declaration to be a true soldier. In fact, it's a moment that Che himself later looked back on as a turning point: "Maybe that was the first time I had to make a practical choice between my vocation for medicine and my duty as a revolutionary soldier."

Che not only took the box of bullets, he took a bullet—in the neck. Two years of training and a lifetime of preparation had brought him to this place, a sugarcane field in southeastern Cuba, and now, as Che laid on the ground covered in blood and deep in shock, he was sure death was imminent. Flashing on an image culled from a Jack London story, "To Build a Fire," in which the main character calmly accepts his fate to freeze to death in the Alaskan wasteland, Che prepared to die. However, another rebel, Juan Almeida, implored Che to pick up his rifle and run. Snapped out of his stupor by his fellow rebel's instruction, Che scrambled onto his feet, applied pressure to the bleeding hole in his neck, and followed the fleeing troops into the surrounding jungle. Che's neck wound proved only superficial, but the experience must have been seminal. Now, more than just believing, he knew that he was prepared to die for the cause.

The assaults on the beach and in the sugarcane field were devastating for Castro and his men. Many of the rebels were either killed in the attacks or executed after being captured by Batista's forces. Among the dead was Ñico López, the first person ever to tell Che about Castro and the Cuban Revolution. When they eventually regrouped in the Sierra Maestra mountains, the initial group of eighty-two would number approximately twenty. Although the exact number of survivors has been a matter of dispute (official reports put the number of survivors at twelve), it is safe to say the group was decimated.

For more than two weeks after the sugarcane field assault Che and a small band of men marched toward the Sierra Maestra, hoping to reunite with the others. With no water and little food, the haggard group lived with the constant fear of another attack. On their journey, they were alternately helped and threatened by peasants they met along the way. The thinly populated and impoverished Sierra Maestra region was controlled by a few land barons who exploited and abused the peasants who worked the land. While many of the peasants helped and supported the rebels, often providing them with directions, food, and shelter, some of them, because of either intimidation or greed, informed the Cuban army of the rebels' actions. Because of this threat, Castro soon adopted a strategy of pretending to be a Cuban soldier when first meeting a peasant, thereby having a better understanding of where his loyalties lay.

Fidel Castro (left) and Che Guevara (right) in the early days (1956) of their guerrilla campaign in the Sierra Maestra Mountains of Cuba.

(*Archive Photos*)

Che and the wandering band of rebels soon decided that it was not safe to trek through the region in the daytime. They would hide out in caves until the sun went down and then head out on foot. Forced to eat raw crabs and drink rainwater, the rebels found themselves wandering aimlessly, sometimes having nothing to eat for days. More than once they happened upon a house, only to detect Cuban soldiers inside. They were able to avoid confrontation, but the threat of being discovered always felt imminent.

After sixteen treacherous and trying days, Che and the small band of rebels reached their target: the farm of a peasant near the base of the mountain range. The other survivors, including Fidel and his brother Raúl, were already there and had sent runners to find the others. Castro, upset at them for abandoning their weapons along the way, severely criticized them for their negligence. They had given up the one and only hope for survival if Batista's men had trapped them. Castro railed that it was not only stupid of them to do, but criminal as well. They were full-fledged soldiers now and would be treated as such. So many of them had been captured and executed, the stakes were higher than ever: There was no room for such stupid mistakes.

Meanwhile, word of the sugarcane field attack on the rebels was spreading fast. Batista's regime was claiming total victory and news reports listed Fidel, Raúl, and Che among the dead. Back in Buenos Aires, Che's family was devastated by the news. Aware that Batista could be bluffing, they desperately searched for confirmation but none was to be found. After days of agonizing uncertainty, word reached the family from the Argentine embassy in Havana: Che was not among the dead or the imprisoned. Elated by the news, the family informed Gadea (still in Mexico and about to leave for Peru with Hildita) of the turn of events. The family soon realized, however, that they could not be certain that Che was truly alive: His body may simply have not been recovered. The Guevaras' New Year looked like it would be anything but happy. Then on December 31, relief came in the form of an airmail letter. Addressed to Celia (*madre*) and postmarked in Manzanillo, Cuba, inside was a handwritten note from Che: He was fine and continuing his work with the rebels. Ending with a tongue-in-cheek request from Che ("have faith that God is an Argentine"), the brief message is signed with his childhood family nickname, "Teté." Needless to say, the Guevaras celebrated plenty come midnight.

Organization of a Revolution

Castro had already returned to the task at hand: organization of the revolution. Peasants proved indispensable in providing contact with urban revolutionaries in cities such as Santiago and Manzanillo. Among these contacts were Frank País and Celia Sánchez, a woman who would come to figure most prominently in both the revolution and the personal life of its leader. Although the rebels had landed alone, they had a network of support waiting both in the mountains and in the urban areas. And although they did not dramatically land on the beach as Castro and his team did, these supporters of the revolution were taking just as many risks for the cause, risking everything to prepare Cuba for the coming struggle.

Soon, more weapons and new volunteers arrived and the rebels began to regroup. (Among these new recruits was a young peasant by the name of Daniel Alarcón, a rebel who, later, would be one of the few to escape from Che's doomed Bolivia campaign with his life.) Within three weeks, they waged a successful attack against the Cuban forces in La Plata. The rebels knew they needed to strike fast if they wanted to be seen as a viable threat to Batista. The military barracks at La Plata, situated on the coast, south of the Sierra Maestra, became their target. The outpost there was small and remote with few guards, perfect for a guerrilla ambush.

Once in the La Plata area, the plan was to kill three of the most despised plantation foremen in the area. By doing so, Castro hoped to shore up support among the peasants in the area. Now an army of thirty-two men (a number continually in flux due to new arrivals and deserters), the rebels were still low on arms with only twenty or so weapons among them.

In mid-January they reached La Plata and staked out the barracks they planned to attack. Informed by a peasant that Chicho Osorio, one of the foremen marked for death, was headed their way, the rebels waited. When Osorio appeared, Castro and the others pretended to be part of the army, there to inspect the camp. A drunk Osorio offered to guide them to the barracks, all the time boasting how the rebels all would soon be killed. After showing off the boots he was wearing that had been taken off the feet of a dead rebel, he even bragged about how he would torture Castro himself if he could get his hands on him. After dutifully pointing out the details of the operation (such as where the soldiers slept and where they kept watch) Osorio was left behind with two rebels as the others went ahead. The orders were to shoot the foreman "the minute the shooting started." The order was obeyed. One has to wonder if Osorio, in his drunken state, ever fully comprehended what he had done.

By the end of the battle, two soldiers were dead and five more were wounded, and three of those soon died from their wounds. The rebels also captured three prisoners along with nine guns, a thousand rounds, helmets, canned food, knives, and clothes. After Che tended to their wounds, the prisoners were released and left with their surviving counterparts. The rebel forces emerged relatively unscathed with no casualties.

It had been an important victory; if they had failed at La Plata, the revolution would have been over before it had even truly begun. As it was, news of the rebel victory soon spread across Cuba, nullifying Batista's reports that they had been snuffed out. Castro knew that soon they would be besieged by Cuban troops and, as the rebels moved into the steepest parts of the Sierra Maestra, began to prepare his plans of ambush. As they made their way into the mountains, a flood of peasants passed the other way, frightened from their homes by rumors of imminent bombing by the army. It looked as though Batista was prepared to devastate the region to stop the rebels.

Che the Executioner

Over the next weeks, the rebels engaged in more combat and wrestled with the harsh conditions of the area. Bouts of swamp fever and diarrhea were common, and Che continued to suffer from asthma attacks. It is during this period that Che killed his first soldier. This must have proven a turning point for him as well. It is one thing to grab a box of bullets but another thing altogether to use them to kill. This man, who in his youth had failed to engage in any kind of tangible political activity other than debating theory, was now killing Cuban military in the midst of a bloody revolution. Even though his account of the incident did not reveal anything more than a clinical observation ("He received a gunshot wound in the middle of his chest, which must have burst his heart and caused instant death"), any doubts about Che's dedication to the cause must have died along with the soldier.

Che was quickly becoming known as a daredevil and often took on the most dangerous assignments. He also grew harder, often demanding death for spies and traitors. Cowardice also infuriated him as his metamorphosis into a true guerrilla fighter quickened. By the end of January, Castro drew the line and commanded that three crimes be punished by death: "desertion, insubordination, and defeatism." Che was pleased by the new hard-line stance and would personally carry out some of the executions to come, his first being that of a traitor in their midst.

Eutimio Guerra, a Cuban peasant who had initially won Castro's trust, had made an agreement with the army troops to betray the rebels. Guerra, whose main function was to serve as a guide, had been captured on one of his expeditions. While held by the army, his spirit and dedication were broken. The troops promised him ten thousand pesos and an army rank for providing information about the rebels' movements and, eventually, for killing Castro. With information Guerra provided, the army was able to burn the homes of rebel-friendly peasants.

When Guerra wanted to sneak away and tell the army of the rebels' campsite near the area of Mt. Caracas, he concocted a story about needing to visit his sick mother. Castro not only believed Guerra, he gave him money to help him on his trip. Soon after Guerra's departure, the air filled with the sound of airplanes. As Che would later describe the scene:

*We suddenly heard the clatter of a fighter plane, the rattle
of machine guns, and, soon after, the bombs. Our experience was very limited back then and we could hear shots
everywhere; .50-caliber bullets explode when they hit the
ground, and when the attackers came close they gave us
the impression they had come out of the brush itself. At
the same time we could also hear machine-gun fire from
the air …*

In a stroke of good luck, the rebels had moved not far from
the original campsite but were still close enough to suffer from the
attack. Once again, the rebels had been reminded of both the
importance of staying on the move and being aware of betrayal
from within. Guerra continued his pattern of deceit, and the rebels
continually faced surprise army attacks.

Eutimio's deception was uncovered in late February when Che
became suspicious of the timing of Guerra's trips. He always
seemed to be absent from the camps when attacks took place. Plus,
Guerra began to foolishly predict to the others when and where
the next attack would take place. When his predictions kept coming true, Che and Castro were convinced and other peasants in the
area soon confirmed Guerra's guilt. In addition, some army docu-
mentation proving Guerra's complicity with them was also found.

Guerra was soon seized and brought before Castro, his guilt too
evident to deny. He fell to his knees and begged for his life to be
ended quickly. While the others hesitated, Che saw no reason to
wait: He fulfilled Guerra's request, shooting him in the head. Che
would later write about the incident in an article called "Death of
a Traitor" (although in doing so, he did not publicly admit that he
had pulled the trigger, but other accounts and his own diary show
that he did). In the article, he writes of how Guerra's last wish was
for his children to be taken care of. Che wrote of how they had
honored his wish, but that Guerra's children would "one day …
have to know that their father was executed by the revolution
because of his treachery."

Nonetheless, Che also wrote how Guerra's children deserved to
know their father accepted his punishment without "a desire for

clemency," and that, as his life came to an end, "he remembered his children and asked that they be treated well."

In a passage filled with imagery and symbolism, Che wrote how, at the moment of Guerra's death, the Cuban sky seemed to open up: "Just then, a heavy storm broke and blacked everything out. The sky was criss-crossed by lightning in an uncommonly heavy rainfall, and the air filled with thunder ... so that none of the comrades nearby where able to hear the gunshot when Eutimio Guerra met his death." The price for treason in the revolution was death, and, as Che wrote it, nature herself seemed to agree.

Che's swift action contributed to his cold-blooded reputation, a reputation that was growing with each passing victory. Guerra may have been the first traitor put to death by Che, but he would not be the last. While one could not call Che "bloodthirsty," it was clear that he was willing to do whatever it took to ensure the revolution's victory.

Important Meetings

Batista continued to wage a propaganda war against the rebels, claiming they were all but annihilated. In a bid to prove him wrong, Castro arranged a meeting with a journalist through an urban revolutionary. He wanted to show the world he was still fighting, and on February 17, Herbert Matthews from *The New York Times* met with Castro. Although Che was not present for the interview, Castro later told him it had gone well. Castro complained to Matthews about U.S. military aid to Batista. He was quick to add, however, that he bore no ill will against the United States or its people. Castro, always wary of being pegged a communist, knew better than to unduly aggravate the U.S. government.

Castro also bluffed about his rebel army and led Matthews to believe it numbered many more than the actual total of twenty. Matthews's account of their meeting, published in a three-part series at the end of February, was favorable. Obviously impressed with Castro and his forces, Matthews concluded, "From the look of things, General Batista cannot possibly hope to suppress the Cuban revolt." The interview spread like wildfire through Cuba, and Batista immediately claimed it was a hoax, demanding photographic proof that the meeting took place. When such evidence was submitted, Batista's earlier claims of victory over the rebels were embarrassingly refuted. Over the course of the revolution, Castro would allow other journalists to come get a firsthand look at his work. In one impressive display a few months later, Castro met with CBS's Robert Taber on top of a mountain peak called Pico Turquino, one of the hardest-to-reach areas of the Sierra Maestra.

Around the same time, Castro held a meeting with his cadre of urban revolutionary leaders, the 26th of July National Directorate. The meeting took place at a farmhouse on the northern side of the Sierra, and over the course of a few days, Castro made it clear that the rebel army was to be the priority. Many of the others had different ideas, wanting to start a second band of rebels closer to Havana and concentrate on raising funds and awareness outside of Cuba. Castro insisted, however, and the others agreed. The 26th of July National Directorate would send more arms and recruits to the rebels while strengthening plans for a national civic resistance. During the discourse, Che hung back, content to size them up in his own way. He found most of them to be insufficiently radical, content to replace Batista with a traditional Western kind of government. However, Che did find much to admire in Oriente commander Frank País, noting that "he had the look of a man totally dedicated and faithful to the cause."

Castro also took the opportunity to address the population directly. In writing his "Appeal to the Cuban People," Castro hyped his plans for the country. Vigorously declaring that, after eighty days of fighting, his rebel forces were stronger than ever, Castro claimed the mountain-area peasants were steadfastly reinforcing his rebels in growing numbers. He called for a national "civic resistance," a general "revolutionary strike," more funding for his guerrilla troops, and economic sabotage. The document was printed up and distributed across Cuba in hopes that its message would begin to take hold.

The Batista forces also had a message for the Cuban people: Help us or die. The army made it perfectly clear that anyone who helped the rebels would suffer dearly. As a result, many of the peasants were caught between the rebels punishing informers and the army brutalizing sympathizers.

In late February, a surprise assault by Batista's forces drove the rebels deeper into the hills. While retreating, Che suffered a brutal attack of his own when an especially severe case of asthma racked his body. He had been afflicted before and would sometimes have to be carried, but he was always committed to keeping up the best he could. Che's persistence in the face of his ever-recurring ailment made him seem all the more valuable to the group. But this time Che was simply too weak to continue on. He would later remember the attack as being "the toughest stage of the war."

A peasant was paid to go to Manzanillo for asthma medication and, as the others traveled on to meet some new recruits, Che and another rebel took temporary refuge and waited for his relief. After two days, the precious delivery arrived. Still far from recovered, Che and the rebel known as "Teacher" eventually made their way to the others: "I walked along from tree to tree, with a rifle butt for support, in the company of a frightened fighter who trembled every time fighting broke out, and had a nervous attack every time my asthma made me cough in some dangerous spot." Even though their rendezvous with the others was a cabin not far away, it was ten days before Che and his nervous companion met up with the others on March 11.

News of an assassination attempt on Batista's life soon reached the rebels. During the daylight attack on the Presidential Palace in Havana by the rebel group Directorio Revolucionario, more than forty people, mostly rebels, died—but not Batista. Although Castro had signed a pact with the rebel group back in Mexico City, in reality, the factions were anything but united. The failed assassination was a clear attempt to wrest power from Batista and replace him without Castro's involvement. Castro knew he would have to keep as close an eye on other rebel groups as he did on the man he longed to overthrow.

With fresh recruits on board, the newly expanded rebel army now had approximately seventy members. It was decided that the men would take it slow and avoid confrontation until they felt ready, rather than throw them into battle right away. However, finding food for seventy proved much more difficult than finding food for twenty. Driven by necessity, stores were looted and cows were stolen. Perhaps as compensation, Che began conducting open medical consultations for the peasants. He could do little for their conditions, but the sight of these people ravaged by overwork and inadequate nutrition only deepened Che's resolve to secure a better life for them.

Che's actions during this period were a tangible example of his idea of the doctor as a revolutionary force—one who served the people both medically and politically. He saw himself as improving both their present (through medicine) and their future (through revolution). Although his book, *The Role of the Doctor in Latin America,* was never finished, the practices he had been writing about were put to good use as he fought in Cuba. The people he helped were a constant reminder of why he was there: "Those long-suffering and loyal inhabitants of the Sierra Maestra never suspected the role they were playing as forgers of our revolutionary ideology."

By May Che was assigned a newly arrived machine gun and his position became one of "full-time combatant." Although still capable of providing medical services, his role was changing and he would soon officially move up in rank.

El Comandante

Che proved his mettle once again after the rebels, proud recipients of a fresh shipment of arms, won at El Uvero in late May. Initially, Che did not want to attack the army barracks at El Uvero. He thought a better choice would be to ambush an army truck entering the mountains. But Fidel was certain the barracks should be their target. He thought it would deliver the right "psychological blow" against the army and garner much attention. An ambush of an army truck could be easily dismissed, while a full-blown assault, if successful, would only enhance the rebels' reputation. Although they disagreed, Che deferred to Castro and later admitted that Castro's plan was best.

The El Uvero skirmish marked the largest battle of the war up to then, as eighty rebels took on fifty-three soldiers. The battle lasted just less than three hours, with the rebels eventually taking the barracks and its supplies. The going was tough, but the rebels knew they had to win this one. If not, most of the ammunition would be gone, and no replenishment was in sight. Che showed uncommon bravery during the attack, although he downplayed his exploits in his written memories. In addition to his ferocity, Che showed his usual concern for the wounded, caring for the army soldiers he had just helped to defeat: "I had to swap my gun for a medic's uniform—an act that, as it happened, consisted of just washing my hands."

Although El Uvero was a victory, seven of the rebels were wounded and six died during battle. In all, approximately nineteen of Batista's men were injured, fourteen were killed, fourteen more were prisoners, and six others escaped. Che summed up the battle by writing, "It was an assault by men who advanced bare-chested against others who were defending themselves in an almost unprotected place. It should be acknowledged that there were displays of courage on both sides."

As it turns out, Castro was right: The victory was psychologically important, both for the attention it brought and the morale boost the rebels felt. Che called it "the victory that marked our coming of age." It was from El Uvero that Che felt the rebels' morale "grew tremendously; and our decisiveness and our hopes for triumph increased also."

For two weeks Che stayed behind with the injured men, attending to their wounds and leading them to safety. Upon their return to the others, Che was promoted to "comandante" and put in charge of the rebels' second column—a designation that made him "the proudest man on earth." With the rebel forces now numbering over two hundred, Che was given seventy-five men to command.

Over the next few months Che helped to lead battles that solidified his position as leader in the force, with his column often marching parallel to Castro and the others. His men were acutely aware of his rigid standards and dedication to the cause, but his troops always seemed to echo each other with the same sentiment about their leader: He never asked more than what he was willing to give himself. Che had shed the "I" long ago and did his best to teach the same outlook to his men.

In one memorable display, Che marched his men past an area that gravely emphasized the price of treason. After two rebels had deserted, only to be executed by fellow rebels, Che "gathered all the men together on the hill at the scene of these macabre events, telling them what they were about to see and what it meant, the reason why desertion was punishable by death and the reason for carrying out a death sentence against all who betrayed the Revolution." Che's insistence on loyalty was well-known, but he still felt the need to provide tangible examples.

In his new position Che also began to take direct part in the leadership of the 26th of July movement. He often disagreed with the direction of the movement, always pushing for the radical ideology. For instance, when Castro signed "The Manifesto of Sierra Maestra" pact with reformist politicians in July, Che strongly opposed. He felt the pact was reformist rather than revolutionary and that the ideas expressed were watered-down versions of the rebels' goals. Of course he was right. But he was learning more from Castro than just how to fight; he was learning how to strategize as well. The pact, like others they had agreed to, was not what they wanted, but it was necessary to continue receiving resources. Che took solace in the fact that the original manifesto outlining the rebels' revolutionary plans could still be considered their mission statement. Still, the friction between the reformists in the cities and the revolutionaries in the mountains continued to be a problem—with Che often the most vocal critic.

In late July 1957 Santiago police murdered Frank País, the Oriente Province contact. His brother, Josué País, had been killed recently as well. In the days following Frank's funeral, several protests broke out in cities across Cuba. Although saddened by Frank's death in particular ("we lost one of our bravest fighters"), Che knew that the riotous reaction to his demise only proved the revolution was taking hold: "New forces were joining in on the struggle and that the people's fighting mood was on the rise."

The 26th of July movement was gaining momentum—and not just in the mountains of the Sierra Maestra.

Batista responded by declaring a state of siege and media blackout. At the same time, the United States took greater notice of the unrest in Cuba. Wanting to protect its economic interests on the island, the United States encouraged Batista to bring about a democratic form of government and hold elections, but the presence of Castro and his ever-growing rebel army changed all that. In response, the CIA, State Department, and Defense Department all formulated plans for the region—plans that did not always coincide with each other's. Generally the CIA and State Department supported the removal of Batista, while the military sided with the Cuban president.

During the course of the conflict, the CIA approached Castro's urban leaders and reportedly provided support and funds for the rebels. They also contacted officers of Cuba's navy who were planning their own revolt against Batista, vowing support for them as well. The insurgent naval men, joined by other like-minded members of the Cuban air force and army, also approached Castro and his people with a plan to join forces in the fight against Batista. Castro was wary of a military-led coup for fear he would be denied power when it was over. Even though he did not accept the offer, it would not have been entirely surprising if he had: Castro had already proven a pragmatic opportunist who used pacts to further his own agenda only to break them later.

Castro was also facing dissension among his own leadership. Growing weary of Castro's iron grip on the movement's direction, some of the 26th of July movement leaders attempted to exert more control. Disagreements over the formation of a second rebel army and which of the other rebel groups they should align themselves with were just a few of the simmering problems. Che often did not help the tension, refusing even to contact Daniel Latour, the rebel who replaced Frank País, when making supply arrangements. Che and Latour would continue to clash in the coming months. Meanwhile, Castro relied more and more on Celia Sánchez as his relationship with the other urban leaders weakened.

She eventually came to the mountains to be by his side, both as rebel and lover.

As 1957 wore on, Che continued to lead his men into inter-mittent battles with the Cuban forces. He continued to enforce strict discipline on his charges, and desertions were frequent. Not everyone admired his tough leadership style. Unfortunately, the mountain area was now home to renegade groups that often con-sisted of deserters and various outlaws who took the opportunity to steal, kill, and rape the peasants in the region. When these "rene-gade rebels" were caught, their punishment was often death. Among those executed was the man known as "Teacher," the "nervous" and "frightened" rebel who had stayed behind with Che during his devastating asthma attack earlier that February. "Teacher" had broken from the rebels and was passing himself off in the region as Che himself, raping young peasant girls.

Rebel forces once again rose up in the cities, often with disas-trous results. In early September, rebel forces seized the naval base and police station in the city of Cienfuegos. Their success was short-lived, however, and soon Batista sent in tanks and American-made B-26 bombers to quell the uprising. As many as three hundred rebels from varying groups, including some urban members of the 26th of July movement, were killed in the ensuing battle. The United States was displeased with Batista's actions. Using U.S.–supplied arms to defend Cuba from hostility within rather than from outside attacks was a violation of defense treaties between the two governments.

By October Che had set up a guerrilla camp in an area called El Hombrito. Among the impressive achievements he spearheaded were a dam that provided hydroelectric power, the founding of a newspaper called *El Cubano Libre* (*The Free Cuban*) used to inform the Cuban people about the revolution, a simple hospital, a bread oven, and even an armory. While there, Che spent a good time of time instructing his troops in areas other than battle. Only a small number of them could read and Che strove to bring literacy to their lives—another example of his across-the-board commitment to the people he fought for and with. The entire operation was destroyed a few months later by Batista's forces: "El Hombrito was razed, with forty houses burned and all our dreams shattered."

The fighting between the rebels and the army continued throughout the Sierra Maestra, with Che once again leading several attacks and ambushes. In the beginning of December, during a bungled ambush, Che was shot in his left foot and, unable to walk, was forced to ride a horse. A doctor removed the bullet a few days later and within a few weeks Che had recovered.

As 1957 came to a close more problems arose between Castro and his National Directorate. Without Castro's consent the leaders had entered the 26th of July movement into what was known as "The Miami Pact." In it the most revolutionary aspects of Castro's plans were given short shrift: There was no clause against foreign intervention or a military-based replacement of Batista. Also, the rebels were to be absorbed into the armed forces once the revolt was over, guaranteeing its nonexistence. To make matters worse, the agrarian reform, arguably the most significant part of the cause for which they were fighting, was diluted almost to the point of being unrecognizable. The pact seemed to be an attempt to pander to United States interests. Not surprisingly, Che was livid, all but demanding that Castro repudiate this open betrayal. In a move that proved symbolic to Che, Castro condemned the agreement openly, declaring, "The leadership of the struggle against the tyranny is, and will continue to be, in Cuba and in the hands of the revolutionary fighters." Che would later write Castro, telling him that his stand "filled me with peace and happiness." He had always been upfront with Castro about his distrust for the majority of the other leaders and even proposed disbanding the national leadership altogether. A major shakeup would, in fact, occur in the leadership, but not for several months.

Castro's open defiance all but shattered the pact and further splintered his support. Still, Castro had spoken and his message was clear: I lead the revolution, with you or without you. As he put it, "To die with dignity does not require company." At the same time, Castro began establishing stronger, yet still covert, ties with the Communist Party of Cuba.

A New Year, a New Strategy

As 1958 began, so did the revolution outside the mountains. Castro's rebels began slowly moving out into outlying cities, effectively spreading the war out of the Sierra Maestra while rebel activities continued across Cuba. In addition, army forces were withdrawing from the mountains: "An armed truce was in effect, a respite. The guerrillas were unable to operate against the army's heavily defended positions, and the army did not feel inclined to climb up the Sierra."

Also of note, the rebels enacted agrarian reform within the mountains themselves. A lawyer sympathetic to the rebels drafted "legislation" allowing the seizing of landowners' cattle for the distribution to peasants and rebels of the region. More than ten thousand cattle were dispersed, only increasing the support of the rebels by the citizens. It was still difficult for the guerrillas to get food, medicine, and weapons, however. Apparently the urban leaders were reluctant to hand over their supplies to the rebels in the mountains. Che continued his criticism of the leadership that he had always found so distrustful. In a letter to Castro, Che wrote, "I have the sneaking suspicion that they are directly sabotaging this column, or more specifically, me personally."

In retrospect, it is doubtful the leadership was sabotaging anyone, not even Che, one of its most vocal critics. While the rebels were faced with encroaching armies in the mountains, the urban leaders had Batista's police force and its constant reign of intimidation to deal with. As Pacio Ignacio Tabio II (*Guevara, Also Known as Che*) wrote:

> Che's view tended to underestimate the role that the struggle in the cities had played and continued to play in the revolutionary political process that had closed in on the dictatorship. By denying that role ... he saw the guerrilla war as an autonomous process, rather than the vanguard of the widespread dissent that it fed, and fed on.

Perhaps Che's attitude toward the leadership and suspicions of betrayal can also be attributed to his exposure to desertion while commanding his own men. Whatever the cause for the dissent,

Che would soon get his wish with the 26th of July National Directorate undergoing an extensive overhaul.

Che had set up another camp in La Mesa, similar to his earlier settlement. Only now, in addition to a newspaper, armory, and makeshift hospital, there was also a radio transmitter. True to his socialist beliefs, informing the Cuban people was of utmost importance to Che. Despite the limited success of the broadcasts (various factors often interfered with the transmission), "Radio Rebelde" became one of Che's pet projects.

Che was also instrumental in the founding of another school for the peasants, rebels, and even captured soldiers. Looking to the future, Che not only taught politics and combat, but history, culture, and literature as well. He knew the revolution would one day be over, and he wanted them prepared not just physically, but mentally as well.

In February Castro led his column in a strike on the army barracks at Pino del Agua. After a long battle in which Camilo Cienfuegos, one of Castro's best fighters and acknowledged heroes of the revolution, was wounded. Despite his injured leg, Cienfuegos hurled himself back into battle, only to be injured again. The operation proved a successful coup for the rebels, securing valuable arms and ammunition. While Che often receives much of the credit and attention for his bravery, prowess, and dedication, he was but one of the many rebels who fought alongside Castro during the revolution.

By March 1958 the United States cut off weapon sales to Batista. His continual breaches of treaties between the two had proved costly. In addition, the likelihood of Batista retaining power was fading, and the United States wanted to keep its options open. The move brought increased rebel activity and appeals for Batista to step down. Sensing an opportunity to strike, Castro and his 26th of July National Directorate, along with other rebel groups, drew up plans for a general strike, hoping for a complete freeze across Cuba: Taxes would not be paid, anyone remaining in government would be classified as a traitor, and new recruits to the army would be branded as criminals. Armed attacks in Havana, the capital of Cuba, and around the country would be enacted simultaneously. Castro hoped for a complete overthrow of the government.

On April 9 the call went out. It failed miserably. The principle reasons for the failure rested with Cuba's major labor organization, the Cuban Confederation of Labor, and its support of Batista. However, the Cuban Communist Party, disenfranchised by Castro's urban anti-communist leaders, also did not participate. Businesses remained open, taxes were paid, and the few uprisings that did occur were quickly stamped out. Despite the Cuban Communist Party's noncompliance, they were becoming more vocal in support of Castro's cause. Meanwhile, more communists continued to join Castro's forces, often finding a place among Che's troops.

Stung by the failure of the strike, serious shakeups were in store for Castro's National Directorate. Castro blamed the urban leaders for the dismal strike and vowed to regain full control of "his" movement. By early May, the entire leadership order was restructured and three of its leaders demoted. The command center was moved entirely to the Sierra Maestra, where Castro assumed his role as "General Secretary." Acting as the final authority on foreign affairs, arms control, and the rebel forces, the urban hubs were no longer considered headquarters, but simply outposts.

Batista had also been affected by the failure of the strike. Now receiving arms from the Dominican Republic, he began to amass his troops for what he hoped would be the final and total elimination of the rebels that had plagued him for more than a year. The stage was set for the final act of the Cuban Revolution.

Beginning the third week of May, Batista launched his all-out offensive on the rebels in the Sierra Maestra. The numbers were staggering: More than ten thousand troops were involved in the attack against approximately three hundred and twenty rebels. On paper it seemed hopeless, but the rebels had come too far and fought too hard to be defeated. The jungle had become their natural environment, and the military's hopes of snaring the rebels in an ever-tightening circle proved fruitless. Estimates put the army's casualties at over a thousand, while the rebels lost fifty of their men during the two-and-a-half-month-long assault. Che was cautiously optimistic: "We had broken the back of Batista's army after that final offensive, but it had to be beaten."

With victory seemingly in his grasp and the Cuban army in a state of disarray, Castro decided in mid-August on a three-pronged attack in which the war would move into central and western Cuba. Che and Camilio Cienfuegos played a crucial part in the deployment of these troops, leading their men to the Escambray Mountains in the Las Villas province of Central Cuba. But Che's column was only one part of the plan: The southern city of Santiago was also to be seized as well as Pinar del Rio at the uppermost tip of the island. Once there, he coordinated other rebel forces whose goal it was to hammer the central region of Cuba until the enemy forces were immobilized.

At the same time, the rebels' numbers ballooned as popular support for the revolution was continuing to grow among the population as well as within Batista's disheartened armed forces. Castro openly courted disaffected members of the Cuban military. As long as they brought their weapons they were welcome in rebel territory and they would continue to receive salaries.

It was in central Cuba that Che met Aleida March, the rebel who would become his second wife. He had sporadic contact with Gadea while in Cuba, and the marriage had been essentially over before he left Mexico. Aleida, young, attractive, and with a white upper-middle-class upbringing, served as his assistant and closest companion during the last weeks of the war.

By late 1958 troops led by Che and Cienguegos were able to inflict much damage while in central Cuba, blocking transportation routes and destroying communication lines, essentially cutting the island in half. Their journey to the area had been arduous to say the least: forty-seven days of hunger, avoiding ambushes, and evading devastating combat. Che—now sporting his trademark black beret and beard—suffered his own damage, too, fracturing his arm. All the while, opposing rebel forces hoping to seize power were jockeying to usurp Castro before he had even unseated Batista. Time was of the essence, and the rebels would have to move fast.

The Revolution Draws to a Close

The greatest battle of the war still loomed ahead and its name was Santa Clara. The capital of the Las Villas province, Santa Clara's population held one hundred and fifty thousand citizens and more than three thousand soldiers. Che had about three hundred and fifty men at his disposal and, by now, the odds did not seem so long.

In late December, after weeks of successful attacks on several army bases in the area, the troops began what would be the last battle of their long struggle, slowly moving into Santa Clara. Once the attack started, Che knew that the biggest obstacle in his quest to take Santa Clara was the armored train that could facilitate the army's departure from the area. Twenty-two cars long, capable of hauling four hundred soldiers, and well-stocked with large stashes of arms, the armored train had to be stopped. In a move that became legendary, Che oversaw the removal of part of the train track leading into the city. Once that was done, the battle began in earnest. The rebels had moved in under the cover of darkness, and the dawn of December 29 found them dispersed throughout Santa Clara. No longer in the mountains, Che and the rebels were fighting for their lives in the streets alongside civilian supporters.

Besieged by tanks and air assault, the casualties (civilian and guerrilla) mounted, but the fighting continued: "Our men were fighting against soldiers supported by armored units; we put them to flight; but many paid with their lives, and the improvised hospitals and cemeteries began to fill up with the dead and wounded." The rebels overtook railway offices and attacked police stations as the tide of victory turned in their favor—the city around them transformed into a combat zone. It must have been a truly horrific sight: airplanes dropping bombs from overhead, armed rebels and soldiers blanketing the streets with bullets, Santa Clara's citizens running for their lives as the world all but exploded around them. It was a scene not unlike one Che had witnessed before in Guatemala City; a scene that prompted him to "smack his lips with glee." Now he was not just a witness, but also an active participant in activities he had once characterized in his youth as "a lot of fun." It is doubtful that Che, in retrospect, would have agreed with this assessment.

With the rebels gaining ground, the commanding officers that had eluded combat sought shelter in the armored train, hoping to ride it safely out of danger, unaware that the track had been removed. In what must have been a cataclysmic roar of human agony and ripping metal, the train's engine and its first three cars derailed. Using Molotov cocktails and flaming canisters of fuel, the rebels turned the train into a giant cooker, forcing the soldiers out in surrender. The rebels were left with a virtual treasure trove of weapons and artillery they quickly dispatched to other parts of the city where the rebel attack continued. These new arms all but confirmed the rebel control of Santa Clara as police stations and government buildings fell under the onslaught.

By New Year's Eve word of army surrenders around Cuba had reached Batista, and he quickly made plans to retreat. At a New Year's Eve party (a scene notably recreated in *The Godfather, Part II*), Batista renounced his power, turning over both the presidency and the military to others. By early New Year's Day, Batista, his family, and a group of his closest confidantes were on a flight to the Dominican Republic, finally vanquished.

Castro, maintaining a command post back in the Oriente Province, ordered Che and the others to advance toward Havana, their work far from finished. The revolution may have been effectively over, but the reconstruction was just beginning. As he drove toward the capital, what was this Argentine doctor/rebel/writer thinking? Considering what history has taught us about Che Guevara, it is very likely that he was thinking about the faces of the poor and disenfranchised he had gazed upon during his strange and wondrous journey to this point in history and what this revolutionary victory would mean for them.

The details of the Cuban Revolution can, and have, filled volumes; the intricate plotting and strategy analyzed and studied in a manner much more thorough than possible in these few pages. Still, it was the perseverance of these rebels against seemingly insurmountable odds and treachery that formed the heart and soul of the Cuban Revolution. What these men and women did changed the course of an entire nation and, in turn, the world. And in midst of all this unbelievable revolution stood comandante Che Guevara.

Chapter 6

The "New" Cuba Takes Shape

We've won the war. The revolution begins now.
—Che Guevara

With the taking of Santa Clara and the flight of Batista out of Cuba, the rebels had won. As word of Batista's departure spread across the island, spontaneous celebrations began almost immediately in Havana with residents flooding the streets and unfurling banners of triumph throughout the city. There were also incidents of looting and vandalism reported at gas stations, hotels, and casinos, as well as sporadic and futile attempts by police to control the crowds with gunfire. More often than not, police stations were merely abandoned by officers. Resistance groups also overran radio and television stations and newspapers sympathetic to Batista. The private homes of those involved with the Batista regime were also attacked.

Santa Clara also saw its share of celebrating as residents danced in the streets and cheered for the rebels who had only recently infiltrated their midst. Freed from a reign of police-led terror, the citizens were ecstatic. Of special importance to them was Che. He had already begun to take on mythic qualities, and it seemed as though everyone wanted to see him or even get to touch him.

In the wake of the Santa Clara victory, Che took note of the citizens' complaints of torture and violence at the hands of officials and signed death warrants for several of Batista's policemen identified by the people as the worst offenders: "I did no more and no less than the situation demanded—i.e., the death sentence for those twelve murderers, because they had committed crimes against the people, not against us."

Although Castro and his regiment of men still had to take the southern city of Santiago, by this point, the outcome of the war was a foregone conclusion. Che's success in central Cuba clinched the revolutionary win. Now the true nature of the revolution would begin to surface. In the coming year, Che would press his own agenda even harder as the "new" Cuba grew more focused. For Che the fighting did not end with Batista's hasty exit, it only changed the battleground as he grappled to gain a foothold from which to reach his ideological goals in Cuba's reformation.

Still in southern Cuba, Castro ordered Che and fellow rebel leader Camilo Cienfuegos (via Radio Rebelde) to advance on Havana right away. Che was dispatched to the La Cabaña military base, and Camilo was sent to the Columbia base. The two were to secure all weapons at the bases and wait for Castro to take a recently surrendered Santiago. Upon his triumph, Castro would then begin the march of his life, a weeklong trek up the entire island—a victory march to end all victory marches.

After Castro's victory in Santiago the rebels were called back into their columns for the march to Havana. Che was adamant that no commercial cars (taken from the streets of the city) be used by the rebels for the trek; he felt to do so would show little respect for the Cuban people: "They were going to Havana—by truck, bus, on foot, but it was the same for everyone." Che was determined to have the rebels be a part of the masses, not above them.

It would take a week to reach the capital, and Castro had very specific ideas about his arrival. Che and Camilo were to keep other rebel forces out of the triumphant celebrations. Castro did not want any members of the Student Directorate or the Cuban Communist Party (among others) to be part of the glorious roll into Havana. Although Che had grown closer to the groups and they played a tangible role in Cuba's liberation, they were to be excluded. It would seem as though Castro had his moment, and it would be his revolution alone.

Che spent much of that week talking to the press, a new experience for him. Many of the comments he made at the time were watered-down versions of his beliefs: "To label 'Communists' all those who refuse to bow down is an old dictator's trick; the 26th of July movement is a democratic movement." Clearly he did not speak with his trademark intensity and instead appeared halting and unsure of himself. Perhaps this was the case. Given all that was going on, it is very possible Che was unclear exactly where he stood in this "new" Cuba. The press also spoke with Aleida March, the woman who had been by Che's side these last few weeks. In one of the few interviews she ever agreed to, March simply stated her dedication to the revolution and said nothing about her growing personal attachment to Che.

There has been much discussion about Castro's decision to send Che to La Cabaña rather than Columbia. Columbia was the capital's military headquarters, La Cabaña simply an extension, secondary in nature. After Che's triumph in Santa Clara and his spectacular prize of an armored train, the assignment almost sounded like a demotion. Chances are, however, that Castro knew exactly what he was doing. Already showing an extraordinary ability to manipulate those around him, Castro's move was undoubtedly politically pragmatic. Perhaps it was because Che was not Cuban-born—his Argentine roots not perfectly suited to the occasion. Or maybe Castro wanted Che out of the limelight at that crucial moment because of his political leanings. After all, Che had already jeopardized the cause before, his outspoken views casting a decidedly "red" pall over the revolution. Castro's politics and communist leanings were still murky, but there was no mistaking Che's loyalty. Camilo, on the other hand, while a strong leader and indispensable to the revolution, was more like Castro. The differences between Castro and Che were always pointed: In essence, Castro was a politician, willing and able to bend (and sometimes completely reverse) his political position to fit the situation, while Che was a dogmatic believer, rarely willing to compromise his dedication for any reason, even political expediency.

Out of the Spotlight

As the world turned its spotlight on Cuba, and more specifically, Castro, the intense and brooding young Argentine man who had done so much to secure the revolution's success was in the shadows, though not totally in the dark. For example, when Castro finally rolled into Havana on January 8, 1959, to adoring ecstatic crowds, Che (having left Havana the night before to meet up with Castro) was in the tank with him. But as the celebrations reached a fever pitch, culminating in a massive rally at Camp Columbia, Che had faded from the foreground. It was as if Castro did not want Che beside him but did not want to hide him either. Perhaps he knew that either move would only draw attention to Guevara.

Whatever the reason for the sidelining, it was most likely that Che understood and accepted the move. After all, Che was not in this for power or recognition, even though he did have an agenda. So it was Raúl Castro and Camilio, both Cuban and outwardly revolutionary, not Che, Argentine and communist, standing at Castro's side when a dove landed on Fidel's shoulder as he addressed a crowd at the Columbia army base: "How am I doing, Camilo?" the shaggy-bearded rebel leader asked his compadre. "You're doing just fine, Fidel," was the response. The incident became legendary, as if nature herself had anointed Castro's revolution.

Although one would never have known it by the attention and celebration surrounding Castro, he was not the official leader of the "new" Cuba. After taking Santiago, Castro appointed Manuel Urrutia, a Cuban moderate sympathetic to the rebels' cause, as the new president. Castro became commander in chief of the armed forces but remained firmly entrenched in his position in Cuba. Continuing the stance he had taken during the war, Castro maintained that the revolution's reform agenda was a moderate one and that he himself had no political aspirations. He maintained that he was merely obeying President Urrutia after obeying the people during the revolution. Even so, the new president only named one person to his cabinet; Castro appointed the rest. While Urrutia was the president, Castro remained the leader.

The tenor of the Urrutia-Castro cabinet was overwhelmingly anti-communist and liberal middle class with most members being capitalist-friendly Cuban political veterans. At first it seemed as though conservatives, both in Cuba and around the world, would be satisfied with the new regime. The new government was quickly recognized as legitimate by much of the world, including the United States and the Soviet Union. However, the "honeymoon" would be short-lived. In 1959 a very different Cuba was taking shape—a Cuba shaped in very significant ways by Che Guevara. In this newly reformed Cuba, Castro may have been the face, but in many ways, Che would prove himself to be the force.

Family Reunions

Soon after the triumphant march into Havana, Che was reunited with his family. Having flown in from Buenos Aires, Che's mother, father, sister, and one of his brothers were overjoyed at the sight of their Ernesto. It had been six years and a lifetime since they had been together. His experiences since leaving home had understandably changed Che, making him harder and tougher. When asked by his father about his future, Che declared that he was done with medicine: "Now I am a fighter who is working in the consolidation of a government. What will become of me? I don't even know in which land I will leave my bones." Despite the changes in their son and brother, Che's family felt a connection with the boy they had seen grow up in Argentina and did their best to accept his new standing as a guerrilla hero.

Two weeks later, Gedea and Hildita arrived from Peru. It was an uncomfortable situation for Che; Gedea's presence was a source of friction as she and Aleida took an immediate, intense, and understandable dislike for one another. Later that year Gedea and Che agreed to divorce, opening the door for him to marry Aleida in June 1959. Tenseness aside, Gedea stayed on in Cuba, and Che attempted to forge a relationship with the little girl he had left behind two years earlier. As his role in the Cuban government grew, she would often spend days with him, playing in his office while he worked.

The Arm of Justice

In stark contrast to the joyfulness of his familial reunions, Che's task while occupying La Cabaña was dismal and dark. The rounding up of war criminals was well underway, and Che was in charge of purging the defeated army. He had always felt that the situation in Guatemala had been fatally compromised by the failure to do just that: It was a mistake to which he was committed not to repeat. Those accused had trials, with Che having final say, and his sentences were invariably swift and often merciless. If found guilty of extreme torture and killing, the offending party received the same: death. In a period of approximately one hundred days, there were an estimated fifty-five executions at La Cabaña. Over the following months, executions of war criminals in Cuba are estimated to have topped five hundred fifty. Che was instrumental in many of these, not enjoying them in a visceral sense, but always accepting the necessity of the sentences. Che had been prepared to die for his cause and expected the same of other soldiers, rebels, and Cuban military alike. It was an extension of the life he had learned to live while in the Sierra Maestra. Che saw little, if any, difference between being a guerrilla and being a civilian: The same rules of loyalty and justice applied.

While most of these cases were given a full trial, there were occasions of savagery. Most infamously, Raúl Castro once mowed down seventy soldiers with a machine gun, their bodies tumbling on top of one another as they fell into a freshly dug trench. Apparently the action was emblematic of the violent and ruthless Raúl. It seemed that behind Castro there were some truly frightening men indeed.

Still, the execution of Batista's men received initial support. Batista's innumerable atrocities had been given plenty of play in the Cuban media, while Castro and his men were treated as conquering heroes. With each new exposure of a hidden grave filled with the bodies of those tortured, raped, and executed by Batista forces, the more loudly the Cuban people seemed to call for justice. Castro compared the Batista trials to those held famously in Nuremberg and his public overwhelmingly agreed. As one Cuban newspaper, *Revolución*, wrote at the time, Castro's trials were the deserved response to "barbarians who had gouged out eyes, castrated, burned flesh or ripped off testicles and fingernails, shoved iron into women's vaginas, burned feet, cut off fingers—whose actions, in short, made for a frightening picture." Any independent move toward retribution was forbidden, however, with Che himself vowing to put anyone taking justice into his own hands on trial as well.

Outside Cuba, however, worries intensified about the legitimacy of these trials. There was rising international concern that the proceedings were not being fairly conducted, and an attempt was made to show the world what was really going on. Still wanting to placate the world at large, Castro decided to hold an especially high-profile case (several top officials of Batista's forces stood accused of extreme cases of murder and torture) in Havana's sports stadium. The move backfired with the undeniably Roman Gladiator–feel of the event. The masses in attendance screamed long, loud, and lustily for blood, and the carnal image was a blow to Castro's carefully orchestrated moderate image. The resulting criticism from the United States brought an incredulous response from Castro: Where were these calls of outrage when Batista's men carried out their crimes? Where was decency when Hiroshima was bombed? How dare they use the word "bloodbath" in connection with the Cuban tribunals when the United States had allowed and even committed the slaughter of innumerable innocent (rather than guilty like Batista's men) people themselves?

Che Calls for Change

Castro's countercriticism did little to smooth Cuban relations with the United States. The United States was already wary of the charismatic and opportunistic Castro and his band of rebels and did not take kindly to his retorts, no matter how logical. Castro also took the opportunity to ratchet up the tension surrounding the others in his regime, alluding to those "more radical" than him waiting in the wings. They would continue the revolution if something were to happen to Castro. It was, in effect, an insurance policy for Castro; Che and others had already been fingered as communist in U.S. intelligence reports regarding Cuba. Castro was betting that the fear of the unknown would play in his favor and deter any plans to eliminate him as the leader-in-effect of Cuba.

Becoming once again truer to his nature, Che became vocal about his vision for the reform to follow the revolution. Near the end of January, in a speech called "Social Projections of the Rebel Army" at a Cuban Communist Party–sponsored event, Che delivered his personal agenda. Having accomplished an "armed democracy," Che stressed that much more needed to be done: Revolutionary agrarian reform, the creation of a strong domestic economy, intense industrialization, radically reduced (if not eliminated) dependence and contact with the United States, and the elimination of the remnants of Batista's army were just a few of the viewpoints he openly shared.

It was also in this speech that Che held up Cuba as an example for other Latin American countries, stressing that the Cuban Revolution could be just the beginning: "There is another [lesson] for our brothers of America who are situated in the same agrarian category as us, and that is to make agrarian revolutions, to fight in the fields, in the mountains, and from there to the cities." Che's words of revolution-for-all were the truest expression of how he felt, the sum of his experience and vision. Unlike Castro, who continued to disavow any communist ties, Che could not or would not sugarcoat his ideas for anyone, not even the United States.

In early February the new government ratified the new Cuban constitution, a document with a special "Che-clause": Any foreigner who fought against Batista for two years or more and held the rank of comandante for a year would now be classified a Cuban citizen. Che was now official. Che used the attention his new citizenship garnered to once again publicly push for radical agrarian reform: "Today, we are set on going to the big landholdings, even on attacking and destroying them ... The rebel army is ready to carry the agrarian reform through to is final consequence." In addition, Che remained dedicated to educating both his troops and the Cuban people, setting up classes and recreation programs that operated directly out of the La Cabaña base. Che knew the future of the revolution rested with the younger generation and held many meetings with children in which revolution and the conflict in the Sierra Maestra were openly discussed. The children also learned how to properly care for guns.

In addition to Che now being an official citizen, a new law was soon passed that lowered the minimum age for holding public office from thirty-five to thirty. Castro and Che, thirty-two and thirty respectively, could now hold such offices. On February 16, 1959, Fidel Castro became the prime minister of Cuba. Granted the power to direct governmental policy by President Urrutia, Castro was more powerful than ever.

An especially severe and prolonged case of asthma brought on a bout with emphysema for Che and, in early March, he and Adelia moved to Tarará, a town by the sea, not far from Havana. The house they moved into had belonged to a high-profile Batista supporter, and Che thought it was much too luxurious. He even felt the need to defend his new lodging in an open letter published in *Revolución:* "I must clarify to the readers of *Revolución* that I am ill, that I did not contract my sickness in gambling dens or staying up all night in cabarets, but working more than my body could withstand for the revolution." Che's pride had been stung by criticism over his move, writing, "The fact that is the home of an old *batístiano* means that it is luxurious; I chose the simplest, but at any rate it is still an insult to popular sentiments." In two months' time, Che did leave Tarará and took up residence in a home on the outskirts of Havana that was much more in line with his "revolutionary posture."

There has been much speculation about the psychological aspects of Che's asthma attacks. A correlation has been made by many between traumatic events in Che's life and his most severe bouts of asthma. If this were true, now would have been one of those times; the revolution was over, and the serious work had only just begun. Adding to the pressure was the presence of his family from Buenos Aires (they returned to Argentina in the middle of February), not to mention a soon-to-be wife and ex-wife, along with a three-year-old daughter he was just now becoming reacquainted with. Spending his days with Hildita and other family members and using his nights to decide the life-or-death fate of hundreds of war criminals must have been strange. It makes sense that his health may have suffered for it.

Still, he was able to keep a sense of humor about himself and his health. Once diagnosed with emphysema, Che had been ordered by his doctors to severely curtail his cigar-smoking (he had become a heavy smoker while in the Sierra Maestra), allowing him to have only one cigar a day. In a famous anecdote, Che's secretary apparently walked in to find him puffing on a specially made Cuban cigar about a foot-and-a-half long. Che simply chuckled and said, "Don't worry about the doctors. I'm obeying their orders—just one cigar a day, no more, no less."

A Shadow Government

For Che, the home in Tarará was not just a refuge in times of ill health; it became a headquarters for the formation of a parallel government. It was here that the "real" Cuban reform was debated, constructed, and prepared for application. All aspects of Cuban life were examined—social, economic, and political—but the main focus was the agrarian reform and the newly formed agency that would put it into action—the Instituto Nacional de Reforma Agraria (INRA). The group was to have far-reaching power in the Cuban government; health care, housing, industrialization efforts, and education of and for the rural areas all fell under its jurisdiction. Che and his group of advisors (left-leaning members of the 26th of July movement, rebel soldiers from Castro's army, and members of the Cuban Communist Party) would work on proposals and plans for the reform while Castro would add his input—and sometimes complete revamping—later. None of the ministers in the "official" government were invited; in fact, none of them knew about the group's existence. Also at this time the rebel army and the Cuban Communist Party were holding talks, working out a plan of unity. Clearly the revolution was not over. It was just beginning.

Che also continued to lead the training of the army. Even though the revolution was over, the army was considered just as vital to the regime, and for good reason. Castro knew they would be his only dependable line of defense when the all-but-inevitable counterrevolutions came. As before, members were not only taught combat or politics, but culture and technology as well. At this time Che also channeled his experiences in the revolution onto the page, starting what would become his first book, *Guerrilla Warfare*. Members of the Cuban Communist Party assisted Che, and U.S. intelligence duly noted the training as further evidence that Cuban leaders, especially Che Guevara, were firmly entrenched in communist ways.

Che also found time to devote to another of his passions: journalism. He was an important figure in both the independent news agency, Prensa Latina (Latin Press), and the magazine, *Verde Olivo* (*Olive Drab*). Latin American journalists who had spent time in the Sierra Maestra ran Prensa Latina, and *Verde Olivo* served as the rebel army's official magazine. Che took an active role in both projects, often attending staff meetings and helping in the operations. The publication of *Verde Olivo* only heightened already existing tensions between Che's brand of revolutionaries and the more conservative factions that existed in Cuba, earning the magazine a nickname: "Olive Red."

In April Castro went to the United States and addressed a forum of American Newspaper Editors. He had had good luck with U.S. journalists in the past and wanted to dispel any negative feelings about his revolution. A Cuban revolutionary press was also established in Havana as a platform for pro-Cuba propaganda distribution.

While in the United States, Castro was in fine form: encouraging American tourism, denying any communist ties, supporting foreign investment in Cuba, reassuring fears about the agrarian reform law, and expressing hope that the United States would buy even more sugar, Cuba's largest crop and main source of income. As usual, Castro may have not convinced everyone, but most could not help but be impressed—the man was charismatic to a fault. With his olive-green uniform, distinctive beard, and trademark cigar, Castro certainly looked different than your average politician, even if sometimes he acted like one.

The United States was not the only world power taking special note of Castro's Cuba: The Soviet Union was also well aware of the developments. Exactly when the Soviet Union became directly involved with the Cuban Revolution remains a muddled question, but Moscow's fast recognition of the new regime and the growing question of communist influence in the region seems to reflect that the Soviets were, at the very least, closely monitoring the situation for quite some time. To have a communist presence in the Western Hemisphere would have been quite a coup, even if the rebels' methods did not always conform to party doctrine.

Armed revolutionary conflicts took place elsewhere in areas around Cuba in 1959 with attempted coups in Panama, Nicaragua, the Dominican Republic, and Haiti. Worried about negative repercussions, even Che issued a denial. He went on television to deliver a statement that the government of Cuba did not sanction these attempts and that Cuba did not export revolution, only revolutionary ideas. Nonetheless, Che was reportedly involved, with all four teams apparently receiving training, direction, and arms from Cuba.

Despite Castro's attempts to woo the United States (including ultimately putting a halt to the tribunals that had resulted in executions), growing concerns over the impending agrarian reform and these suspected Cuban-assisted attempts at revolution only heightened tension between Castro and the United States. In addition, upper- and middle-class Cubans were becoming nervous about the radicalization and leftward swing of the government; many of them left Cuba, most going less than a hundred miles away to Miami.

When Castro returned to Havana in early May, the agrarian reform bill was signed into law, and the INRA was up and running. The bill called for the expropriation of major sugar and rice plantations, with compensation not in cash but long-term bonds. The United States quickly denounced the bill, warning Cuba that any American landowners involved in the expropriation process should be paid quickly, and cattle ranchers in the Camaguey region of Cuba were also incensed by the plan that benefited the peasants. In the uproar that followed the signing of the bill, President Urrutia resigned (replaced by Osvaldo Dorticós, an equally benign choice), and moderate politicians were forced from office, only to be replaced by people more in tune with Castro's ever left-leaning regime.

Che once again publicly declared his hope that Cuba serve as a revolutionary beacon to the rest of the world, specifically Latin America. In an article published in June by the Brazilian magazine, *O Cruzerio*, he wrote:

> *We are now placed in a position in which we are much more than just factors of one nation; we are now the hope of unredeemed Latin America. All eyes, those of the great oppressors and of the hopeful oppressed, are now turned our way. The development of popular movements in Latin America will depend to a great extent on the future attitude we display, on our ability to solve manifold problems, and each step we take will be watched over by the ever-present eyes of the great creditor and of our optimistic Latin American brothers.*

Che knew that Cuba was standing at a crossroads and desperately wanted the decisions made about the island's future to be in agreement with the intent of the revolution.

Counterrevolution

As 1959 wore on, the tension about Castro and his new regime continued to rise, not only from sources outside Cuba, but from within the 26th of July movement itself. A military commander by the name of Huber Matos soon gained attention as a figurehead within the 26th of July movement's more moderate wing who opposed Castro's communist bent. Matos publicly complained about the communist influence within the armed forces and the INRA. He was hardly alone, as the factions within the organization grew more and more divided.

Counterrevolution quickly became a buzzword for Castro, and he ensured that it was a "crime" that could be punishable by death. Of course the definition of "counterrevolution" was open to interpretation, but it was only Castro's interpretation that mattered in the end. Threats continued to thrive as an attempt to reclaim Cuba by the "Anti-Communist League of the Caribbean" was launched from the Dominican Republic and an assassination plot against Castro was revealed in Havana. In addition, a sugar plantation had been bombed and a small band of counterrevolutionary rebels rounded up.

The conflict between Castro and Matos finally came to a head in September, with Matos demanding a meeting of the National Directorate to address the communist influence in the movement. Matos, aligned with the upset ranchers in the Camaguey area, had real influence, and his protestations carried considerable weight. Nothing came of the meeting, and Matos sent Castro his resignation in October, accusing Fidel of killing the revolution. Along with Matos, a handful of his officers followed suit. Castro, accusing Matos of treason and betrayal, clamped down hard and, by December, Matos had been arrested, tried, and sentenced to twenty-plus years in prison while many of his men suffered similar fates—all for the crimes of conspiracy and "counterrevolution."

Another thorn in Castro's side was Pedro Díaz Lanz, Cuba's air force chief. After defecting and leaving the island, Díaz Lanz appeared in front of a Senate committee in Washington to bemoan the influence of communists in Cuba's armed forces. Díaz Lanz appeared again to irritate Castro in October, this time in the skies. Piloting a B-26 bomber, Díaz Lanz flew over the heads of more than two thousand travel agents gathered in Havana (they were there as part of a convention to promote tourism to Cuba from the United States). Pamphlets urging Castro to eliminate the communists from his group were dropped from the plane and into the midst of the travel agents. Díaz Lanz managed to elude the Cuban air force planes and anti-aircraft efforts from the ground and returned safely to the United States. Castro quickly called the stunt a "bombing attack" and claimed lives had been lost. Díaz Lanz admitted to his flyover but insisted he dropped nothing but paper. Whatever the truth was, the incident gave Castro even more fodder for his determination to squelch counterrevolution wherever it reared its head.

Near the end of the year Castro also stepped up pressure on the media in Cuba with charges of "counterrevolution" flying fast and furious if they printed or reported something opposing Castro's will. Eventually the regime shut down any offending Cuban news agency that did not toe the revolutionary line. As Castro swung to the left, the price to pay for dissention became a high one.

On the Road Again

In June Castro sent the newly married Che on what the government called a goodwill tour. The idea of the trek was to strengthen diplomatic and commercial relations between Cuba and areas of the Middle East, India, and Japan. There were rumors at the time that Castro was actually expelling Che, the communist influence, from the government. Che's men were especially suspicious, fearing this was a demotion for Che—or worse. Of course these rumors could also have been plants to give that exact impression. With Castro one never knew what was really going on. Although Che and Castro were undeniably close, their continual differing rhetoric and the pressure on Castro to contain any communist influence (from both inside and outside Cuba) must have been a source of unease for Che. He had seen how Castro could turn on those he relied on the most. Would it be any different for Che? Had he outlived his usefulness?

Whatever the intentions, Che followed Castro's command (leaving Aleida behind). He was gone for three months and visited fourteen countries, touring exotic areas and doing his best to shore up support for Cuba in as many areas as possible. The most vital destinations included Egypt, India, Yugoslavia, and Indonesia. Japan, a heavy sugar importer, was also highly prized. While on his sojourn, Che also made covert contact with Soviet representatives about sugar sales. Although the Soviet Union had bought from Cuba before, in the political climate at that time, it was not advisable for the Cubans, especially Che Guevara, to advertise any contact with the Soviets.

Along with Che was a small group including a sugar expert, a bodyguard, a reporter, and a member of Cuba's National Agricultural Development Bank. With the reform bill about to be announced, it was important to find new markets for Cuba's exports. In fact, soon after Che's team departed, Castro let it be known that Cuba was looking to expand its main customer base, no longer wanting to rely so heavily on the United States.

Che thought it was important to not isolate the revolution and took the trip seriously. For someone who loved to travel as much as he did, the trek also offered a chance to reconnect him with his love of the road. Crowds greeted him warmly, heads of state welcomed and respected him, and important inroads of diplomatic and trade relations were forged. The mission was a success.

Still, his view from planes and official caravans was very different from the one he had from the back of a broken-down motorcycle. In a letter to his mother, Che wrote, "My dream of visiting all these countries has come true in such a way as to thwart all my happiness." He goes on to complain that all he does is, "talk of economic and political problems," and "throw parties where the only thing lacking for me to do is put on a penguin suit." Left with precious little time for sightseeing, Che writes, "I forsake untainted pleasures like dreaming in the shade of a pyramid or over the tomb of Tutankhamun." Clearly he would have preferred to be an anonymous visitor to these great lands, scampering over landmarks and writing poetry inspired by their beauty. But instead, this traveling Che was a diplomat with official business to attend to.

In light of his experience, Che had a personal revelation: "A sense of the big picture as opposed to the personal has been developing in me. I am still the same solitary person who continues to seek his path without any help, but now I have a sense of my historical duty." Even with all that had happened to him, all the revolutionary change he played a part in, Che still felt alone but purposeful.

Che goes on to write more about the direction his life had taken and where he expected it to end: "I feel not just a powerful inner strength, which I've always felt, but as though I'm doing something in life; I feel that I have a capacity to give something to others and an entirely fatalistic sense of my mission, which makes me quite fearless." His assessment of himself is telling: It would seem that this sense of fatalism, knowing that he would never make it out alive, is what Che believed gave him the drive to keep fighting in the face of seemingly insurmountable odds and fueled his revolutionary fervor.

In closing this powerful letter, Che grows a bit dismissive ("I don't know why I'm writing all this; maybe I just miss Aleida"), but it is too late; he had already opened his soul and allowed his mother to peer inside. In the end, his impressions were right: Che's "historical duty" and need to move would get the better of him, but not yet.

Back in Cuba

In early September, Che returned to Havana. Things had changed quickly in Cuba with Castro's cabinet reshufflings occurring during his absence. Back on staff at the INRA, Che ran the Department of Industries with his wife as his assistant. The post had expanded, and Che was now responsible for many of the sugar mills seized under the agrarian reform act. Che's experience with societal industrialization while in the jungles of the Sierra Maestra and his dedication to the military made him an obvious choice for the job. In addition to the INRA position, Che kept his military rank and duties. The dream was for a Cuban society in which everyone was a soldier, and Che was a perfect example. Despite attempts to keep Che's involvement with Cuba's most valuable economic asset under wraps, the United States knew of Che's rising prominence.

Che also became even more involved with education. He began a series of speeches and debates at Cuba's three main universities that served as forums about the gap between the revolution and Cuba's institutes of higher learning. He often urged the students and faculty to join in the revolution, even at the risk of losing their autonomy: "Why can't the university march ... on the same road as the revolutionary government and in step with it?" He stressed a need for students to pursue useful vocations that would benefit the revolution as a whole and not simply their own desires. He used himself as an example and cited how he had gone from studying to engineering to medicine to military strategy and, ultimately, economics. These calls for solidarity were harbingers of official changes yet to come for the schools.

Eventually, self-direction by the educational institutions was ended; the state took on the task of study planning. To fulfill the goal of mass industrialization, Cuba needed people trained in agriculture, science, and technology, and Cuba told the students what they would study. In defending the decision, Che bluntly acknowledged that it was "dictatorship" but that the students should join the legions of those who take action and not just talk.

Before the radical changes, Che was awarded an honorary teaching degree from the University at Las Villas, which he accepted with humility ("all the teaching I've done has been in guerrilla camps ... setting a tough example"). In addition, he became a student himself, taking a series of advanced math classes in order to better perform his official duties.

At this time, a Soviet agent, Alejandro Alexiev, came to Cuba under the guise of a journalist. After contacting the Cuban Communist Party, a meeting with Che was arranged through a third party. During their late-night discussion (Che was famous for being in the office far into the night), the two spoke openly about Che's personal desires for Cuba to form a real relationship with the Soviets. As always, Che was very open about his respect and admiration for the Soviet Union, but when asked what Castro thought, Che only stressed that the opinions he was expressing were his own. Alexiev pursued the matter and secured a meeting with Castro himself in hopes of seeing where he stood in relation to Che. During the meeting, Castro appeared open to the idea of cultural, commercial, and domestic relations between Cuba and the Soviet Union but warned that they must go slowly, so as not to alarm the Cuban people. Once again Castro may have been straddling the fence. Although Castro did not commit to the word "socialism," Alexiev nonetheless felt that he and Che were of like minds. The most tangible result of the meeting came with an agreement that a Soviet industrial exhibit would come to Havana and be officiated by the Soviet Deputy Prime Minister Anastas Mikoyan in February 1960. It was but the first step toward an official Cuban–Soviet relationship.

Near the end of October, Camilo Cienfuegos (the rebel who stood by Castro's side during the revolutionary celebration) disappeared without a trace. He had been flying from Camaguey to

Havana when his plane just vanished. There were no obvious reasons for a crash (the weather was clear, the pilot seasoned), and no wreckage was ever found. Rumors quickly sprang up about Camilo's fate, one of the most resilient ones being that Castro had the likeable rebel killed out of suspicion or jealousy. Like most rumors, there is little evidence to back the claim up, but perhaps more important, the duplicitous nature of Castro seemed more and more apparent. After all, the rumor would most likely have not taken hold if Castro's character had not suggested that it could be true.

Che had his own ideas about what happened to Cienfuegos, certain he had been killed: "The enemy killed him, and they killed him because they wanted him dead ... his character killed him, too. Camilo had no respect for danger; he had fun with it, played with it. It attracted him and he handled it. To his guerrilla-like mind, a cloud could not stop or twist a charted course." A month after Cienfuegos's disappearance, Che enacted a day of voluntary labor to help build an educational complex to be named after his fallen rebel brother.

Che the Banker

How Che got the job as director of Cuba's National Bank has become a joke: The legend goes that Castro asked a group of his assembled cohorts who was an economist. Che raised his hand, only realizing later that Castro said "economist" not "communist." Whether that is true or not, his appointment was not funny to the business community: A communist running the bank? It was not funny at all, and the appointment was serious. Che was in charge of fiscal policy, foreign fund reserves, and economic strategy. Che, unfamiliar with the banking world, quickly threw himself into the position, stepping up his study of economic theory and advanced mathematics. According to legend, even Che's father had something to say about Che's appointment: "My son Ernesto handling funds for the Republic of Cuba? Fidel's crazy. Every time a Guevara starts a business, it goes bust."

On Che's part, he would later describe the appointment as simply necessary, not because of his prowess, but because the revolution demanded it: "economic programs and the drive toward rapid advancement of the revolution were being strangled ... [I] knew nothing about banking but operated according to the revolutionary government's guidelines." In his new position, Che was more powerful than ever—but probably not happier. He would admit years later that he never really liked running the bank, preferring the industrial management he did with the INRA.

The move was just the latest in a string of cabinet changes that demonstrated that Castro was firmly in control of Cuba. As Jorge G. Castaneda wrote in *Compañero: The Life and Death of Che Guevara:* "The moment was also ripe for Fidel to send a message to the United States and the Cuban oligarchy about who was running the country, and how." In addition, Fidel's brother, Raúl (already notorious for his cruelty), had been appointed defense minister. As 1959 drew to a close, the Cuban regime was sporting a very different look than had been promised.

Chapter 7

Growing Tensions and Emerging Ties

... [O]ur road to liberation will be opened up with a victory over the monopolies, and concretely over the U.S. monopolies.

—Che Guevara

With Che now the director of Cuba's National Bank, 1960 brought even more tension to the island's relations with the United States. Things quickly went from bad to worse as Cuba's socialization became more and more radical. The United States was upset over the noncompensation for the appropriation of American-owned land during the agrarian reform, and in January Castro responded by expanding the reform's reach. Cuba expropriated virtually all the large ranches and sugar plantations in Cuba, including those owned by Americans. Further complicating matters, the CIA was facilitating bombing raids by unidentified airplanes from the United States and was preparing a group of Cuban exiles to launch a counterrevolution against Castro.

Meanwhile, Che was making major changes within Cuba's National Bank, many of which were designed to control foreign currency reserves. Soon after taking office, he put into effect a series of controls regarding import licenses, foreign currency transactions, the import/export of currency, and the purchasing of dollars by tourists and others from abroad.

Che's style and reputation gave many in the Cuban banking community pause. One famous anecdote has a worried executive telling others that, "the chairman's waiting room is filled of long-haired people with guns." Of course, these "longhaired people with guns" were some of the rebels that had been so faithful to Che during the revolution. He was determined to keep himself surrounded by people he felt he could trust.

Che also sent ripples of concern through the banking industry when his signature began appearing on the currency. Much like the secretary of treasury in the United States, it was customary for the director of Cuba's National Bank to have his signature printed on each bill. But what was unique about Guevara was the manner in which his appeared: It simply read "Che." For many this lack of formality was a sign that the economy, banking industry, and money in general were far from the most important priority to the new Cuban government. They were right. As Che himself put it, "I'm still more of a guerrilla than a bank chairman."

In addition to his banking duties, Che continued a steady stream of writing. The first of several articles about his experience during the Cuban Revolution (eventually published collectively as *Episodes of the Cuban Revolutionary War*) had been appearing in various magazines. Plus, Che had written an article (published in *Humanismo*) titled "America from the Afro-Asian Balcony," that underlined his commitment to radical change and the worldwide spread of revolution. Cuba had been invited to attend the Afro-Asian People's Conference, and Che took the opportunity to share his dream of an international alliance to destroy imperialism:

> *Cuba is not an isolated event, merely the first signal of*
> *America's awakening ... I am one brother more, one*
> *more among the multitudes of brothers in this part of the*
> *world that awaits with infinite anxiety the moment [that*
> *will allow us to] consolidate the bloc that will destroy,*
> *once and for all, the anachronistic presence of colonial*
> *domination.*

Che's new position at the National Bank gave his fiery words even more bite as Cuba's intentions became clearer to the world. Now Che had an opportunity to project himself and his vision of Cuba onto a global stage and he seized the moment.

In 1960 the tiny island ninety miles off the coast of Florida was getting more and more attention in the United States, especially because it was an election year. Vice President Nixon made Castro and Cuba one of his campaign issues, warning that if Castro did not behave, Cuba would lose its biggest sugar consumer. On the other hand, Democratic candidate John F. Kennedy came to accuse the Eisenhower administration of doing nothing about Cuba and vowed to restore democracy to the nation. As the year went on, Nixon and Kennedy broached the topic of Cuba often, each promising to be tougher on Castro than the other. Eventually it would be up to Kennedy to go up against Castro and his supporters. His efforts would meet with varying degrees of success.

Despite halting attempts to end the squabbling, Cuba and the United States' crash course to confrontation was intensified by the arrival of the Soviet Trade Fair in Cuba in which more than one hundred thousand Cubans marveled at the examples of Soviet technology and industry. Soviet Deputy Premier Anastas Mikoyan accompanied the Trade Fair, continuing to strengthen the growing bond between Cuba and the USSR. Mikoyan's son, Sergo, was also along for the trip.

Meanwhile American-supported planes continued to bomb Cuban sugar plantations. Although Cuban opposition to Soviet and communist ties was still strong (protests were mounted outside the Trade Fair), on the surface, the USSR must have seemed the far more benevolent of the two superpowers to the Cubans. After all, it was not bombing Cuba's fields in night raids; the USSR was showing Cuba how advanced its society was under communism. In retrospect, it all fit quite snugly into Castro's spin that the United States was pushing Cuba toward the Soviet Union with its aggressive and imperialistic actions.

In light of the Soviet Trade Fair's relative success, Cuba came clean about trade relations with the Soviet Union: Over the next five years, the Soviet Union would buy four and a half million tons of sugar from Cuba, but for the first four years they would not pay them in cash. Instead, Cubans would receive goods and products from the Soviets, especially oil. Cuba also received a hefty loan from the Soviets: a one-hundred-million-dollar line of credit at the staggeringly low interest rate of two and a half percent. Cuba would use the funds to industrialize the nation, an integral part of Che's vision. Buildings, machinery, and factories were but a few of the tools Cuba now hoped to obtain as the reform efforts continued. Poland, East Germany, China, and Czechoslovakia also solidified trade agreements with Cuba. This expansion of relations was yet another step toward the fulfillment of Che's dreams for Cuban reformation.

The growing closeness of Cuba and the Soviet Union must have seemed inevitable to many in the United States government who had long suspected Castro of communist ties. However, as before, many of Castro's decisions would be spun by Cuba as reactions to United States policy, not as an overt attempt to turn Cuba into a communist nation. Che's influence and Castro's continual shift toward socialism cannot be ignored, however, and it seems highly unlikely that Cuba was forced to turn to the Soviet Union because of the United States alone. In fact, according to Jon Anderson Lee (*Che Guevara: A Revolutionary Life*), Sergo Mikoyan (the son of the Soviet deputy premier who visited Cuba at the time of the Soviet Trade Fair) remembers hearing a conversation between his father, Castro, and Che:

> "It was a very strange chat," said Sergo Mikoyan. "They told [my father] that they could survive only with Soviet help, and they would have to hide the fact from the capitalists in Cuba ... [Then] Fidel said, 'We will have to withstand these conditions in Cuba for five or ten more years,' at which Che interrupted and told him: 'If you don't do it within two or three years, you're finished.'
> There was this difference [of conception] between them."

It seems clear that Cuba was moving in a direction that was not being accurately represented to its own people or the rest of the world.

Arms deals soon followed from Cuba's growing trade relations with other nations. Castro secured some weapons from Belgium and Italy, but the United States refused and other countries followed suit. The issue of arms in Cuba soon took a dangerous turn and forever altered the state of Cuban–U.S. relations.

An Icon Is Born

In early March 1960 a French freighter, *La Coubre*, exploded in a Havana harbor. More than one hundred people were killed and hundreds more hurt. The freighter had arrived with weapons from Belgium, and Castro quickly assigned blame for the deadly blast to the CIA. Whether or not the tragedy was by chance or design is apparently unknown, but the memorial that followed firmly solidified Che as the face of rebellion. Photographer Alberto "Korda" Diez was in Havana for the memorial service for the victims, in which Castro and other revolutionaries took the podium and poured their outrage into the world. While Castro fumed and ranted, Che sat silently behind him, his quiet anger etched deep into his face. Korda caught the moment and the photo eventually became "the" picture of Che, a symbol of rebellion that resonated around the world. The image is, indeed, an indelible one. His steely gaze seems fixed on a distant horizon, his chin defiant and his resolve strong. A black beret with a single gold star rests upon a tangle of thick black hair, and his eyes reflect both anger and pain. It is an amazing photo, and one that would later appear on T-shirts, posters, and propaganda material all over the world. Some would see righteous anger while others saw cold calculation, but it seemed everyone saw something burning deep within the Argentine rebel who had given so much for Cuba and the socialist cause.

More than thirty years later the Korda photograph would be at the heart of a bitter lawsuit between the photographer and a London advertising agency. The picture of Che had become so ubiquitous that it was often being used without Korda's permission or approval. The situation came to an end after the image turned up in an ad for Smirnoff vodka. Billboards were erected in the United Kingdom that touted Smirnoff's new spicy vodka. The image of Che was used along with the Soviet symbol of a hammer and sickle, except that the sickle was replaced by a chili pepper. Korda was incensed, saying that he was not against the use of the photo by those who wished to celebrate Che and use the photo in the pursuit of social justice, but to use it in this manner "or for any purpose that denigrates the reputation of Che" was unacceptable. Korda sued the ad agency over the use of the photo after his ownership of the image was proven in a London high court.

In many ways the use of the image was the ultimate slap in the face to Che's memory. Here was a picture capturing the very essence of Che and his righteous anger at the continued aggression against Latin America being used to sell vodka. The tragic irony here was that Che, thirty years after his death, was suddenly a pitchman against his wishes. It is hard to imagine anything more distasteful to Che, a man who fought so hard against materialism and corporate greed. To be used in such a manner not only demeaned Che has a man, it trivialized his entire life, reducing him to a cartoon.

In September 2000 Korda's lawsuit against the ad agency was settled out of court for an undisclosed sum. Korda was vindicated, but the result has been a clampdown on the photo, making the rights to it difficult to obtain. Nonetheless, it remains the most famous image of Che and one that seems to capture his very essence.

The explosion of the boat in Havana's harbor only fueled Castro's desire to secure more weapons, and he soon turned again to the Soviet Union. The explosion seemed to be the harbinger of more violence to come, and a desire rose to arm the people and to turn all of Cuba into a rebel army. Che fueled this call to arms in a televised speech called "Political Sovereignty and Economic Independence." While not expressly calling for arms, Che spoke of how, "In order to conquer something we have to take it away from somebody ...." Although he was speaking about reclaiming the economy, his words, as always, carried the ringing of armed revolution.

Castro's anger over the explosion led to the first step toward a global nuclear showdown. He contacted Alejandro Alexiev (the Soviet agent already in Cuba) and, for the first time, apparently spoke openly about receiving arms from the Soviet Union. According to Alexiev, Castro asked him to send a message to Khrushchev, suggesting that the arms could be brought in by submarines and hidden in caves off the coast of Cuba. According to Alexiev, the reply from Khrushchev came the very next day:

> Fidel, we share your worries about the defense of Cuba
> and the possibility of an attack, and we will supply you
> with the arms you need. But why do we have to hide them
> and take them in a submarine if Cuba is a sovereign
> nation and you can buy whatever arms you need without
> hiding the fact?

In early May 1960 diplomatic ties with the Soviet Union were announced, and weapons would soon arrive, albeit covertly at first. Castro was still wary of U.S. pressure and was not yet willing to provoke a conflict. Still, Castro and Che were closer to achieving another aim.

While many upper- and middle-class Cubans poured out of Cuba, others were heading to the region. The revolution was a work-in-progress, and intellectuals, communists, and emerging third-world leaders converged on the island to see it firsthand. There are parallels with the situation in Guatemala, except this time Che was a leader and not just an observer.

Among the interested throng were the French existentialist philosophers and authors Jean-Paul Sartre and companion Simone de Beauvoir. Although not an existentialist himself ("I think one has to constantly think on behalf of the masses and not on behalf of individuals"), Che had studied and admired Sartre while growing up, and he was just one of the many philosophers that shaped his intellectual worldview. Meeting Sartre and having the revolution studied by him must have been almost surreal for Che. After Che's death, Sartre was widely quoted as saying Che was "the most complete human being of our age."

Existentialism

Existentialism is a philosophy emphasizing individual choice and freedom. It was Sartre who gave the term existentialism much of its import when he used it to name his own philosophy. He believed existentialism to be a form of humanism, the emphasizing of humanity and dignity of the individual. Sartre did not find Marxism at inherent odds with existentialism and tried and reconcile his beliefs with a Marxist analysis of society. Sartre came to believe that individual power and freedom could only be obtained by use of group revolutionary action, but he never officially joined the Communist Party himself.

Che's first book, *Guerilla Warfare*, was published in April 1960 and served as a handbook for the type of fighting that had served his men so well in the Sierra Maestra. Outlining the basics of survival, weaponry, and tactical strategy, Che emphasized that popular forces can not only win against an army, they also can spark the revolution by their actions alone. The necessity of containing the initial fighting in the rural areas (specifically in Latin America) was also given importance. The book would become a bible of sorts for like-minded fighters around the world. Che's desire to inspire similar revolutions was now not only a dream, but a tangible manual. An unintended result may have been that several of the counterrevolutions being formed around Cuba now had access to Che's strategies, and the CIA continued to support such movements, using the radio to send anti-Castro propaganda messages into Cuba.

Growing Army, Growing Fears

By May 1960 Cuba's army was estimated to number more than one hundred thousand, including trained citizens. U.S. fears of Soviet-supplied arms were heightened and all but confirmed by a massive military May Day rally held by Castro. Although May Day in the United States is thought of being in honor of the Haymarket Square Riot in Chicago, the day has special resonance in communist countries as well. It marks the first congress of the Second International in 1889, an assembly of socialist and labor parties.

Soon Castro finished off the opposition media in Cuba, taking over selected independent newspaper offices and staffing them with his own loyalists.

May Day

Although May Day celebrations probably stem from the rites practiced in honor of Flora, the Roman goddess of spring, the day has taken on a political resonance. In 1886 May Day was a call for eight-hour workdays by thousands of striking workers in many American cities. Today May Day is mainly associated with events immediately following the strike: the Haymarket Square Riot, a confrontation between police and protesters that took place on May 4, 1886, in Chicago. On May 3, 1886, police shot several men (on strike from the McCormick reaper works in Chicago) during a riot at the plant. A meeting was called at Haymarket Square on May 4 as a protest against police violence. The police attempted to disperse the meeting, and in the ensuing riot a bomb was thrown, which triggered another gun battle. Seven policemen were killed and many injured, as were many civilians. Although the identity of the bomb-thrower was never established, eight protestors attending the meeting were arrested and charged with being accessories to the crime, on the ground that they had publicly and frequently advocated such violence. They were found guilty, and seven of them were sentenced to death and one to imprisonment. The eight became infamous in some circles as the "Haymarket Martyrs." The event continues to serve many as a day to protest and remember the importance of laborer solidarity.

Che, in his position as National Bank director, again stepped up his call for economic independence. Despite advances in agrarian reform and a substantial cut in utility rates and rents, Che bemoaned what he saw as continued American control of much of Cuba's economy in regard to oil, chemical, and mineral interests. His radical agenda had not been tempered by the reforms so far, only strengthened. In fact, it was oil that would soon prove to be a breaking point in U.S.–Cuba relations.

In early April the first oil shipments from the Soviet Union began arriving in Cuba. Che used the shipments as leverage in a move designed to fail. Behind in payments to American-owned oil companies in Cuba (Esso and Texaco), Che made them an offer they *could* refuse: If the companies would buy three hundred thousand barrels of the Soviet oil and process them, only then would he pay the debt. The companies had been using oil from Venezuela and were owed more than fifty million dollars by Cuba for the island's supply. The American government strongly advised the companies not to play ball, and they agreed, just as Che expected. Their refusal paved the way to Cuba nationalizing the refineries, a move that weakened relations with the United States while strengthening ties to the Soviet Union.

In retaliation to Cuba's seizure of the oil plants, the United States quickly halted their acquisition of Cuban sugar. The United States was the world's largest sugar consumer, and its quota was an estimated three million tons every year, making it the island's biggest customer. For years this relationship had ensured that American interests in Cuba were given precedent above all others. By late August, Cuba nationalized the remaining sugar plantations, further angering the United States. Cuba now controlled the oil refineries, sugar plantations, and utility companies such as telephone and electricity. Che had long railed against the sugar-quota system (an agreement over the amount of sugar Cuba was legally allowed to import into the United States) as imperialistic blackmail, and this was just the latest in what seemed to be victories for his plan for Cuba's massive industrialization.

Castro, picking up the U.S.-thrown gauntlet, called the cancellation of the sugar sales an act of "economic aggression" and spoke out about the imminent arrival of weapons for his army, essentially confirming the threat of a Soviet arms deal. Nikita Khrushchev, the Soviet Union's prime minister, spoke up and vowed to purchase the remainder of the United States' sugar quota for the year. He ominously added that, if need be, the Cuban people would be supported by Soviet missile fire. The statement was categorized as a figurative one, and Castro and Che both downplayed its significance. However, the meaning was crystal clear: Cuba now possessed an oil refinery industry and a powerful ally in the Soviet Union.

In addition to running Cuba's economy, writing books, and overseeing much of the army, Che was ushering in a new family. In late 1960 Aleida gave birth to a daughter while Che was out of the country. Alberto Granado also reappeared in Che's life, coming to Cuba to visit his now famous friend and former traveling companion. It must have seemed a lifetime ago that the two had knocked around Latin America on *la poderosa,* wondering where their next meal was coming from. While not as passionate as Che, Granado and his family eventually stayed on in Cuba.

Che: His Own "New Man"

Che continued his passionate defense of the Cuban Revolution and reformation, speaking publicly at numerous conferences, on television, and at various forums. His rhetoric, spurred by the support of the Soviet Union and the increasingly socialist leanings of Castro, became even more radical. In a particularly chilling speech to the First Latin American Youth Congress in late July 1960, Che saw fit to speak of Cuba as a whole, saying that "if they [the Cuban people] should disappear from the face of the earth because an atomic war is unleashed in their names ... they would feel completely happy and fulfilled ...." The threat of atomic annihilation would soon be a very real one—not just for Cuba, but in essence, the world. For Che, the promise of spreading revolution seemed worth the sacrifice of every Cuban, an assessment doubtfully echoed by every one of the people he claimed to represent.

On a similar theme, Che began openly advocating the elimination of the individual in Cuba, formulating an ideology that would become his trademark—the "new man"—a concept that may well be Che's most important contribution to philosophy and political theory. (For more on Che's concept of the "new man," see the essay by Ted Henken in Appendix D, "Che Guevara's 'New Man.'") This "new man" would work solely for society, not for profit. He began to reference the communist and socialist influence in the revolution but insisted it became relevant to their struggle during, rather than before, the revolution. By doing so, Che deemed socialism to be the result, rather than the cause, of the uprising. Che also continued to apply his message to Cuba's universities, using himself again as an example, serving as a witness to the importance of submitting to the will of the revolution. Che's dedication to this concept of a "new man" was also exemplified in his continued participation in the practice of voluntary labor. On Sundays, Cubans were encouraged to pitch in cooperatively to build schools and housing projects. Che was a constant presence at these functions, invariably working harder and longer than the others. Much like his days in the Sierra Maestra, Che never asked for more than he was willing to give.

In the end, Che's faith in others may have been his undoing; socialism works on paper but the human element seems to muck it all up. While Che may have been a "new man," the cold hard truth was that he was often a new man alone. His intensity and passion for his cause ran deep and was rarely matched by others. The Cuba he envisioned depended on everyone sharing his innate desire to better life for everyone. In light of the capitalist conception of human nature—that people work best when motivated by self-interest—Che's outlook may seem naïve, but it was what Che fervently believed. If Che had been the rule instead of the exception, it just might have worked.

Cutting Ties

Meanwhile, the United States stepped up its efforts to halt Cuba's move to socialism with an economic blockade, passing bills imposing sanctions against countries that purchased Cuban sugar with U.S. loans and stopping security backing for those that gave Cuba any support. The United States also hammered out an agreement with the Organization of American States (OAS) that clearly denounced any interference by the Soviet Union on behalf of Cuba. By October the United States had declared a trade embargo on Cuba. Attention in the States was high as Nixon and Kennedy continued to use Cuba in their campaigns. *Time* magazine even ran a cover story on the Cuban Revolution, characterizing Che as its "brain," Fidel as its "heart," and Raúl as its "fist."

After the United States' moves against Cuba, Castro fired back with an explosive declaration that the island was a revolutionary example and that Cuba would continue to fight against the evils of capitalism and imperialism—in short, the United States. If the United States did decide to attack Cuba, Castro made it plain that

Cuba would gladly accept the help of the Soviet Union, regardless of the consequences.

Castro soon went to the United States to attend the United Nations General Assembly. (While there he also spent time in Harlem, expressing a common brotherhood with oppressed African-Americans.) During the United Nations General Assembly, Castro and Khrushchev made a grand show of solidarity, hugging and supporting each other's statements condemning the United States. As the two leaders lambasted the United States for its aggression and called for a more nonaligned United Nations, it was quite clear to all watching that Cuba and the Soviet Union were closer than ever.

As Castro faced the United Nations, Che faced the embargo head-on and addressed the economic problems it would bring to the island. While admitting that the resulting shortages would not be overcome easily, he expressed optimism and an abiding faith in Cuba's ability to adapt. He insisted that any counterrevolutions attempted would only serve to strengthen the resolve Cuba had amassed since the day Batista fled. Once back in Cuba, Castro tightened his grip as a national network of neighborhood groups ("Committees for the Defense of the Revolution") was established to provide support for Castro's regime. A new round of urban reform laws also went into effect, banning Cubans from owning more than one home and absorbing all rental properties into the state. Castro was now a landlord with thousands and thousands of tenants.

Labor camps were set up to contain those deemed insufficiently dangerous to require imprisonment but requiring state supervision. It was not just political rebels who found themselves interred in these camps but social rebels as well. For instance, homosexuals were among the groups that soon found they had no place in Castro's Cuba. Independent media was effectively silenced; criticism of Cuba's revolutionary policies was not welcome either.

Rebel opposition was growing quickly and, perhaps following Che's example and writings, counterrevolutionary groups formed in the mountains. Not to be outdone at his own game, Castro saw to it that the rebels had no peasant support, one of the key factors in his rebels' success. Not surprisingly, the U.S. embassy continued to urge all American citizens to leave Cuba. The air was thick with tension, and confrontation seemed increasingly inevitable.

Mission to the Soviet Union

In late October, Che embarked on yet another journey, this time to see communism in action for himself. Gone from Cuba for two months, he traveled all over the communist bloc, including Prague, Moscow, Leningrad, Shanghai, Beijing, and East Berlin. His mission was to arrange the sale of sugar not already spoken for by Moscow. Along the way he secured many economic coups for Cuba, including a twenty-million-dollar loan (an amount later doubled) from Prague to build an automobile factory in Cuba.

While on his mission, Che also came face-to-face with a man from his past, Nikolai Leonov, the Soviet agent he had met years earlier in Mexico. Leonov served as Che's interpreter, an ironic role given that Leonov had been one of the first to introduce Che to Soviet life. Now Leonov was Che's literal gateway to the Soviet Union, not just his symbolic one. The two spent a great deal of time together during Che's trip. Leonov later remembered Che telling him that whether or not the Cuban Revolution succeeded, he would not be a refugee in an embassy somewhere. Instead, he would "go out with a machine gun in my hand ... I'll keep fighting to the end."

Che visited Lenin's tomb in Moscow and lobbied hard for Soviet support of his plans to build a steel plant in Cuba. The idea did not fly; Cuba was ill-prepared for such an undertaking, and Che was disappointed. He felt Cuba needed not only to think big, but to act big as well. He was against the idea of starting small and working up; his plans for industrialization were too important to compromise.

While in Moscow, Che attended the celebrations in Red Square commemorating the forty-third anniversary of the October Revolution. He found himself at a place of honor, standing next to Khrushchev overlooking the military displays. After years of study and rapt devotion, Che was standing directly above the red marble tomb where the embalmed body of the man he so admired,

Vladimir Lenin, laid in state. As adoring crowds cheered for Cuba and chanted his name, Che must have been overwhelmed at the course of his own life and humbled by the opportunity to forge a "new man."

Even though the trip impressed Che, it appears much of his itinerary may have been engineered to steer him clear of the downsides of socialism in the Soviet Union. He was not afforded much opportunity to see how "real" people lived, and his experience was primarily limited to official business with leaders. Or perhaps Che was aware the Soviet Union had failed to fully live up to the socialist dream but was holding out hope for Cuba to do better. Or maybe he was simply awestruck by the pageantry and hype of his visit. Regardless of the reasons why, whether due to Soviet calculation, blindness brought on by his own enthusiasm, or a steadfast faith in socialism as a concept, Che nonetheless held on to his ideology and respect for the Soviet Union. It would be some years before Che realized how far from his ideal the USSR truly was.

Making his way to China (as well as North Korea), Che found success with the sale of one million tons of sugar, as well as a line of credit worth more than fifty million dollars toward the purchase of Chinese goods. The Soviet Union, at ideological odds with China at the time, upped its commitment to Cuba and arranged to purchase an additional two-and-a-half million tons of sugar.

It was also during this trip that Che met Tamara Bunke, a young German-Argentine woman, in East Berlin. Raised as a communist in Argentina, Bunke served as an official interpreter in Berlin but longed to return to Latin America and help foster communism. By May 1961 Bunke (soon to be known as "Tania") made her way to Cuba and ultimately found herself fighting alongside Che during his last campaign in Bolivia.

Back in Cuba Che's trip was hailed a success. The advancements he had brokered while touring the socialist homeland further strengthened Castro's resolve to stand tough against the United States. That resolve would soon be tested. After Castro paraded newly acquired Soviet tanks and weapons through the streets of Havana, President Eisenhower ended the United States' sixty-year relationship with Cuba. On January 3, 1961, practically on his way out the White House door, Eisenhower terminated diplomatic relations with Cuba. The new president, John F. Kennedy, would have to deal with the aftermath.

Chapter 8

Conflicts in Cuba

*The victory of the Cuban Revolution will be a tangible
demonstration before all the Americas that the peoples are
capable of rising up, that they can proclaim their independence in the very clutches of the monster. It will mean the
beginning of the end of colonial domination in Latin
America, that is, the beginning of the end of U.S. imperialism.*

—Che Guevara

Early in 1961 Che found himself with even more responsibilities. In February the Cuban government founded the Ministry
of Industry, an organization responsible for the hundreds of nationalized companies on the island. Che was named Minister of the
Department, a position that virtually placed the entire Cuban
economy in the palm of his hand. His recent trip to the Soviet
Union had been formative for him, and he had already begun to
prepare the Cuban people for the coming changes. In a televised
speech after his return, Che announced, "Of course, for a Cuban
living in the twentieth century, with all the comforts that imperialism has accustomed us to in the cities, [the socialist countries
abroad] may seem even to be lacking in civilization. They are
countries where every last cent has to be used in production for
development."

The deficiency Che witnessed can be summed up in an exchange Che apparently had while in the Soviet Union. Remarking that Cuba lacked some raw materials for items like deodorant, Che was reportedly told, "Deodorants? You're used to too many luxuries." Quality of goods was about to take a real downswing for Cubans, and Che wanted them to be ready. But for a people already accustomed to "luxuries" like deodorant and razor blades, the shift from good to poor would be hard to accept.

In the coming months Che continued to stress the need to adhere to the principles of socialism, urging, "In the new stages of the revolutionary struggle, there will be no privileged officials or plantation owners. The only privileged people in Cuba will be the children." By now the importance of the next generation was a familiar theme for Che. For him, the importance of their dedication to the revolution could not be overstated.

Che was also upfront about the Cuban Revolution and the mistakes they made. In a February 1961 article titled "A Revolutionary Sin," he observed that revolutions "are never perfect," but products of "passions or improvisations by men in their struggle for social justice." Remarking specifically on the fractured nature between the leadership of the revolution, Che also wrote, "[The revolution] made mistakes, and some of those mistakes are being paid for dearly." Sarcastically thanking the Cuban exiles who had already made their way to Miami, Che also expressed his disappointment over what he saw as their continued commitment to Batista.

In looking at the problems facing post-revolution Cuba, Che found three areas that contributed to the problems the island was facing: lack of awareness, lack of organization, and lack of technical knowledge. He was steadfast in his belief that the Cuban people could (and would) unite in the face of these shortcomings and prevail, using the period during the actual revolutionary war as an example: "When the country was bracing itself to resist the enemy onslaught, production did not fall, absenteeism disappeared, problems were solved remarkably quickly."

For Che, it was vital for the country to continue to operate as if still at war. Without that solidarity, the necessary changes would be made even more difficult, and Che did his best to keep a sharp focus on what was most important for the Cuban people: "At the end of the day, you cannot eat soap and stuff; we must first ensure food supplies for people, because we are at war." Although Che was speaking metaphorically (referring to an economic war), Cuba would soon find itself balancing precariously between two superpowers in a nuclear standoff.

Even though Che was dedicated to fulfilling the needs of the revolution, he had already begun to think beyond Cuba. Soon after assuming his new position as Minister of the Department of Industry, he told his secretary that he would "stick this out for five years" and then take off to fight a new guerilla war. A combination of familiar wanderlust and a desire to improve the revolutionary efforts already undertaken in Cuba was calling Che. It was a call that would ultimately lead him to his death.

The Bay of Pigs

The tensions between the United States and Cuba rose to a new level in 1961. In late January, Che arrived in the Cuban military zone of Pinar del Río, which was placed on red alert following the inauguration of U.S. President John F. Kennedy. He acknowledged the threat of a U.S. invasion with a sobering address to the troops there: "We all hope the successor to our well-hated enemy Eisenhower is a little more intelligent and does not allow himself to be so influenced by monopolies." But as many predicted, an attempt to overthrow Castro was soon launched. President Kennedy had inherited the Cuban situation, and plans to remove Castro had been in the works for months. Cuban exiles were being trained in Central America, specifically Guatemala, and the long-simmering confrontation took off in earnest in mid-April 1961.

On April 15, B-26 bombers, piloted by Cuban exiles, launched an assault on the Cuban air force base in Santiago. The mission was a success, decimating much of Cuba's already small air force. Castro had early warning of the plan, and Che had been dispatched to the western section of the island (once again, Pinar del Río) where he would lead the area's forces in case of armed invasion. While there, Che addressed the troops, reinforcing the need to be ready for a full-scale invasion by the United States, leading them in a rallying cry of "Homeland or Death!"

The CIA quickly denied involvement in the air strike, insisting the planes were Cuban and that the attack, the result of growing Cuban dissatisfaction, was launched from within. On April 16, at the funeral for victims of the bombing raid, Castro publicly announced for the first time the socialist nature of the revolution. Although hardly surprising, Castro's declaration was an ideological turning point for the revolution and Che's hopes for a new Cuban society. A socialist Cuba was no longer whispered rumors and shrouded intent, but rather a stated objective. Che, never one to mince words or hide his dedication, surely felt vindicated.

The move by the United States, while obviously frightening, must have also excited Che. He had long advocated radical opposition to the United States, and the opportunity to flex Cuba's military muscle in the face of American intervention was something he undoubtedly welcomed. In addition, the growing support of the Soviet Union only strengthened his faith in the Cuban regime's ability to defend itself. As Paco Ignacio Tabio II (*Guevara, Also Known as Che*) wrote:

> *For a man who liked to leave scorched earth behind him in his personal history, a man well suited to metaphors of burning boats and bridges behind him, it could have been no less than a moment of glory when a country opened a door to heaven or hell and closed the rest.*

In the early morning hours of April 17, fifteen hundred men landed on the shores at Playa Girón on the Bay of Pigs situated on the south coast of Cuba. Armed with U.S. weapons, the so-called Liberation Army hoped to find support from the local population—one of many miscalculations that doomed the operation from the start.

Intending to cross the island to Havana, the exiles were quickly stopped by Castro's army. Out of supplies and outmaneuvered at every turn, the exiles were put down before they even really began. In the battle, one hundred sixty Cubans were killed, while the exiles lost more than one hundred men. A total of approximately twelve hundred exiles were captured by Castro's men, a coup that would later net Castro more than fifty-two million dollars in food and medicine from the United States in return for their release.

The Bay of Pigs was an unmitigated disaster for Kennedy and the United States. Initially designed as a starting point for the gradual buildup of anti-Castro forces within Cuba, the plan had quickly spiraled out of control in both scope and cost. The budget for the operation had ballooned from four billion dollars to over forty-six billion and U.S. involvement was to be key to the mission's success. Perhaps in an effort to fulfill campaign promises or due to simple inexperience, President Kennedy had agreed to the plan, and his administration would now have to pay the price.

Many blamed the dismal failure on the Kennedy administration for not giving the invasion adequate air support. After the initial air attack had proved successful, Kennedy postponed a second air strike, a move that conceivably ended the invasion before it began. Apparently, the decision was prompted by a desire to minimize obvious involvement by the United States. The result yielded the opposite effect with the United States ostensibly sending the fifteen hundred men to inevitable defeat. Counting on air support that never arrived, the Liberation Army never stood a chance.

In 1998, thirty-seven years later, an internal CIA secret audit concerning the Bay of Pigs invasion was released to the public. The document blamed a series of mistakes made by the agency in the planning and execution of the invasion for its failure. Among its many findings were that the CIA failed to provide for adequate security measures in the training and preparation of the mission. In addition, the impending invasion was anything but a secret. The plan was leaked to the media and also reached Castro, who was well-prepared for the attack. Perhaps the biggest mistake, however, was the overestimation of popular support in Cuba for such an operation. Pockets of resistance were still active in Cuba, but there was no clear organization and no discernable plan to unite the counterrevolutionaries. Despite CIA assurances to Kennedy that the support was there, there was no network of resistance waiting for the men who landed at the Bay of Pigs—only Castro's men and ignominious defeat.

For Castro, the Bay of Pigs was vindication of the highest order. Che's insistence that the population be armed had paid off with over two hundred thousand militiamen on their side. In a public speech given months later, Che would sarcastically thank the Kennedy administration for giving the Cuban Revolution a seminal event that reinforced their cause. In Castro's eyes, he had faced down Washington and won. Che attributed the victory to revolutionary fervor and an empowering sense of social justice: "You can't expect that a man who was given a thousand acres by his father and just shows up here to get his thousand acres back won't be killed by a countryman who used to have nothing and now has a terrible urge to kill the guy because he wants to take his land away."

In the wake of the Bay of Pigs, Castro's regime clamped down even harder on dissidents in Cuba. A new one-party system was conceived (but never fully realized) that would bring together the 26th of July movement, the Revolutionary Student Organization, and the Popular Socialist Party. It appeared that the Cuban Revolution was stronger than ever, at least in spirit.

Although Che had not seen any action during the Bay of Pigs, he was, nonetheless, wounded. While in the western part of Cuba, Che had accidentally dropped his firearm. It went off and wounded him on the cheek, landing him in the hospital for twenty-four hours. Apparently, he had been very lucky; a slight difference in trajectory and Che would have been killed: The bullet came within an inch of entering his skull.

Back to Business

After the Bay of Pigs, Che quickly resumed his work at the Ministry of Industry, hoping to magnify the momentum gained by the turn of events. Meticulously organized and detailed, Che was determined to turn Cuba's economy around. Acknowledging that Cuba was a work in progress, Che forged ahead despite the problems that continued to plague the island. Che's dedication to voluntary work remained a priority as he often spent rare days off in communal labor.

Che was determined to make the newly created Ministry of Industry work, but the task at hand was fraught with problems: Lack of technology, hopelessly outdated facilities, and conflicts within the increasingly centralized department were just a few of the hurdles facing Che that would prove insurmountable. Rationing would soon begin in Cuba with many necessities (meat, milk, shoes, and toothpaste) being handed out with care. Che was fanatical about adhering to the ration system in his own growing family (two more of his children would be born by 1963), insisting to Adelia that they never take advantage of his standing.

Many of the problems facing Cuba stemmed from the economic blockade spearheaded by the United States. Approximately seventy-five percent of Cuba's foreign trade had been halted due to the action. Canada, Belgium, and France were but a few of the countries that bowed to U.S. pressure when dealing with Cuba.

In light of the falling economy and ever-mounting problems, Che dug his heels in and insisted to the Cuban people that to succeed together, they would have to suffer together. Che never whitewashed the situation, often admitting that times were hard and likely to worsen. He blamed his own department, the Ministry of Industry, for failing to include worker (iron and steel workers, in particular) input early on: "We can see clearly now that the people had nothing to do with drawing up the plan, and a plan with no worker participation runs a serious risk of failure." Che believed that if the workers in the factories had been consulted, problems such as a lack of raw materials and a shortage of spare parts would have been detected earlier.

Still, his passion and faith remained steadfast as he tried his best to untangle the many problems that plagued the Cuban economy. To him, the greatest antidote to the crisis, to *any* crisis really, was enthusiasm and dedication to the revolution. However, very real problems—such as lack of materials, inferior and untimely supplies from the socialist bloc, and dwindling foreign reserves—could not be overcome by revolutionary fervor, no matter how brightly it burned.

Alliance for Progress

In August 1961 Che traveled to Uruguay for an economic conference where President Kennedy's "Alliance for Progress" plan was detailed. The twenty-billion-dollar development package was designed to aid Latin American countries over the next ten years. Not surprisingly, Che was unimpressed: "… the Alliance for Progress is not for Cuba but against her," declaring the plan to be little more than an attempt by the United States to downplay the importance of the Cuban Revolution in Latin America. Che strongly asserted that the United States funneled resources into Latin America and supported only minimal social and political reform to keep those countries from following Cuba's example.

Buoyed by revolutionary momentum, Soviet assistance, and his own faith, Che insisted that Cuba's economy would eventually be proof that socialism was the answer to Latin American woes. He drew sharp contrasts between the U.S. plan and the Soviet aid to Cuba, perhaps hoping other countries would follow suit:

> Don't you get the impression, just a little bit, that your leg
> is being pulled? You are given dollars to build highways,
> you are given dollars to build roads, you are given dollars
> to build sewers. Gentlemen, what do you build roads
> with, what do you dig the sewers with, what do you build
> houses with? You don't have to be a genius for that. Why
> don't they give dollars for equipment, dollars for machin-
> ery, dollars so that our underdeveloped countries, all of
> them, can become industrial-agricultural countries, at one
> and the same time? Really, it's sad.

All in all, however, Che's appearance at the conference reflected a more moderate and conciliatory Cuban stance. After the Bay of Pigs invasion, the tone set by Cuba was surprising; the exact opposite had been expected. Che even went so far as to "guarantee that we will not export revolution." Promising that "not one rifle will be moved from Cuba, that not one weapon will be moved from Cuba for fighting in any other country in Latin America." In reality, Cuba (and Che in particular) was already deeply involved in exporting revolution to other Latin American countries, specifically Venezuela.

The message appeared to be that Cuba, not included in the Alliance for Progress agenda, really just wanted to be left alone to live up to its potential. Still, Che insisted that Cuba did not want the Alliance for Progress to fail: "We are not interested in it failing, if and insofar as it means a real improvement for Latin America in the standard of living of all its two hundred million inhabitants."

Che even met with Kennedy advisor Richard Goodwin and appeared to be willing to set up a dialogue with Washington. It may have been that economic worries prompted the meeting. Or perhaps he wanted to show the Soviet Union that Cuba had exhausted all means of communication with the United States, furthering Soviet involvement with Cuba. Or maybe it was just another example of Castro's tendency to play both sides of the fence, hoping for a short-term political advancement that would benefit the country in the long run. Like much of Cuban rationale, the truth may never be fully understood.

The meeting, while garnering much media attention, brought little in the way of tangible results. With the Cold War an ever-present concern, and especially in light of the Bay of Pigs fiasco, President Kennedy appeared to have little interest in compromising with Cuba. In fact, the Cold War soon came to a head with Cuba smack in the middle of a crisis that found the world staring into the abyss of nuclear war.

Another meeting in August 1961 brought attention to Che when he met with Argentina President Arturo Frondizi. Secretly traveling to his homeland, Che met with Frondizi at Los Olivios, the president's official residence. Apparently the two discussed Cuba's future with Argentina and Frondizi's hope that Cuba would not enter into a "formal alliance" with the Soviet Union. Che maintained Cuba's independence, as long as the United States did not attack them. Word of Che's visit soon leaked out, however, and Frondizi's foreign minister (who initially denied the meeting took place) was forced to resign because of the scandal it caused. Frondizi also found himself ousted seven months later following a military coup buoyed by public concerns over his clandestine meeting with the rebel leader.

A similar fate befell Brazilian President Janio Quadros. After a meeting with Che, Quadros publicly declared support for Cuba and decorated Che with high government honors. Five days later, Quadros was ousted by his own military. It seems Che was such a powerful symbolic force in Latin America that even a few hours in his presence had a shattering effect. Tabio (*Guevara, Also Known as Che*) summed it up nicely:

> Che was dangerous in Latin America then; his very touch
> polarized opinions. Despite the projected image of the
> Alliance for Progress as democratic and progressive, Latin
> America seemed to face a choice between the relatively
> small and radicalized group of Cuban revolutionaries or
> the military jackboots supported by the United States.

The economic situation in Cuba, despite an ideological push following the Bay of Pigs invasion, continued to slide downward. By 1962 a shortage of raw materials, a lack of convenient and affordable imports, trade deficits with the USSR, and continued rationing were all dragging Cuba's economy down. Che's insistence on rapid and radical industrialization did not produce the desired results, perhaps because he refused to aim low. The Cuban economy was all but collapsing, due largely to Che's grand plans.

In the end it was mostly about sugar. By 1963, due to drought and government policy, Cuba's sugar crop dropped to just under four million tons (in 1961 it had topped off at just under seven million tons). Essentially, the economy suffered from a cyclical problem: To industrialize, Cuba needed to stop relying so heavily on sugar production. However, to acquire foreign reserves with which to industrialize, Cuba had to sell sugar. With the United States no longer an option for any import or export products, let alone sugar, Cuba often found itself stuck in a spiral. Still, Che announced a plan to double the standard of living in Cuba by 1965. He wanted Cuba to produce the goods normally imported to the island—at least the basics.

Beyond economics, Che also set out to vastly improve education and healthcare for all Cubans, an area in which he found considerably more success. By 1961 school attendance in Cuba had risen dramatically—by more than fifty percent, cresting somewhere around eighty percent (in 1959 the figure had been around sixty percent). Literacy rates also shot up, and by 1965 the percentage of children in school rose to more than fifty percent over the Latin American average. Healthcare took a similar upswing as new hospitals and clinics combined with massive vaccination drives vastly improved conditions for all Cubans. Che took great comfort in the tangible results these efforts generated, no doubt feeling the revolution had made a radical difference for many Cuban peasants. But of course all these social improvements cost money—money Cuba was rapidly running out of.

Ever-growing demands put ever-greater strains on Cuban domestic goods and services while the island's foreign reserves were being gobbled up by the cost of imports. Necessities became increasingly scarce as the rationing became increasingly pronounced. By March 1962 rationed products included rice, eggs, milk, fish, chicken, beef, oil, toothpaste, and detergent. Che admitted publicly that many of the problems could be attributed to ill-conceived plans—his plans.

As for Soviet assistance, the deal did not prove as illustrious as Che once thought. The USSR was either unable or unwilling to continue to fund Cuba's reformation indefinitely. The one-hundred-million-dollar, five-year credit had gone quickly, and it was widely perceived that Cuba had been extravagant with the funds, trying to do too much too soon. And when products did arrive from the Soviet Union and other socialist bloc countries, they were often late or of poor quality.

Cuba was feeling the cost of socialism in material ways, and Che's policy of massive centralization only made matters worse. The centralized structure required companies to funnel all resources to the Ministry of Industry. Funds required by businesses to continue production and investments were then parceled out from the Ministry, allegedly to foster the entire Cuban economy. In addition, all monetary dealings between the companies themselves were banned, resulting in no internal market for the island. Although he was trying his best, Che was having a very hard time making the Cuban system work. Many of his ideas and policies were based in Marxist economics, and the strong centralization of industry created levels of bureaucracy that seemed only to stifle the Cuban economy.

Che was often his own strongest critic: "The main cause of our errors was our lack of a sense of reality at a given moment." Realizing his plans were initially simplistic, he admitted that many of the Ministry's decisions had resulted in shortages for the Cuban people, a realization that must have been painful for him indeed. At the same time, Castro would often deny there was a production crisis in Cuba—one of the few times the two publicly disagreed. But through it all, Che held steadfast to his belief that revolutionary passion would see Cuba through the dark economic times: "Quietly and full of wrath, the working people will go forward until some day, some place, the spark will ignite and a new revolutionary flame will be lit in the Americas." Che never stopped believing that Cuba was the example for the rest of Latin America.

Paradoxically, Che often fought fire with fire, heaping more of the same policies into the fray, hoping to turn it around. At the same time, CIA-endorsed guerila acts of sabotage and revolt—collectively known as "Operation Mongoose" and designed to overthrow Castro—cost Cuba dearly. According to Paco Ignacio Taibo (*Guevara, Also Known as Che*), seven hundred sixteen acts of terrorism were committed by the CIA between February and October of 1962. Needless to say, the problems inherent in the Cuban economy during Che's tenure as Minister of Industry are multi-layered, complex, and impossible to cover in detail here.

On the Brink of Nuclear War

By mid-1962 the Kennedy administration had stepped up efforts to contain Cuba with the trade embargo—only medical supplies were allowed passage. The Organization of American States suspended Cuba's membership and banned arm sales to Cuba by its members. Colombia, Panama, Nicaragua, and El Salvador had all broken ties with Cuba; "Operation Mongoose" was in effect; and forces were being trained. And the Alliance for Progress measure was making its presence felt throughout Latin America. Meanwhile, Castro strongly reiterated his ties to communism, and

Cuba struggled to make economic headway. In the midst of all this tension, Cuba soon found itself at the center of a global firestorm of nuclear proportions.

Che continued to vocally criticize the Alliance for Progress ("an imperialistic attempt to halt revolutionary impulses") and made allusions to approaching violence: "Latin America today is a volcano. It is not in eruption, but is moved by the immense subterranean rumbling that heralds [the revolution's] approach." Che clearly felt another conflict would prove to be the catalyst needed to cement Cuba's revolutionary policies. He continued to underscore Soviet involvement, an involvement that would soon be severely ratcheted up.

Near the end of May 1962, Khrushchev called upon the Soviet ambassador to Cuba and inquired about the possibility of secretly placing nuclear weapons in Cuba. Khrushchev said he wanted to help Cuba, to save the revolution. Actually, Khrushchev was aware that the United States had placed nuclear weapons in Turkey that were pointed toward the Soviet Union. Still, he was concerned as to what Castro's reaction would be. The assumption was that Castro would be resistant to the plan. After all, Castro wanted Cuba to be an independent entity, regardless of his socialist agenda. To replace a U.S. presence with a Soviet one would just be replacing one "master" with another, not to mention that such a move would undoubtedly place the Cuban people in the highest possible danger. Despite concerns that Castro would refuse, the offer was nonetheless put on the table.

During their meeting with Castro, Soviet envoys explained that the missiles and troops were purely a last resort. Along with forty-two missiles, forty-two thousand Soviet troops were also slated to arrive in Cuba if the deal was accepted. The troops would be entirely under Soviet control. Another attack on Cuba by the United States was thought to be inevitable, and it was doubtful that the Americans would repeat the same mistakes that had plagued the Bay of Pigs invasion. The nuclear missiles would only be revealed if no other methods of persuasion worked. The missiles would be the ultimate deterrent—a nuclear ace-in-the-hole to ensure Cuba's survival.

Upon hearing the plan, Castro, in typical fashion, neither rejected it nor accepted it outright. After all, this was the most serious decision of his life. Had he launched a revolution, overseen massive reform (no matter how successful), and forever altered Cuba's political landscape to end up a pawn in the Cold War? Was this truly the only way to ensure Cuba's security? He said he needed a day to think about it. He needed a day to talk to Che.

The following day, Castro accepted the Soviets' offer. Che was present at the meeting and was very involved in the discussions. It was clear that Cuba only wanted the missiles to keep the United States from invading. As to the gravity of the decision, it was Che who offered the most succinct opinion: "Anything that can stop the Americans is worthwhile" (Lee, *Che Guevara: A Revolutionary Life*). Years later, Castro would continue to insist that it was only concern over Cuba's defense that led him to make such a serious call.

Castro wanted a military pact to seal the deal: an agreement over what Cuba would demand from the United States once knowledge of the missiles was made public. Among other points, Castro wanted assurance that the United States would not invade Cuba and that the military base at Guantánamo Bay would be disbanded. The Soviets tentatively agreed, and the pact was to be drawn up in the coming weeks. Raúl Castro went to Moscow and met with Khrushchev to hammer out the deal. When asked what the Soviet Union would do if the United States discovered the missiles being delivered into Cuba, Khrushchev promised to "send out the Baltic Fleet in a show of support."

Once Raúl returned to Cuba, more haggling over the pact ensued. Even so, the first shipment of missiles was making its way to Cuba from the Soviet Union, carefully hidden aboard cargo ships. Castro insisted that the pact spell out that any attack on Cuba would be the same as an attack on the Soviet Union. In no way did Castro want Cuba to serve as a sacrificial lamb. The revised agreement was sent back to Moscow in late August, this time delivered by Che.

The CIA took special note of Che's trip and documents from that time reveal their concern that his "delegation may have a broader mission than [that of] his announced agenda, which pertains to industrial matters." Che was coming under increased CIA scrutiny, a pattern that would continue until his death.

When Khrushchev agreed to the wording of the pact but declined to sign it officially, Che pushed for the agreement to be made public. Insisting on total secrecy, Khrushchev again said Cuba could count on the Soviet Union's full support should the United States prematurely discover the operation. Despite the possibility of a double-cross, Che returned to Cuba, hoping his faith in the Soviet Union was not unfounded. Che seemed to be convinced that the Soviets' resolve and nuclear power were either equal to or greater than that of the United States. He was wrong on both accounts.

By the time Che arrived home to Cuba, the secret was already out. U.S. U-2 spy planes spotted the Soviet military buildup in Cuba, but not the nuclear presence. The planes had discovered the building of both ground-to-ground missile sites as well as coastal defense missile installations, but no sign of the true nature of the weapons. President Kennedy was informed that national security was not in peril, but he was nonetheless understandably concerned. Cuba had long been a sore spot and was under constant observation. Determined to avoid another Bay of Pigs fiasco, Kennedy put out a public statement about the Soviet buildup in Cuba. He said that the placing of offensive (i.e., nuclear) weapons in Cuba by the Soviets could lead to the "gravest issues." Soon Congress called up one hundred fifty thousand military reservists, and the United States planned military training exercises in the Caribbean. Cuba braced for an invasion while the Soviets continued to insist the weapons were merely for Cuba's defense. The tension was mounting and would soon break open the Soviet–Cuba agreement to a stunned and frightened world.

President John F. Kennedy's address on the Cuban Missile Crisis (February 11, 1962).

(Central Press)

On October 16 the truth was revealed when U.S. intelligence officials presented Kennedy with photographs showing nuclear missile bases under construction in Cuba. From the photos it appeared that preparations for two types of missiles were underway: medium-range ballistic missiles (capable of distances of about thirteen hundred miles) and intermediate-range ballistic missiles (capable of distances of about twenty-five hundred miles). With Cuba's close proximity to the United States, these missiles could reach most major U.S. cities, including Los Angeles, Chicago, and New York. Virtually every major city in the United States was now within range of a possible nuclear attack. The photos also suggested the presence of nuclear-capable bombers.

A ballistic missile base in Cuba, the evidence with which President Kennedy ordered a naval blockade of Cuba during the Cuban Missile Crisis.

(Keystone)

A Time of Grave Decision

Kennedy knew he had no clear choice of action to take against the Cubans and Soviets. Attacking the Soviet installations in Cuba could lead to a global nuclear war, killing many millions of people, but doing nothing was a huge risk as well. He had to make good on his pledge to oppose "offensive" weapons in Cuba. If he did not, he ran the risk of invalidating every U.S. pledge.

Another U.S.–Soviet standoff was underway as well, this one over the city of West Berlin, Germany. Following the allied victory in World War II, Berlin had been divided into East and West Berlin. The East section was controlled by communist East Germany, and the West belonged to capitalist West Germany. Khrushchev had threatened to take over West Berlin earlier that year, telling Kennedy he was willing to go to war over the city. (The situation never came to that. The Soviet Union eventually accepted the city's division and backed off.) Khrushchev had set a deadline of November 1962 for the resolution of the issue. Now Kennedy had the Soviets encroaching even closer to the United States, about ninety miles off the coast of Florida.

In all likelihood, Khrushchev had Berlin as much in mind as he did Cuba when he decided to place the missiles on the island. Whether it was over Cuba or Berlin, Kennedy would have to respond to the Soviets' overtures. Before the Cuban missile crisis began, it was thought that U.S. nuclear superiority would keep the Soviets in check. But the reconnaissance pictures told a different story, convincing Kennedy and his men that the weapons might have been placed in Cuba to keep the United States from intervening on behalf of West Berlin. In addition, Khrushchev had no desire to lose Cuba to a U.S. invasion. The loss would have been devastating to the Soviets, showing the world they could do little but make empty threats.

On October 16, the first day of the crisis, Kennedy and most of his advisers agreed that the only reasonable thing to do was to conduct a surprise air attack against Cuba. A blockade and an invasion could follow, if need be. A change in plans occurred the following day, however, and it was decided that the blockade would come first. The reasoning was twofold: First, the blockade would serve as a kind of ultimatum, a warning shot to Khrushchev. Unless the missiles were pulled out of Cuba, some kind of military action by the United States would follow. Second, the blockade would serve as an opening to negotiations. While decisions were made at the highest level, the U.S. military began moving soldiers and equipment into position for a possible invasion of Cuba.

On October 22, 1962, in what had to be the most important address of his life, President Kennedy went on worldwide radio and television to announce the discovery of the missiles. After demanding that Khrushchev withdraw them, Kennedy announced the formation of a naval quarantine zone around Cuba. U.S. naval forces would intercept and inspect ships to determine whether they were carrying weapons (the blockade was called a "quarantine" because international law defined a "blockade" as an act of war). Kennedy warned that if Khrushchev fired missiles from Cuba, the result would be "a full retaliatory response upon the Soviet Union." There it was: the threat of nuclear war. The two biggest superpowers in the world were locked in a standoff, and Cuba was smack-dab in the middle.

The next day, October 23, 1962, battle stations were again prepared across Cuba. Che was once more dispatched to Pinar del Río where he set up headquarters at the Los Portales Cave on the banks of the San Diego River. He quickly initiated the buildup of ammunition and delivered morale-boosting speeches to the Cuban people. He was certain that an invasion by the United States was just around the corner.

In the days following, the word "tension" took on a new meaning. What would the Soviets do—honor the blockade/quarantine or initiate a military confrontation at sea? For several days Soviet vessels on their way to Cuba avoided the quarantine zone while Khrushchev and Kennedy communicated via diplomatic channels. In Cuba the army continued to mobilize and prepared for the worst. As in the Bay of Pigs maneuvers, Che remained in western Cuba to lead the area's forces should war break out.

On October 26 Khrushchev sent a message to Kennedy that seemingly offered a withdrawal of missiles from Cuba in return for a U.S. pledge not to invade the island—something Kennedy had already volunteered more than a week earlier. Before Kennedy could respond, Khrushchev delivered a public message saying the withdrawal of the Cuban missiles had to be accompanied by the removal of "analogous" U.S. weapons in Turkey along the southern border of the USSR. Although the missiles in Turkey were considered obsolete and expendable, nearly all of Kennedy's advisers advised against caving in to Soviet demands.

Meanwhile, the blockade continued and skirmishes occurred. Low-flying U.S. surveillance aircraft encountered hostile fire, and on October 27, the Cubans shot down a U-2 plane, killing its pilot. The Kennedy administration decided not to retaliate for fear of escalating the crisis.

Despite his willingness to remove the missiles from Turkey, Kennedy did not want to be perceived as rolling over for the Soviets, at least not publicly. Kennedy decided on a public reply that would only address Khrushchev's first offer to withdraw the missiles in exchange for a pledge not to invade Cuba.

At the same time, however, Kennedy planned to privately inform Khrushchev that the United States would remove the missiles in Turkey. The president's brother, Attorney General Robert Kennedy, paid a secret visit to the Soviet embassy in Washington, D.C., and conveyed the president's pledge and its terms: If the Soviets revealed the pledge to remove the missiles from Turkey, the missiles would not be withdrawn. Robert Kennedy also warned the Soviets that time was running out and that an attack on Cuba was imminent.

As it turned out, Khrushchev had already decided to pull the missiles out of Cuba. The concern over nuclear war was simply too great: Castro had sent Khrushchev a message saying a U.S. invasion was imminent and that Khrushchev should be ready to launch the missiles. To use Secretary of State Dean Rusk's familiar phrase: "Khrushchev blinked." Sensing that he had pushed Kennedy too far, Khrushchev decided that Kennedy was serious and that both an air attack and an invasion of Cuba were at hand. Unwilling to back the pledge to defend Cuba as part of the Soviet Union, Khrushchev agreed that the missiles be withdrawn from Cuba.

On October 28, in a worldwide radio broadcast, Khrushchev agreed to remove offensive weapons from Cuba in return for a U.S. pledge not to invade. He also called for United Nations inspectors to verify the process. Castro was furious over the announcement. Not only had the Soviet Union failed to follow through, he had not even been informed of the turn of events beforehand and was left out of the decision-making process entirely. Apparently Castro learned the news over the radio, along with the rest of the world. Che was equally upset, his confidence in the USSR forever shaken. In the end, Cuba had been a pawn in the global chess game known as the Cold War.

An indignant Castro quickly lashed out, refusing to allow UN oversight of the dismantling process. There were also protests that broke out in the streets of Havana marked by the rallying cry: "Nikita, little sissy, what you give you don't take back!" Eventually an agreement was reached: The bombers would be removed within thirty days, and the missiles and other "offensive" weapons would be evacuated in the open so that U.S. surveillance aircraft could observe their removal.

For most of the world, Khrushchev's capitulation was a relief. For Che, it was a crushing disappointment. In a perfect example of his willingness to sacrifice himself and others to the revolutionary cause, Che characterized the Cuban people as "prepared to be atomically incinerated so that their ashes may be used as the foundations of new societies." Expressing his disappointment in the Soviet Union, Che continued, "And when, without consulting [the Cuban people], a pact is made to withdraw the missiles, they do not breathe a sigh of relief or give thanks for the truce. Instead they arise to give voice to their willingness to fight, theirs, and their determination to fight alone, if they must."

Once again, Che seemed to be making a huge leap of faith. He may have been perfectly willing for Cuba to serve such a sacrificial purpose, but his dedication and resolve was most likely not shared by most. Perhaps it is no surprise that the revolutionary zeal that burned so brightly within Che would soon lead him away from Cuba and back into full-time guerilla warfare.

Part Three

Exporting Che

Chapter 9

Looking Beyond Cuba:
Exporting Revolution

*Other nations of the world summon my modest efforts of
assistance .... I carry to new battlefronts the faith that you
[Castro] taught me, the revolutionary spirit of my people,
the feeling of fulfilling the most sacred of duties: to fight
against imperialism wherever one may be.*
—Che Guevara

For Che, Cuba was becoming less and less a place he wanted to be. After the tension of the Cuban Missile Crisis and the subsequent Soviet back-down, Che's desire to "export revolution" outside Cuba became even more pronounced. Cuba had long supported other revolutionary attempts, but since its expulsion from the Organization of American States in 1962, Cuba had become even more involved with the covert fostering of armed revolutionary conflict. Before long, Che found his homeland, Argentina, beckoning him.

Relations between Cuba and the Argentine Communist Party were tense in 1962. Cuba's (and Che's) support of revolutionary violence was a main source of friction, as it so often was. Argentine communist leaders were certain that factions within the party were being trained by Cuba in hopes of overthrowing not only Argentina's government, but the leadership of the Communist

Party there as well. Che was certain that revolutionary armed struggle was the only way to tame Argentina's army and oligarchy. In an address to Argentines living in Cuba as well as representatives from the Argentine Communist Party, Che, referring to socialism as "the symbol of the future," spoke of all of Argentina's revolutionary forces joining together: "We believe we are part of an army fighting in every part of the world." Che tried to unify those gathered before him, but the task proved too difficult to accomplish. The communists were opposed to unifying with the Perón supporters, and Che's calls for warfare and violence were unsettling and disturbing. Finding no place within the official Communist Party in Argentina and in the light of fading Soviet support of armed revolution, Che launched a campaign that attempted to recreate Cuban revolutionary success in his homeland.

Che was still dedicated to his duties in Cuba, however. He was happy to see that production had increased during the Cuban Missile Crisis. To Che, it was proof that the Cuban people worked best in the face of danger. He continued to press for the Ministry of Industry to enact a fairer pay scale for workers and to provide the people with more technical training. In February 1963, Che wholeheartedly threw himself into the testing of a new sugarcane-cutting machine. He had long thought the mechanization of cane-cutting would prove invaluable to Cuba. Che spent many long, backbreaking hours in the fields with the machine, helping to repair it when it broke down and, once again, proving that he was always willing to do more than his share of physical labor. The machine, while not perfect, certainly was able to help, but the sugar harvest that year still fell far short of projected (and badly needed) totals.

In addition to the disappointing sugar numbers, Cuba was also suffering from a lack of support from other socialist countries. When shipments did arrive from the socialist bloc, the quality of goods was usually very poor. Che was also seeing a clearer picture of the USSR and wondering why, forty-five years after its own revolution, production was so often in a state of disarray and inefficiency there. He also expressed concern over the growing net of red tape that was consuming the Cuban government: "We carbon-copied the experience of brother countries and that was a mistake … [that] made a dangerous contribution to one of the phenomena that must be fought most in a socialist revolution, that of bureaucracy." Che fought Cuba's bureaucratization the only way he knew how—by remaining as hands-on with the workers as ever. His commitment to volunteer labor continued, as well as his visits to various factories and plants where he would walk amongst the workers, attempting to connect with them on a basic level. In fact, whenever photographers and journalists followed Che into a field or a factory (as they often did), Che would insist, if they wanted an interview or to take photos, that they pitch in and contribute physical labor as well. No one was exempt from Che's call for solidarity and sacrifice.

Even so, Che was disheartened by the lack of response he saw from many of the workers. Production meetings held in factories between workers and supervisors were often poorly attended: "Where does the responsibility for workers' lack of participation and their apathy lie? Simply in that they see the meetings as an obligation to someone, not as a place to sort things out." Che, continuing to stress the importance of moral incentives over material ones, desperately wanted to strengthen the bond between the government and workers. He knew that it was this concept that was the backbone of his goals.

Homeland Revolution

Still, the thought of fostering revolution in Argentina consumed Che. Despite revolutionary failures in Venezuela, Nicaragua, and Guatemala, Che was determined that Cuba not be the exception to the rule that it was turning out to be. He took his theory of guerrilla warfare and intensified it, insisting that a revolutionary force could invent itself without relying on any preexisting conditions that all but demanded its creation. If revolution was nonexistent, then Che was determined to bring it life, no matter what the cost.

In part, Che's fervor may have been stoked by the publication of *Reminiscences of the Revolutionary War*, his second book. The response to the book in Cuba was tremendous, with people lining up for blocks to get a copy. The book apparently did quite well. Che refused to make any personal profit from the sales, choosing instead to funnel it back into Cuba's revolutionary goals. Undoubtedly this kind of support only strengthened Che's resolve that the people who could make revolution work just needed to be focused.

Jorge Masetti, an Argentine journalist who interviewed Che while he was stationed in the Sierra Maestra, proved to be instrumental in Che's revolutionary hopes for Argentina. Masetti had been an important player in post-revolutionary Cuba as one of the founders of Prensa Latina, the Cuban news agency. When Cuba began supplying Algeria with arms in its own revolutionary struggle in the early 1960s, Masetti played an integral role. Che would find himself personally involved in African revolution soon enough, but for the time being, Argentina remained his main focus.

Ideally, Che wanted former Argentine leader Juan Perón, exiled from the country in 1955, to be behind his campaign for revolution. When that failed to materialize, Che moved ahead with plans to form his own band of revolutionaries who would liberate his homeland.

Masetti was put in charge of assembling and recruiting those willing to fight in Argentina. Not finding enough Argentines willing to join, Masetti was joined by several Cubans, including Che's driver, Alberto Castellanos, his bodyguard, Hermés Peña, and José Martínez Tamayo, one of his personal aides. Peña would eventually die during the Argentine operation, and Tamayo would meet his demise later in Bolivia, only a few months before Che. Castellanos would be captured in Argentina and receive a four-year prison sentence. Also on board was Cuba's current Minister of the Interior, General Abelardo Colomé Ibarra, known as "Furri." Determined to be an active revolutionary once again, Che seemed intent on joining the group when the time was right, probably late 1963 or early 1964. It is unlikely he would have sent such a trusted group of his closest associates had he not been certain of his own forthcoming personal involvement with their actions.

Immediately prior to the Argentina operation, Che's mother Celia had her own brush with Argentine forces. After visiting Che and his family for three months, Celia returned to Argentina in April. Upon her arrival, she was arrested and charged with carrying Cuban communist propaganda. The authorities accused her of being a spy—guilt by familial association. Celia had undergone a political change of sorts, professing a belief in socialism but not communism. Despite her political beliefs, Celia had obviously been singled out for one reason only—because she was Che's mother. There appears to be no real evidence that she was doing anything that substantially furthered her son's goals. While not mistreated in prison, the experience could not have been a pleasant one. Released early in early June, Celia continued her defense of both her son and the land he had come to call his own.

In the summer of 1963 the group made its way to Bolivia, from where they planned to enter northern Argentina. While there, the group ventured into Argentina hoping to shore up support, supplies, and troops for the operation. By the end of the year, the small, ill-prepared outfit moved into Argentina and tried to set up operations. The group was always too small and proved to be nothing more than a slight annoyance to the Argentine government. They were devoted, but unlike Castro's group, they were never able to overcome a number of obstacles. A similar, but even smaller, operation was launched in Peru earlier that year and quickly defeated. Che's hopes for spreading revolution across the continent seemed to be dimming.

The Argentina-bound group was fractioned from the start and lacked the cohesion of a charismatic leader like Castro or Che. Many of the group's members were executed on orders of Masetti. Holed up in the jungles of Argentina, the group quickly fell victim to the punishing environment, the army's offensive, and their own internal weaknesses. To make matters worse, Argentina had recently become a representative democracy. Che's assertion that revolution could be forced upon an area that did not call for it seemed false.

By early 1964 it was all over. Following the capture or execution of his troops, Masetti simply disappeared into the Argentine jungle, presumed dead. The connection to Che was always suspected but never proven until after Che's own death. The failure of the mission undoubtedly hit Che hard: Many of these men had died fighting what was essentially Che's war, pursuing his dream under his direction. For a man so inextricably linked to his own ideology, these realizations must have been painful to bear. He had always thought of himself as a foot soldier in the revolution, but now others were dying for the cause while he was far away in Cuba. He soon remedied that situation and took himself out of the relative safety of Cuba and threw himself back into the heart of armed conflict.

Following Che's wholehearted participation in guerilla activity throughout Latin America, the man who had been instrumental in the construction of Soviet–Cuban ties soon found himself a target of suspicion himself. The Soviet Union and China had long been embroiled in what was known as "the Sino-Soviet split" and Che was increasingly identified with the Chinese, rather than the Soviets.

The Sino-Soviet Split

In 1956 Soviet Prime Minister Nikita Khrushchev began a major rift between Communist China and the USSR by denouncing his predecessor, Joseph Stalin, at the 20th Soviet Communist Party Congress. China was outraged, insisting that it and other communist states should have been consulted beforehand. Other conflicts over domestic, foreign, and defense policies, economic relationships, and ideological differences quickly developed.

The Sino-Soviet split did just that to International Communism, dividing it into two basic factions. All European national parties (except Albania) sided with the Soviets while Yugoslavia remained neutral. The Asian parties (except those of India and Mongolia and, later, Vietnam) stood with China. The Cultural Revolution, the major Chinese political movement that consisted of an attack on bureaucracy and privilege, only deepened the rift between China and the Soviet Union. In 1967 diplomatic relations between the two were broken, but the 1980s saw a shift by both countries toward a compromise on many of the points in dispute.

As the Sino-Soviet split widened, both China and the Soviet Union were determined to sway the communist parties of the world to their side. Almost all of the Latin American communist parties, including Cuba, looked to the Soviet Union for economic support, virtually guaranteeing their siding with the Soviets. Up until the early part of 1963 Cuba had remained officially neutral on the split, but the crumbling state of Cuba's economy more or less tipped Castro's hand. After his trips to Moscow in 1963 and 1964, Cuba and the Soviet Union seemed tighter than ever. The visits appeared to have healed the wounds between the two caused by the Cuban Missile Crisis. In reality, the two needed each other: Cuba needed Soviet assistance, and the Soviets needed Cuban ideological support in their attempts to one-up China.

In return for Cuba's support of socialist unity and the pursuit of peaceful coexistence with the United States, Castro was able to procure new Soviet subsidies for the island. Reports even began to filter out about Castro's desire to reestablish friendly ties with the United States, despite the United States' steadfast refusal to do so. Che managed to stay relatively quiet about Cuba's stance, but he could not have been more opposed. The differences that had always existed between Che and Castro grew more pronounced: While Castro seemed ready to compromise in an effort to keep both Cuba and his own political future afloat, Che's determination to infect Latin America with revolutionary fervor burned brighter than ever.

Che may have once been seen as the portal to good Soviet–Cuban relations, but now he seemed more of a hindrance than a help. After all, peaceful coexistence could hardly be obtained by igniting armed guerrilla conflicts wherever he could. His writings continued to fan the flames of continental revolution but relied less heavily on communist ideology and terminology. In addition, Che refused to stop funding, training, and arming communist dissidents—no matter what Moscow wanted. More and more it seemed he was at odds with Cuba's declaration of support for the Soviet Union.

For the Soviets there was growing concern that Che's continued guerrilla activities would pull the Soviet Union into another standoff with the United States. In the wake of the Cuban Missile Crisis, Che had publicly said the Soviets should have used the missiles and fired upon the United States. It was a stand echoed in China—that the Soviets had cowardly betrayed Cuba at the worst possible moment. It was that kind of rhetoric and potential confrontation that the USSR wanted to avoid. In keeping with his dedication to honesty at all costs, Che had often publicly lauded the Chinese for what he saw as their "truer" sense of the socialist mentality and criticized the Soviet Union for not being stronger. Che was afraid that the capitulation by the Soviets would hinder the chances of the fulfillment of his most deeply held goal: revolution elsewhere in Latin America. Che was now a liability, and KGB agents were assigned to keep an eye on him.

Disillusioned by Castro's compromising and the Soviets' deference to the United States, Che was ready to move on. Cuba's economy was riddled with problems, and Che's direction of Cuba's fiscal policy was under increasing attack. Che's vision of Cuba's massive industrialization had been ill-conceived and overreaching, and Cuba soon found itself falling back on agriculture (specifically sugar) as its main source of production—something Che never wanted. He saw Cuba's return to heavy reliance on agriculture as a betrayal of his dreams of industrialization. He resisted the move away from centralization and "moral" incentives toward a system based more on "material" incentives and self-management. In light of Cuba's return to agriculture as its main objective, it was decided that the sugar industry would have its own ministry, a ministry that was, perhaps tellingly, *not* run by Che.

Even without these factors of division, disillusionment, and disagreement, it is quite possible that Che would have wound his way out of Cuba and back into full-time revolutionary work anyway. His heart had always been on the battlefield, and his wandering soul had been too long confined to the same area. The failure of his Argentine forces only reinforced his desire to put himself back into the middle of the fray. His theories had yet to be proven outside of

Cuba, and he longed for another revolutionary success in Latin America. Even his dedication to volunteer work seemed to falter, not necessarily in hours spent, but in the passion he felt. The time was drawing near for Che to say good-bye to Cuba and Castro.

Che the Diplomat

Che continued to represent Cuba diplomatically even as his influence in the country was diminishing. In 1963 Che attended an economic conference in Algeria, and in Geneva in March 1964 he represented Cuba at the first United Nations Conference on Trade and Development. In his speech, Che reiterated his concern for the poor of the world and those who continued to fight for their liberation, stressing fairer trade policies that would benefit everyone involved, not just industrialized countries: "We clearly understand and frankly say that the only solution to humanity's problems at the moment is to completely suppress the exploitation of developing countries by developed capitalist countries."

In contrast to earlier speeches, he barely mentioned the Soviet Union. While in Geneva Che felt disenfranchised from other socialist delegates and was rarely, if ever, included in their meetings. In addition, relations with representatives from Latin American countries were just as tense.

Another trip to Algeria brought Che closer to the struggle for liberation in Africa. Che was certain that a rebellion was at hand in the Congo, where a similar effort had been beaten down in 1961. He was right, and in the summer of 1964, revolutionary efforts in the Congo were in full swing. The Congo soon played a crucial role in Che's life and provided him the impetus to leave Cuba.

Che and the Congo

In 1960, the Congo, newly independent from Belgium, was the site of a massive power struggle that found Soviet, Belgian, American, and United Nations powers all supporting a variety of groups. (For more on the Congo see Appendix B, "Relevant Struggles and Histories.") The area was rich in minerals mined for the United States, and American officials were afraid the USSR was trying to snag the region as its own. Patrice Lumumba, prime minister of the Congo and symbolic revolutionary leader, had first called upon UN forces for help in maintaining order and was now asking the USSR for military backing. Before a CIA-backed plot to remove Lumumba (by any means, apparently) could succeed, he was captured by Congolese rivals and executed. Che had looked upon Lumumba as a brother in revolution, and his death was marked in Cuba by a three-day period of mourning.

The battle in the Congo continued to rage on as U.S.-backed powers in the capital of Leopoldville (now known as Kinshasa) tried to wrest complete control from Lumumba-inspired rebels in the northern city of Stanleyville (now Kisangani). The situation seemed to be hopeless, with no solution in sight. Che, always in search of fellow revolutionaries, kept a close eye on the situation and watched its development closely. In it he found yet another example of American imperialism at its worst and began to use the Congo in his writings and speeches. In Africa, he began to see one of the best chances for exporting revolution: "Africa represents one of the most important battlegrounds, if not the most important." All over the continent, rebel forces were fighting to overcome colonial powers: The Portuguese-controlled areas of Angola and Mozambique, white-ruled South Africa, and especially the Congo remained hot spots.

In November 1964 the rebels in Stanleyville had been effectively ejected from the city after Belgian paratroopers were flown in via U.S. planes, leaving hundreds of Congolese rebels dead in their wake. Che characterized the action as "imperialist bestiality" and compared the operation to those of Hitler. In his address to the United Nations in December, Che lambasted the organization for allowing Western imperialism to win yet another victory in its quest for domination. He foreshadowed his own commitment to the revolution in the Congo: "All free men throughout the world must make ready to avenge the Congo crime."

In November 1964 Che returned to Russia to attend the anniversary of the Russian Revolution, a Russia without Khrushchev. In October 1964 Khrushchev's critics, including Leonid Brezhnev (Khrushchev's successor as head of the Communist Party and eventually top leader of the USSR) accused him of acting with disregard for the best interests of the state and for wielding power in an arbitrary, capricious manner. Clearly the trip, in light of all he had learned, was but a dim reflection of Che's first foray to Moscow in 1960 when he stood above Red Square, awestruck by not only what he imagined the Soviet Union to be but by what he envisioned for Cuba. Four years later, a disillusioned and disheartened Che must have felt very differently as he watched the flashy but meaningless parades and pageantry.

In December 1964 Che headed to New York, where he addressed the Nineteenth General Assembly of the United Nations as the head of the Cuban delegation. During his speech, Che covered familiar ground as he spoke of Cuba, and he expressed outrage at the turn of events in the Congo. Che also supported the call for nuclear disarmament, the main reason for the conference. In doing so, however, he struck a cautious tone:

> ... [W]e believe it necessary to also stress that the territorial integrity of nations must be respected and the armed hand of imperialism held back, for it is no less dangerous when it uses only conventional weapons ... Cuba reaffirms once again the right to maintain on its territory the weapons it deems appropriate, and its refusal to recognize the right of any power on earth—no matter how powerful—to violate our soil, our territorial waters, or our airspace.

Che was just as wary of nonnuclear weapons and their ability to suppress and destroy: "Those who murdered thousands of defenseless citizens of the Congo did not use the atomic bomb. They used conventional weapons. Conventional weapons have also been used by imperialism, causing so many deaths ...." In referencing the Congo, Che was signaling the area in which his revolutionary focus would soon be pointed.

It was over the situation in the Congo that Che found support in one of the United States' most well-known political figures, Malcolm X. Both of them drew parallels between white racism in the States and in its actions abroad. The two never met face to face, but Che did send a note of solidarity to Malcolm X, which

Malcolm read to his followers at a rally in Harlem. Che's hopes for sparking revolution all across Latin America was also in full view: "I would be prepared to give my life for the liberation of any country in Latin America, without asking or demanding anything from anyone or exploiting anyone." Che soon made good on his promise.

Profile portrait of Ernesto Che Guevara with cigar (December 17, 1964).

(Bob Parent/Archive Photos)

While in the States, Che appeared on the CBS program, *Face the Nation*. His appearance was marked by his trademark defense of the Cuban Revolution ("the best thing would be for the U.S. to forget about us") and his growing interest in the Third World. His appearance brought protests from other Latin American governments over what they perceived as unfair publicity for Cuba.

After his trip to New York, Che traveled to Africa again and took a quick spin around the continent. It was a glimmer of the "old" Che as he held talks with leaders of liberation groups, journalists, and students and toured guerrilla training camps. While in Africa, Che offered Cuban help to the rebel leaders and shared his own revolutionary experiences with them: "A revolutionary soldier was made in war. I proposed to them that their training should take place in the Congo, where the fighting was going on—against imperialism in its neocolonial form." He left them with the promise of mobilizing black Cuban volunteers to come help in the Congolese struggle.

The Congo was an area ripe with conflict and already in the throes of revolution. With visions of a tri-continental revolutionary force forming (Asia, Africa, and Latin America), Che had decided to throw himself into the heart of Africa and its revolutionary fight.

After leaving Africa, Che went on to Algeria for another economic seminar where he raised the hackles of the socialist bloc by insisting that national liberation struggles in places such as Vietnam and the Congo be funded by the socialist countries:

> Arms cannot be commodities in our world. They must be delivered to the peoples asking for them to use against the common enemy, with no charge and in the quantities needed and available. That is the spirit in which the USSR and the People's Republic of China have offered us their military aid. We are socialists ... The reply to the ominous attacks by United States imperialism against Vietnam or the Congo should be to supply those sister countries with all the defense equipment they need, and to offer them our full solidarity without any conditions whatsoever.

In the speech, he effectively broke his ties with the Soviet Union, bitterly criticizing the Soviet bloc for showing what he called "tacit complicity with the exploiting countries of the West." Che felt that by pursuing "mutual advantage" trade, socialist countries were exploiting the very people they were supposed to be helping. How was socialism served when some countries "sell at world prices the raw materials that cost backward countries infinite sweat and suffering, while they buy at world market prices the machines produced in large, mechanized factories"?

By accusing those he trusted so much of "imperialistic exploitation," Che was burning the very bridges he had crossed to arrive at this point in his life. But as he had proven time and time again, Che was committed to speaking his mind. Castro was obviously unhappy with Che's strident stance, a factor that most likely contributed to Che soon leaving Cuba. Also on this trip, Che would visit China (where he tried to explain the Cuban stance over the Sino-Soviet split, to no avail), Paris, Ireland, and Egypt.

Home to Cuba, but Only Briefly

Che returned to Havana in March 1965. In his absence, Aleida had delivered her fourth and final child with Che, a little boy named Ernesto. She had undoubtedly become accustomed to her husband's long absences, but the longest one yet was about to begin. Che was met at the airport by Castro—a show of solidarity amid growing rumors that the two were not on good terms. In fact, the two soon had a marathon meeting, forty hours is the figure bandied around, but the exact details of their conversation are unknown. Obviously Che's desire to go to Africa must have been figured prominently in their talks. Years later, Castro confirmed that Che's desire to continue his revolutionary work was indeed the topic at hand. It was apparently during this meeting that Castro decided that Che would be put in charge of the forces to be sent to the Congo. Of course, Che's determination would have made any other outcome highly unlikely.

Che quickly began to assemble his team for his excursion to the heart of Africa. The Congo promised to be a base for Che, a flashpoint for revolution in all parts of Africa and leading to a massive

Third World revolution. The guerillas had cleared a large area in the heart of the Congo and were well-stocked with Soviet and Chinese arms. He moved quickly, writing letters of farewell to be released after his departure. He began to give away personal belongings and gave his final talk as Minister of Industry to his staff. He focused on Africa but gave no solid indication of his future there. His plans were wrapped in secrecy as he began slowly to withdraw from the public eye. The official line was that Che was going to cut sugarcane in the region of Camaguey. In fact, his appearance at the airport with Castro was the last time the Cuban people at large saw Che before his departure.

His last few days in Cuba were undoubtedly bittersweet for Che. The revolution had come so far and yet seemed to have so far to go. Clearly, Che felt his usefulness had come to an end. He was, at heart, a revolutionary and traveler, not a banker or minister of industry or diplomat. It was time to do as he had always done—hit the road in search of himself. Still, the tone of his farewell letter to Castro and the Cuban people (released to the public after he left but read by Castro before Che departed Cuba) is one of gratitude, dedication, and love. Che could be a deeply personal writer, a man unafraid to express the richness of his experience, and one evocative section in particular seems to embody his state of mind as he prepared to leave the land that had come to mean so much to him: "I will say once again that the only way that Cuba can be held responsible for my actions is in its example. If my time should come under other skies, my last thought will be for this people, and especially for you."

Chapter 10

Che's Congo

I have learned in the Congo. There were errors I will not commit again; maybe others will be repeated and I will commit new ones. I have come through with more faith than ever in guerrilla warfare, but we have failed.

—Che Guevara

Che was headed back into revolution, but he would never recreate the success he had found with Castro in Cuba. The struggle in the Congo was born from hundreds of years of conflict, both external and internal. As much as he wanted it to succeed, his determination would prove no match for the obstacles that waited for him deep within Africa.

Che had left his family behind before, and Aleida probably always knew this day would come. Che promised to send for her when he could, and he hoped that sooner or later the Congo would be a suitable place to move his wife and four children. Of course it never was. Che's second marriage, much like his first, was a lower priority than his politics and revolutionary passion; he and Aleida were far from close. He had also sent word to his first child, Hildita, reassuring her that she would always be on his mind. In the years since the Cuban Revolution, he had made a sincere effort to be close to his firstborn, often taking her to work with him where she would play on the floor as he conducted his economy business.

After the CIA-backed storming of Stanleyville in July 1964, the revolution in the Congo was all but over. The rebels would continue to survive for years to come in little bands, but Che was coming to the battle late in the game. Still, incensed by what he considered yet another Western-led slaughter, Che felt driven to fight what was essentially a losing battle. His goal of centralizing the rebel forces into a coherent army would never be realized, and his hope of unifying Soviet and Chinese support would remain unfulfilled. Despite his disagreement with the Soviet Union and the Sino-Soviet split, both the USSR and China were supplying arms to the Congo, albeit in an effort to usurp each other.

One has to wonder if, after four years of post-revolutionary life in Cuba, Che was not ready to fight anywhere, no matter what the odds. He had tired of sending others into battle (the failed attempt in Argentina was undoubtedly weighing heavy on his mind) and was determined to send himself this time. Moreover, there was the Cuban situation. As evident in his writings and speeches, Che was finding it harder and harder to condone the shift back toward agriculture that Castro was supporting, among other changes. There was simply less for Che to do in Cuba, a reality that drove him to want to do more elsewhere.

Internally, Che may have been the same man who had sailed aboard the *Granma* and fought so successfully from the Sierra Maestra, but externally, the four years had taken a toll. His asthma attacks had continued while in Cuba, and the medicine he took, combined with the natural progression of age, had added considerable weight to his frame. Perhaps it was this passing of time and the deterioration of his physical condition that also led him to take on the Congo, fearing that sooner or later he just would be unable to fight.

As Che headed into Africa he felt certain that the continent would prove to be the world's prime spot for radical change and a major blow against imperialism. In what must have been very reminiscent of his South American trip in his youth, Che had been touched by the poverty and oppression he encountered during his trip through Africa in late 1964 and early 1965. It had always been the plight of the common man that inspired Che; the sight of suffering spurred him to action. But as Che soon found out, the people were different in Africa. There was a level of division and internal conflict between tribes that made unification nearly impossible. It was but one of several lessons he would learn the hard way while in Africa.

Conflict in the Congo

For obvious reasons, most of the Cuban volunteers who were sent to the Congo were black. There was much concern that Che would not be readily accepted (if at all) by the Congolese rebels because he was white, and a dark-skinned force behind him was required. In truth, Che's Congo forces, chosen for less than sound military reasons, were far from ready. In all, about one hundred fifty Cubans were initially sent to the Congo, some with Che, some ahead of him, and some to follow.

Ready or not, Che and his men arrived in Tanzania in mid-April 1965. Che had furtively left Cuba on April 1 and taken a circuitous route to Africa. Soon the group made their way to Kigoma, a village to the east of the Congo. As Che was heading into the heart of Africa, his mother, Celia, was starting a journey of her own, a journey that would be her last. Celia was in a Buenos Aires hospital, dying of cancer. She did not yet know her son was in Africa; his plans were kept secret, even from her. Castro would not announce the truth about Che's actions until months later, in October 1965. Despite Aleida's attempts to reach Che (she did not tell Che's family in Argentina about Che's African quest), he did not learn of his mother's condition until it was too late. She died in mid-May, her family—minus Che—by her side.

Others shared the Guevara family's curiosity concerning Che's whereabouts. Rumors about his "disappearance" (some of which were planted by the CIA in hopes of flushing out the truth) were flying fast and furious. Some of the most oft-repeated stories had Che expelled from Cuba by Castro, even executed, for his public stances against Cuban policies. While Che and Castro had grown apart and a rift had developed, there seems to be little evidence that such a plot by Castro was ever developed. In fact, it seems likely that Castro preferred to have Che in Africa rather than in

Latin America. He feared for Che's life and thought U.S. intervention (and assassination attempts) would be less likely if Che were fighting in the Congo rather than in Latin American countries.

Other rumors had Che fighting forces in Vietnam or the Dominican Republic. Still others suggested that he had gone insane and was convalescing in a Cuban sanitarium. There were also tales that he was in the United States, secretly waging his own war in his own way. Like many popular figures throughout history, Che was everywhere and nowhere. In the rumors and stories one can see his transition into a cultural icon beginning before his death. It was almost as if the world needed to see Che, to know where he was, to know what he was up to. And if the world could not know for sure, it would dream about it. The rumors had one thing in common though: Che was still in battle. Whether it was for his people or his politics, or for his sanity or his life, Che was already cast in the public eye as a fighter, a warrior of his own making.

Meanwhile, Che was quickly realizing that the situation in the Congo was far from what he had hoped for. Despite reports to the contrary, the forces there were poorly commanded and unruly. Often they were more interested in getting drunk and frequenting whorehouses than they were in revolution. Che was dismayed and upset to learn that little had been done to prepare for his arrival. The leader that Che had been in contact with, Laurent Kabila, was not present, and Che soon found himself dealing with various commanders who seemed to be at odds with their own ranks.

Equally dismaying was the state of the troops. Most of them spoke only in their varied native tongues, further widening the gap between the commanders and themselves. Whereas the Cuban rebels had shared a common culture and goal, the Congolese rebels were bound by little more than circumstance. Deeply superstitious, the fighters believed in witchcraft, specifically in the concept of "dawa." Dawa was thought to be a magic potion that rendered the men invincible to gunfire. One can only imagine Che's incredulity when one of the commanders himself extolled the virtues of dawa to him, claiming that several bullets had simply dropped off him, causing no wounds. For a man like Che, such talk of magic and witchcraft must have seemed a recipe for disaster: "I always feared that this superstition would turn against us—that the Congolese would blame us for some failure in combat that left many dead."

Still, Che maintained his steadfast belief that Africa would be the birthplace of great change and that he could help guide the Congo toward its destiny. Various commanders told him exaggerated (or untrue) stories of their troops stationed elsewhere and how they numbered in the thousands. Immediately formulating a training plan for the men, Che was eager to move forward with the operation. He was met with little support, only evasion and delay.

Waiting for Revolution

As days went by with little tangible action, Che found himself in a familiar role—that of a doctor. Many of the rebels had been wounded by gunfire, not in battle, but by mishandling weapons or simple horseplay. His hands were also full treating the seemingly endless cases of venereal disease the men were plagued with. In addition, local peasants not involved in the fighting began to show up, hoping for medical attention. He soon found himself fighting off cases of malaria and other tropical diseases, not to mention the decaying morale of his own Cuban forces.

While waiting for Kabila to arrive Che also began holding classes for the men, trying to educate them in a common language and culture. He was determined to make his Congo mission work. In a way, it is emblematic of Che's unshakeable belief that what had worked before could do so again, even if he had to do it all by himself. And once again, if more people had been like Che, there was probably nothing he could not have accomplished.

Eventually a leader arrived, Laurent Mitoudidi, who agreed with Che's plan to move the troops farther into the wild. It was an area Che undoubtedly felt would be safer; their current position was too close to established areas. Once at their new encampment, far up a mountain (familiar terrain for Che), he began to set up a village, much like those he had established in Cuba. Huts were built and classes taught, all in an attempt to forge order and discipline.

Soon, however, the doctor himself was ill, as were most of the other Cubans. The tropical infections in the area wreaked havoc on their bodies, leaving them listless and plagued by high fever. Che's asthma did not help the situation, and the better part of a month was spent simply recuperating from the effects of a new environment. For those not afflicted with sickness, the monotony of waiting took its toll. They had come to fight but had yet to see any action.

Finally, on May 22, Che received the order from Mitoudidi to prepare for battle, an attack on a town called Albertville. It could not have come at a worse time. The men were sick and unfocused, but Che, not wanting to appear unwilling, went along. More Cuban rebels arrived, along with sad news. Although she had already died on May 19, it was then that Che learned of his mother's hospitalization. He soon knew for sure that Celia had died: "I had to spend a month in sad uncertainty, waiting for an outcome that I had guessed at, but with the hope that there had been some mistake in the news, until the confirmation of my mother's death reached me."

Especially upsetting for Che was the knowledge that she would never know the contents of the farewell letter he had left for his parents. In it he had written, "It is possible this is the end ... if it should be so, I send you a final embrace. I have loved you very much, only I have not known how to express my affection." In his closing he referred to himself as "your obstinate and prodigal son." Knowing that Celia never got to read his good-bye must have only deepened his sorrow over her passing. In the end, the "final embrace" was not from him to her, but from her to him.

Celia had written a letter to Che in her last days, a letter that reached him only after her death. In it she wrote about his abrupt departure from Cuba and the pain it had brought her. A perfunctory letter from Che (not the "farewell" letter) about his going to cut sugarcane for a month only deepened her concern: "the result [of Che's letter] has been a sea of confusion, and even greater anxiety and alarm." She went on to speculate as to his true reasons for leaving Cuba ("there must be reasons I don't know"), wondering if there were, as rumors suggested, a permanent rift between Che and

Castro. In the end, Celia still supported her son, writing that she was simply an "old woman who hopes to see the whole world converted to socialism."

In closing Celia simply said, "Yes, you'll always be a foreigner. That seems to be your permanent fate." It is an assessment Che himself would have had to agree with. She knew his wanderlust and his devotion to adventure firsthand. Despite the worried and somewhat reproaching tone of the letter, it is clear that Celia was only concerned for her beloved son, not mentioning her own health. Although continents separated them at the end, the mother and son shared an understanding of each other, an understanding that must have given them both a sense of peace. Celia may not have understood the details, but she clearly understood and loved the nature of her wandering son. Even so, Che must have questioned, at least in his darkest hours, the choices he made that had led him to be in the heart of Africa instead of at the side of his mother's deathbed.

Battle at Last

Che was able to convince Mitoudidi that the best plan was to wait for their initial attack. Che wanted to get a better idea of the layout and situation before diving in. Sending men out to various front lines, Che waited for their assessment. Although some of the forces were adequately armed and able to attack, overall the situation was dire. Commanders drinking to the point of incapacity (in front of their troops, no less), virtually no training, chronic laziness, and constant intimidation of the peasants by the rebels were but a few of the deadly mistakes made with alarming frequency among the native men. The differences between the Congolese and the Cubans could not have been more pronounced. To make matters worse, the internal fighting between the different rebel forces in the area had not abated, further confusing exactly who was fighting whom in this war.

Exploration efforts continued through June, with little good news reported. Besides, without the approval of Kabila, Che was not allowed to take any action on his own. Kabila remained out of touch, communicating with Che only through sporadic messages:

"Every day it was the same litany: Kabila didn't come today, but tomorrow without fail, or the day after … If the order of the day was not changed, the Congolese revolution was irrevocably doomed to failure."

Arms continued to arrive, mainly from China and the Soviet Union—arms that Che knew were essentially being wasted. Soon Mitoudidi, Che's only real contact with a serious rebel leader, mysteriously drowned, further complicating the operation and depressing Che. According to witnesses, Mitoudidi had fallen from a boat but managed to stay alive for ten to fifteen minutes. Despite efforts to retrieve him, those present told Che of "some magic power [that] seemed to prevent it [the boat] from approaching Mitoudidi." At least one of the others dived in to try and save him, only to drown himself. Che's prediction that Congolese superstition would prove deadly had come true: "So a man lost his life in a stupid accident just as he was beginning to achieve some organization amid the terrible chaos at the Kibamba base." Another liaison would be sent by Kabila, but he proved to be a poor substitute for the man Che had come to rely on. In a suggestion that must have only confirmed Che's worst fears, the new liaison suggested moving the camp in an effort to rid the troops of Mitoudidi's ghost.

The end of June finally brought action Che's way. Kabila sent word that Che and his men were to attack a military base at Fort Bendera. Che was mistrustful because the base was apparently heavily guarded, and he suggested starting smaller. Overruled, and not allowed to go himself, Che mobilized a force of approximately two hundred men and sent them to what turned out to be a disaster. Not only did a third of the rebels flee before fighting even began, but four Cubans were killed, and a diary was confiscated— a diary that alerted the opposing forces of the Cubans' direct involvement. Among those fighting the rebels were anti-Castro Cubans sent to Africa by the CIA. Any secrecy Che had hoped for was lost.

Morale following the pathetic attack quickly bottomed out. The Cubans were disgusted at the behavior of the Congolese fighters, outwardly questioning the logic of fighting for people who would not fight for themselves:

*Every one of our fighters had the sad experience of seeing
troops going into battle break up the moment the fight
began, dumping their priceless weapons anywhere so as
to escape faster. They also saw the lack of comradeship
among the fighters. The wounded were also abandoned
to their fate; terror took hold of the soldiers ....*

Che may have been committed, but his men did not share his enthusiasm or dedication. After three months in Africa, many of them expressed a strong desire to go home. Che did not take their appeals lightly and strongly criticized their attitudes, still hoping he could turn the fight around through sheer will. Still, several Cubans opted to leave when Che gave them a final chance to do so. In time, Che would do the same, but not until he felt he had no other choice.

After weeks and weeks of promises and delays, Kabila finally arrived to see Che in early July. But after only a few days, Kabila left, throwing the temporarily inspired Congolese rebels back into an ineffectual haze: "The soldiers in charge of the trenches said they were not going to work that day as the chief had gone away." Kabila's visit did little to lift spirits, and the rebel forces seemed to be in more disarray then ever.

Internal power struggles within the various rebel forces continued to eat away at any power base left as more and more fighters deserted. The few attacks that were launched produced spotty results at best, leaving Che disheartened and frustrated. Che had yet to be allowed to go into battle himself. By August, he admitted to some of his remaining troops that the situation was growing hopeless. The situation was nothing like the Sierra Maestra, and morale was continuing to spiral downward despite the arrival of fresh troops from Cuba. Che could not even convince the other commanders to send their men to him for training. How could he make a difference in these conditions? By September, counter-rebels had begun to seriously plague the area, making it even harder to trust anyone.

In the meantime, Castro was sending Che messages of good will and encouragement, reminding him that the Cuban Revolution had also had dark days. Che responded by letting Castro know how dire the situation was: "I can assure you that if I was not here, this beautiful dream would have dissolved long ago in the general chaos." He implored Castro not to believe any positive reports he had been receiving, that they "don't have anything to do with the truth."

Che was rapidly coming to the end of his rope, but continued his revolutionary efforts despite his own misgivings. He organized a course in fighting that only succeeded in strengthening his own frustration with the unresponsive Congolese fighters. To top it all off, malaria and other exotic maladies continued to ravage the Cubans, including Che himself.

A Turn for the Worse

In the middle of October, the government began to step up its offensive, further weakening the rebels' position. To further complicate matters, a settlement had been reached between the Congolese government and the rebel backers: The government would recall the ruthless mercenaries they had sent in if the foreign nations backing the rebels, including Cuba, pulled their support. Although the settlement did not go off as planned and the mercenaries stayed, the atmosphere was clearly one of approaching defeat. In fact, several of the rebel leaders were negotiating with the government—to their own benefit, of course.

Ironically, at roughly the same time, Castro announced to the world exactly what Che had been up to all these months. Back in Cuba, Castro had formed the Central Committee of the Communist Party, a committee that featured the glaring absence of Che Guevara. The public reading of Che's farewell letter served as an explanation for Che's absence from both the committee and Cuba; people had demanded to know where he was.

The letter is moving and eloquent and one of Che's most famous. In it he expresses love and respect for Cuba and its leader, even as he declares his desire to leave both:

> *I formally resign my positions in the leadership of the party ... and my Cuban citizenship ... I have lived magnificent days, and at [Castro's] side I felt the pride of*

*belonging to our people in the brilliant yet sad days of the
Caribbean crisis. Seldom has a statesman been more brilliant than you were in those days.*

Hearing news of the reading of his letter, Che knew more than
ever that he was a true foreigner, not even able to go back to Cuba.
He had left them, renounced the party and his citizenship, and was
now fighting a losing battle deep in the heart of Africa.

Perhaps buoyed by the finality of his letter being made public,
Che desperately tried to rebound in the Congo and continued his
futile efforts to whip the troops into fighting form. Acknowledging
the defeats they had suffered, Che nonetheless promised that
November could be the turning point. Indeed, November was the
turning point, but not in the direction Che wanted: Tanzania, an
important rebel backer, pulled its support. Soon, a letter arrived
from Castro telling Che to do what he thought was best: If he
wanted to stay and fight, Castro would send him more men. If Che
thought it best to leave, he would support that as well. Above all
else, Castro wrote, "avoid annihilation."

In the end, it was not Che who decided to give up, but the other
rebel leaders: "We would abandon the struggle only if the
Congolese themselves asked us to for some good reason or in overwhelming circumstances, but we will fight to prevent that." In the
face of all the hopelessness and imminent defeat, Che still wanted
to fight—"Cuba does not renege on its promises and cannot flee
shamefully, leaving brothers at the mercy of mercenaries"—that is
just who he was.

In mid-November 1965, after seven months of attempted revolution and now under explicit orders from Cuba to make his
escape, Che began his withdrawal from the Congo. The Cuban
troops had to be furtive about their plans, unsure of the Congolese
reaction to their leaving. Che led his men to a nearby lake where
one boat lead them out of the Congo and another took the
Congolese to a nearby village. Even as the evacuation was underway, Che had doubts, entertaining thoughts of staying behind
while his men made their escape. Perhaps he thought he had
nowhere else to go. In the end, he left with his men, taking a few
of the braver Congolese with them. Those left behind figured out

what was happening and begged to be taken along. Despite every-thing, Che was moved by their display: "I had to reject men who pleaded to be taken along. There was not a trace of grandeur in this retreat, nor a gesture of rebellion."

As the boat sailed away and the cries of abandoned Congolese fighters filled the air, Che must have reflected on another November boat ride, one that delivered him to revolutionary vic-tory in Cuba. Now, nine years later, another boat carried him away from a defeated revolution to destinations unknown.

Chapter 11

Che's Last Stand

I believe in armed struggle as the only solution for those peoples who fight to free themselves, and I am consistent with my beliefs. Many will call me an adventurer, and that I am—only one of a different sort: one who risks his skin to prove his truth.

—Che Guevara

Although the Congo revolution was far from what he hoped, Che was in no way ready to give up the fight. The only question was the one that had seemingly always haunted him: Where to next? The first stop for Che and his men was in Dar es Salaam, the capital of Tanzania, situated on the eastern coast on the Indian Ocean. There Che and his men regrouped, waiting to return to Cuba. Che would not accompany his men back to Havana, despite Castro's desires to the contrary. Perhaps Che felt he could not return so soon after his declaration to leave Cuba, especially having failed in the Congo. A handful of Cuban troops chose to remain with Che; they were ready to fight with him wherever they were led.

While at the city's Cuban embassy, Che found a place to collect his thoughts and reflect on his last seven months spent in the Congo. In an effort to make sense of his Congo experience, Che threw himself back into writing, feverishly compiling and honing the diaries he kept while there. He was planning a book on the Congo operation, a book that would not be published while he was alive. Concentrating on writing also gave him a chance to recoup physical losses. He had lost a good deal of weight while in Africa, his asthma and bouts with tropical diseases taking a serious toll on his health.

Applying his trademark honesty, Che assessed the operation with candor and self-criticism: "This is the story of a failure." He knew that chances had been slim for the realization of his hopes for the Congo, but he also recognized how some of his own actions contributed to the mission's eventual demise. First, he had been thrust into the midst of the Congolese rebels with no warning, a move that only fostered distrust of him within the troops and their leadership. He also felt he had not found a way to effectively communicate the importance of their work to the Congolese troops and that he had been too harsh on them, even exhibiting erratic behavior out of frustration: "For a long time I maintained an attitude that could be described as excessively complacent, and at other times, perhaps due to an innate characteristic of mine, I exploded in ways that were very cutting and very hurtful [to others]."

He berated himself for not learning Swahili quickly or well enough. He now realized that his ability to communicate with the leaders (mainly in French) had not been enough; he had lacked the ability to relate to the troops themselves, in their own languages. Che's power-base had always been common people, both those he fought with and for. He also wrote of how his tendency to withdraw into his own world invariably made him seem outside the operation (for example, when he had spent hours alone with his books and writing, as he had in his childhood).

Second, Che recognized that he had never been able to instill in his Cuban troops the same dedication and passion he felt for the Congolese people: "At the beginning I tried to use moral coercion and failed. I sought to make my troops have the same point of view as I did regarding the situation and I failed; they were not prepared to look optimistically into a future that had to be viewed through a gloomy present."

Finally, he also felt that the timing of the revelation of his "farewell to Cuba" had been unfortunate: "The letter made the comrades see me—as they had many years ago when I began in the Sierra Maestra—as a foreigner among Cubans." Che felt that his official departure from Cuba severed ties with his troops, undercutting his ability to appeal to a commonality that had previously been such a powerful unifier.

By undertaking such serious self-reflection, Che was obviously hoping to understand why he had failed in the Congo so that certain mistakes would not be repeated in the future. But where would that future play out? The conflict in the Congo was not to be retested, and Che needed a new battlefield in his never-ending revolutionary quest. Che remained in Tanzania until February 1966 (Aleida came at one point for a six-week visit), at which time a plan began to form that would put Che in yet another revolution, fighting in yet another South American country. This time, it would be his last.

The CIA had always been interested in the Cuban Revolution and, in particular, Che Guevara. But in late 1965, while Che was in the Congo, an intelligence memo was circulated titled "The Fall of Che Guevara and the Changing Face of the Cuban Revolution." In it, a CIA analyst by the name of Brian Latell analyzed Che's standing in Cuba and the reasons for his apparent loss of power. Latell blamed Guevara's "persistent opposition to the practical policies recommended by the Soviet Union" for his fall from grace.

As the CIA saw it, Che's slide from power was a direct result of Castro's unwillingness to support Che in two of his most important goals:

> Guevara, who has been considered Cuba's most militant revolutionary spokesman, disapproved of Castro's alignment with the USSR in the Sino-Soviet dispute and of his willingness to diminish Cuba's role as a catalyst and supporter of revolution in Latin America and Africa.

Calling Che's attempt at industrialization "Guevara's greatest failure," Latell blamed Che for the "disastrous effects" of the revolution's early policies. The nine-page memo analyzes Che's situation further, noting that Castro had called for "the decentral-ization of local administration, and announced that extensive reforms would begin to organize a completely new administration apparatus." For Latell, this was undeniable proof that Che was on his way out: "Another of Guevara's cherished theories had been abandoned." In addition, other reasons for and evidence of Che's apparent ousting include his growing tensions with others in the movement and Castro's recent emphasis on material (rather than moral) incentives.

If the CIA knew at this point (October 1965) that Che was fighting in the Congo, this memo does not reveal that information. It does, however, prove insightful about Che's nature: "Guevara never wavered from his firm revolutionary stand, even as other Cuban leaders began to devote most of their attention to the inter-nal problems of the revolution." The CIA's tracking of Che would pick up steam upon his detection in Bolivia and continue until the confirmation of his death.

Latell ends the memo by looking to Cuba's future ("from now on Cuba will probably pattern both its domestic and foreign poli-cies more in accord with Soviet advice") and seeing no sign of Che: "With the fall of Guevara and the general acceptance of Soviet advice in domestic and foreign policies, the Cuban Revolution has entered a new phase." Despite the outward appear-ance that Che was completely out of the picture, he was preparing to embark on a new phase of his own.

Bolivia Beckons

Che soon found himself heading to Prague, staying in a Cuban safe house where he continued to recover both psychologically and physically from his Congo expedition. It was important for Che to get farther away from Africa. The CIA—as well as other agencies eager to rid the world of Che—was all too aware that he was in the area, heightening concerns that he would be killed. While in Prague, Aleida returned, realizing that her prideful husband would not return to Cuba anytime soon, even though Castro (fearing for Che's life) was still encouraging Che to do just that. But Che refused. Pride aside, he knew that he could do more good for Cuba outside its borders. The rift that had grown between the Soviets and him would have proven a liability for Castro. Still, Castro had begun to speak again of the importance of "solidarity" among the guerrilla fighters waging revolution around the world. Castro used his appearance at the "First Tricontinental Conference" to declare 1966 "The Year of Solidarity," proclaiming to the hundreds of delegates from over eighty different Latin, Asian, and African states (as well as the Soviets and the Chinese) his continuing support of the war against imperialism. The search was on for a place Che could venture to in the name of liberation as a revolutionary emissary of Cuba.

For Castro, perhaps deploying Che killed two birds with one stone: Not only did the prospect of a guerrilla mission appeal to Che's rebel nature, but the distancing of Che from the Cuban regime (as noted in the CIA memo) would most likely improve Cuba's internal problems as well as its relations with the Soviet Union. Of course there's speculation that Castro sent Che to Bolivia on a suicide mission, knowing full well that he would never make it back alive. By making Che a martyr, Castro would be able to invoke Che's legacy without having to deal with Che's policies. Like many details of the Cuban Revolution and the ensuing decades, Castro's logic is open to interpretation. But regardless of Castro's reasoning, one thing is absolutely certain: Che was neither sent against his will nor coerced into the mission. He wanted to go.

After considering missions in Peru and Venezuela, Bolivia became the site of Che's next foray into battle. (For more on Bolivia, see Appendix B, "Relevant Struggles and Histories.") The conditions there seemed right (a recent government coup had unseated a revolutionary party from power) and the Bolivian Communist Party was relatively strong and well-structured, with several of its younger leaders having strong ties with Castro's Cuba. By going to Bolivia, Che hoped to foster conditions that would usher in revolution across South America, specifically in Argentina. Essentially a man without a country, Che still longed to make a difference in his true homeland. Even though Bolivia would be his first stop, Argentina was his true destination.

Still, there were no armed rebel forces waiting for Che. He and his men would be igniting a revolution, not reinforcing one. Che had long advocated that outside rather than inside forces could foment a revolution. True, the Bolivian Communist Party appeared to be willing to support such a move, but as time would tell, its approval proved tenuous at best and duplicitous at worst.

In fact, the country's Communist Party leaders did not altogether endorse Che's arrival in Bolivia to lead an armed uprising. Castro's revolutionary designs had alienated Cuba from many Latin American countries, and Bolivian party leaders were less than supportive at first. They soon seemed to agree, however, but perhaps not to revolution. Mario Monje, the Secretary-General of the Bolivian Communist Party, later claimed that he agreed only to allow Che to use Bolivia as a home base and passage down into Argentina, not to begin his own guerrilla war in Bolivia. As Monje later remembered it, Castro told him, "a mutual friend wants to return to his country, someone whose revolutionary caliber nobody can question. And nobody can deny him the right to return to his country. And he thinks the best place to pass through [to get there] is Bolivia. I ask you to help him pass through your country." Monje obviously knew who this "mutual friend" was and says he agreed to help Che in his passage. He insists that Castro assured him, "We are not going to intervene in your affairs." Of course, intervention was exactly what was planned.

After Che's death, Castro accused Monje of initially supporting Che's revolutionary expedition, only to later change his mind. According to Castro, Monje's change of heart was a betrayal that directly led to Che's death. Che evidently felt the same way, describing Monje in his Bolivian diary as a traitor.

It is not clear whom to believe, Castro or Monje. On one hand, Castro could have misrepresented the true nature of Che's mission. As history shows, Castro had proven himself adept at operating in the political short term, not hesitating to say whatever it took to get what he wanted, only to change his position later. Of course the opposite seems just as possible: Castro may have been upfront with Monje about Che's plans for launching a guerrilla campaign in Bolivia. Another possibility is that Castro believed all along that Che would merely use Bolivia as a passageway to Argentina. And yet another equally plausible scenario is that both Monje and Castro were less than forthcoming with the other.

Whatever the details regarding the Bolivian operation, troops for the expedition (primarily men who had fought with Che before, including Daniel Alarcón who had fought in both the Sierra Maestra and the Congo) were assembled in Cuba, a group far more skilled and prepared than that sent to the Congo. Other than that it was of the utmost importance, they were told little of their mission, not even of Che's involvement. In anticipation of their coming trek, some better-informed Cubans went ahead and located a training camp in southeast Bolivia, near the foothills of the Andes. Tamara Bunke (the agent known as "Tania") was already in Bolivia, her purpose being one of a deep-cover courier who could pass between countries undetected to aid the hoped-for revolutionary movement across the continent.

A Changed Man Returns to Cuba

In July 1966 Che returned to Cuba under extreme secrecy and underwent a remarkable physical transformation. Upon receiving his troops, they did not recognize him. His hair had been plucked out on top, leaving him looking naturally bald. In place of his trademark green fatigues and black beret, he was sporting a suit, tie, and glasses. Calling himself Ramón, Che began berating the men, loudly complaining that they were clearly unfit for guerrilla warfare. For several minutes he continued to have fun at the troops' expense until finally he deliberately let some details slip about previous operations. Initially dumbstruck by their masquerading leader, the men were overjoyed at the return of their beloved "comandante."

Now back in Cuba, Che spent his time preparing his troops for Bolivia; he did not want to repeat the Congo fiasco. The men would have to be ready in every way, and there could be no dissension or doubt. A rigorous and exhausting environment was established for the men, with Che overseeing their training. In light of his failure in the Congo, Che was like a man possessed, more determined than ever (if that was possible) to wage a successful revolution outside Cuba.

By the fall of 1966 Che and his men were on their way to Bolivia, taking leave of Cuba in small groups. Before Che's departure, however, in what may be the most heartbreaking twist in his revolutionary life, he had an emotional reunion with his wife and their four children. Aleida knew that Che was back in Cuba, and she had been out to see him several times. However, his children had not. They were too young to be trusted; it was all too feasible that they would tell everyone that Daddy was home. The radical transformation for his foray into Bolivia not only fooled Che's men, but did the same to his own children as well.

When four of Che's five children were brought out to see him (Hildita was simply too old and the risk that she would see through his disguise was too great), Che was introduced to them as their "Uncle Ramón." He talked to them of their father, telling them how he had sent Ramón to see them to relay his love. They had lunch together—the last one ever as a family in what must have a gut-wrenching situation. Che had to check his speech and behavior so as not to reveal his true identity. He had to temper his love and affection, behaving like an uncle (an unknown uncle, at that) and not a father. This must have been very difficult for him: It had already been a year and a half since he had last seen them, and now, forced to be distant, he had no choice but to check his emotions.

Maintaining an emotional distance from his children was the price Che had to pay, the cost of doing what he thought was right. He fully and passionately believed he was doing what was best for his children, making the world a better place. Still, as he sat with these four little people and his wife, his restraint and deception must have hurt him deeply. Giving "Uncle Ramón" a kiss for him to take to their father, the children were soon gathered up and taken home. It was the last time he ever saw any of them.

Meanwhile, the situation in Bolivia was not coming together as neatly as hoped. Monje and the Communist Party leaders had begun to withdraw their support, citing their unwillingness to allow Bolivia to be used as the center of Che's guerrilla activity.

Monje was complaining that he had been misled and that Che and his men were to use Bolivia as transit only, not as ground zero. Still, complete support was not withdrawn, and Castro seemed to think he could maneuver his way around any obstacle. After all, the younger leaders appeared to be behind the plan, but of course, they were not making the final decisions. Despite conflicting messages from the Bolivian Communist Party, the operation continued as planned. Che undoubtedly felt, as he almost always did, that revolutionary zeal and fervor would carry him and his men through. However, the lack of support from the Bolivian Communist Party leadership eventually proved crucial in setting the stage for Che's death.

Into Bolivia

In an effort to keep their plans as secret as possible as they made their way into Bolivia, Che and the twenty men accompanying him all assumed different identities, posing as citizens of Uruguay, Peru, and Bolivia. They hoped to connect with Bolivian fighters recruited for the cause.

First on Che's plan was to set up a training center that would serve as a headquarters. A call would be sent out to other revolutionary leaders in Latin America who, in turn, would send representatives to the center where they would take part in advanced training and practice missions. Then Che would establish a main column of fighters that would fan out, heading to other countries to receive additional training. Bolivia was to serve as the first combat mission, and Che planned to have the group attack a military base as a way of announcing their presence to the world.

By early November Che was in La Paz, Bolivia, disguised and posing as "Adolfo Gonzalez" (an economist from Uruguay), which he pulled off without a hitch. (For a map of Bolivia, see Appendix C, "Maps: Che on the Trail.") While in a La Paz hotel, Che took a photo of himself as Gonzalez. The resulting image is quite striking: Looking into a mirror and holding the camera between his knees for support, Che is unrecognizable. With his smooth scalp and slumped posture Che looks like any other middle-aged businessman, only his intense gaze hints at the real man behind the mask. It is eerie in a way, this photo of Che posing at an age he would never reach. And the fact that it was taken in a mirror gives it an even more surreal quality: It is Che looking at himself, but it is also someone who is "not" himself, someone he would never grow to be.

Che soon hooked up with the confidantes sent before him, and the men made their way to the base set up in the Ñacahuasú area of southeastern Bolivia. Once the rebels arrived, Tania served as a liaison, moving back and forth between La Paz and the camp, bringing necessary visitors to see Che.

This was a new base, chosen by Monje in an apparent attempt to force Che and his troops into Argentina instead. Monje was determined that Bolivia would not be a breeding ground for revolution, despite what Castro and Che wanted. The area was no place to wage a war and could very easily turn into a trap. Che was aware of the inherent dangers of the area, but his impatience and commitment convinced him to make due with the choice.

Once in Bolivia the situation became increasingly clear to Che: He had once again been misled into believing that the waiting conditions were better than they actually were. Monje had reluctantly agreed to have twenty Bolivian volunteers at Che's disposal, but the men were not there. There was a shortage of weapons, and the inappropriateness of the site became more apparent upon arrival. The mountains around them were bereft of cover, and no settlements were close by to which to appeal for peasant support. Still, Che soldiered on, believing that he could make it work.

Che seemed especially concerned that his forces did not have enough of a Bolivian contingent. He felt that to succeed, the revolution had to be Bolivian in nature. He arranged to meet with Monje in hopes of procuring more Bolivians for his troops. Che also planned to ask both the Soviet Union and China for support. Despite his criticism of the Soviets, Che, perhaps idealistically, wanted to bring the two socialist powers together in the heart of South America for the cause, eventually taking on the capitalist nations of the world in battle. He saw Bolivia as a kind of sacrifice, a spark that would ignite revolution throughout South America and spread to engulf the entire world. For Che the battle was not just about establishing socialist countries, but rather establishing a socialist planet.

Upon meeting Monje, Che met with opposition. Monje apparently demanded that he, not Che, be the ultimate leader of the Bolivian conflict. In addition, Che was not to align himself with the pro-Chinese communists of the country. Che agreed to not enlist the communists in question, but stood firm on his insistence that he be the movement's leader. In light of his experiences in the Congo, Che would not allow someone else to direct his men: "I'm already here and they'll only get me out over my dead body." Faced with Che's insistence, Monje then appeared to agree and even went so far as to say that he would join Che's troops as a simple foot soldier.

Had Monje been won over by Che? Was Monje now wholeheartedly behind the armed movement? Hardly. Before he left the camp, Monje gathered together the few Bolivians in the troops, informing them that if the party did not support this operation and if they stayed, they would be expelled from the party's ranks. Monje quickly left, but the fighters stayed. Soon Monje was spreading the word to Communist Party members across the country that the armed struggle was going to happen, even without their support, and that they should either go into hiding or leave the country altogether. A letter was sent to Castro withdrawing virtually all Bolivian Communist Party support of Che's mission in Bolivia. Monje had played his final hand, leaving Che and his meager band of twenty-four rebels high and dry.

Any other leader might have given up right then and there, cut his losses, and retreated to review the situation and formulate a new plan, perhaps even move on elsewhere—but not Che. He decided the best plan was to appeal to the pro-Chinese communist groups for more men, swelling his ranks a little. Che also believed that Castro would be able to smooth over the difficulties with Monje and arrive at some sort of understanding. The operation continued, and the men forged a formidable headquarters, much like those Che established in the Sierra Maestra. However, his tenacity would not be rewarded; the long slide toward defeat and death had effectively begun.

Lost in Bolivia

In early February 1967 Che and about thirty of the men set off on a training mission designed to acclimate the rebels to adverse conditions. The mission, which was supposed to last only a few days, turned into a harrowing six-week hell in which the men became lost and quickly ran out of food. As days turned into weeks the men became famished and unruly. The situation quickly worsened: "People are more and more discouraged, with the end of our provisions in sight, but not the end of the road." At some point the group was detected by the Bolivian army and thought to be drug smugglers rather than revolutionaries. A search was mounted but the rebels were not discovered; however, their true intent and the identity of their leader were soon discovered. Days turned into weeks as at least two of the men lost their lives in drowning accidents while the group battled pummeling rainstorms and unknown forested areas full of vicious insects. The group, badly beaten and fatigued, finally made it back to the camp near the end of March.

Upon their return a badly decimated Che found that any hopes of covert cover had been blown. While they were away, some of the new recruits had grown weary of rebel life and deserted. Alerted by suspicious Bolivians in nearby areas, the sloppy moves of visitors coming to and from the base, and tipped off by CIA and Bolivian intelligence operatives, the Bolivian army was already closing in on Che's camp. The deserting rebels were picked up and quickly told all they knew. The conflict was about to be underway, ready or not.

Electing to stay and fight (apparently fleeing was never an option for Che, even in the worst conditions), Che and his men were able to win the first skirmish with the Bolivian army. On March 23, Che dispatched an ambush team that quickly overtook an army unit, killing seven soldiers and taking about fifteen more captive. The ambush also netted Che and the rebels considerable firepower and, undoubtedly, gave them a morale boost. Of course, this was just one battle. In the larger picture, the war had now begun, a war Che and his men (now called the National Liberation Army) were simply not ready to fight.

Che circa 1967.

(Central Press)

On the Run

Soon all of Bolivia knew about the guerrilla uprising, and the army ratcheted up its attempts to squelch the rebels. The CIA also began to reappear on the scene, dispatching two agents to La Paz to inquire as to whether or not Che Guevara was behind the rebel movement. The CIA had been alerted by the Bolivian military and interrogated two of the rebel deserters. And in April 1967, the

Second Ranger Battalion was established with the backing of the United States. The official purpose of the outfit was to "produce a rapid reaction force capable of counterinsurgency operations." The U.S. government also provided arms and other supplies to the Bolivian troops before the arrival of the Second Ranger Battalion.

As declassified documents from the time attest, the actions of Che Guevara were of notable importance to the United States. Initially, after his "disappearance" from Cuba, the United States believed Che to be dead. But once identified as the man behind the Bolivian uprising, Che was again the subject of U.S. scrutiny. In May 1967 a memo was sent to U.S. President Lyndon B. Johnson about "the first credible report that 'Che' Guevara is alive and operating in South America." In response to the suspicions, a new group of CIA advisers (including an agent by the name of Felix Rodríguez) came to the area and began enacting reconnaissance missions to create accurate maps of the area. The report was soon confirmed.

Due to radio equipment limitations and failure, communications to all outside support, including Havana, was nonexistent. In the midst of all this, there were new visitors to the camp. Among them was Ciro Bustos (a journalist from Argentina) and Régis Debray, a Frenchman serving as a messenger and liaison between Che and Castro.

After months of networking efforts Tania arrived at the camp, eager to become a full-fledged guerrilla. She had abandoned her home in La Paz and rushed to join Che. Speculation about an affair between her and Che has always run high (but supported by nothing more than hearsay), and her rash decision to be by his side lends support to speculation that she was enamored with more than just revolution. Her presence infuriated Che; any inroads she had made as a covert presence in the urban areas of Bolivia were now lost. To make matters worse, she had left behind a cache of evidence pointing to her involvement with the revolution. Faced with an encroaching army presence, Che soon got his band of rebels on the move. Radio reports spoke of more than two thousand army troops closing in, and there was little time to waste.

Back in Cuba, a fresh band of rebels were ready to be dispatched to Bolivia, but without radio contact with Che, there was no way to make it happen. While it may appear that Che and his men were abandoned by Cuba, the truth was that Che had placed himself in this situation. No matter how desperately Castro wanted to help, he knew Che was doing what he wanted to do. In a way, Castro may have simply let history take its course. It must have seemed clearer every day that the situation in Bolivia was going to end in disaster. Still, Che had been lucky so far, avoiding death several times in somewhat similar circumstances. Perhaps Castro was holding on to the hope, no matter how slender, that Che would survive his time in Bolivia as he had elsewhere.

While on the run, Che's band of rebels managed to pull off a few more successful ambushes. In the process, a few rebels were killed as well. While these successes were invigorating and most likely giving the Bolivian army pause, the rebels were not launching major offensives or taking military bases. In short, no major dents were made, and there was virtually no peasant support. In the entire Bolivian operation, not one peasant took up arms alongside Che and his men. The rebels were feared and mistrusted by the populace, their motives questioned and never understood: Who were these men anyway? And why have they come to our country to make war? Che's theories about creating revolution where none existed were proving false. Although there were spikes of rebel success, the Bolivian operation never enjoyed the same level of peasant support the Cuban Revolution did. Without that they were severely limited.

By April the Bolivian army had found and taken over Che's original camp, thereby recovering scads of evidence that had been left behind. After revealing documents and photographs of the troops were recovered (another blunder attributed to Tania, a camera-buff) it was becoming increasingly clear that Che Guevara was at it again in Bolivia. CIA operatives in Bolivia confirmed Che's leadership of the rebels and the Second Ranger Battalion (led by Ralph Shelton) were on the job: Che was a thorn in their side they had every intention of plucking out.

Split in Two

Meanwhile, Che had more obstacles to overcome: The rebels needed a new base of operations and a support network in areas outside those of rebel activity, as he had in Cuba during the revolution. This was a crucial difference between the Bolivian and Cuban experiences for Che. He needed people on the outside to shore up foreign support and relay messages to others, especially Castro. With Tania's rash decision to leave her covert work behind, Che's options were limited.

At roughly the same time, Che's final public message was being broadcast to the world. Che's "Message to the Tricontinental" (written before his final departure from Cuba) called for more revolutions and escalating conflicts: "Since the imperialists are using the threat of war [in Vietnam] to blackmail humanity, the correct response is not to fear war. Attack hard and without letup at every point of confrontation—that must be the general tactic of the peoples." Even though Che was out of the public eye (the message was billed as coming from "somewhere in the world"), his words were still a viable force.

In the address, Che went on to assess Africa, Asia, and Latin America and their potential for revolution. Calling for solidarity, he said, "It is time to moderate our disputes and place everything at the service of the struggle." Che was advocating a global war against imperialism in general, and the United States in particular.

In Che's mind, the situation in Vietnam, which proved so divisive for the United States, was not to be feared, but replicated:

How close and bright would the future appear if two,
three, many Vietnams flowered on the face of the globe,
with their quota of death and their immense tragedies,
with their daily heroism, with their repeated blows against
imperialism, forcing it to disperse its forces under the lash
of the growing hatred of the peoples of the world.

Che's dedication and passion in his address burned brighter than ever, even as his own prospects in Bolivia dimmed rapidly.

In mid-April, while searching for a new area to base operations, he took his remaining troops and divided them in two. In retrospect, the decision seems foolhardy: The forces were already too small, and there was no way for them to communicate once they had separated. Still, Che thought the split was for the best. For one, he desperately wanted to deliver Bustos and Debray back into the urban areas, hoping that they (especially Debray) could facilitate the rebels' efforts from there, supplying the much-needed outside support. By splitting up, Che hoped to move faster and not run the risk of losing all his fighters to an enemy attack. Plus, many of those left behind were sick or injured, leaving the more able troops to make the journey with Che. The two groups were supposed to meet back up after Bustos and Debray were safely deposited in the city of Muyupampa. Unfortunately, things did not turn out that way. The two groups were unable to locate one another, and Bustos and Debray would both be arrested before they could make a difference for the rebels. Neither one would be released until after Che's death.

With no communication or pre-arranged backup rendezvous site, the two bands of rebels searched for each over the next four months. Instead of fighting to free oppressed peasants, Che and his band were now simply fighting to find their other half. Some have attributed Che's poor strategic planning to his deteriorating health and morale. His asthma was returning fiercer than ever, his daily bouts so severe at times that he had to be carried by the others. Any medicine Che had was lost when the first camp was abandoned, and subsequent attempts to secure more were met with defeat. In his journal he wrote about his recurring struggles with the disease as well as dark periods of depression.

Wandering had become a metaphor for Che's rebel operation in Bolivia—first on the training mission and then on the run from the army while searching for the others. On the heels of his failed efforts in the Congo, Che's experience in Bolivia could not have bolstered his spirits either. As days dragged on and Che contemplated the last years of his life—how he had spent them trying to recreate the Cuba success—it is worth wondering whether he might not have thought the missing element to have been Castro. After all, the Cuban Revolution had succeeded where Che's "solo" efforts had come up short. The reasons for the Cuban success may never be fully comprehended, but Castro's personal guidance and charisma had been its backbone. In Che's waning days, the warmth of the Cuban people, his family, and Castro must have seemed far away indeed.

The Beginning of the End

At the end of August the deathblow against the other wandering band of rebels was delivered as they attempted to cross Bolivia's Rio Grande. Their plans betrayed by a peasant, the Bolivian army ambushed the rebels as they waded into the water. Ten of them were killed instantly, including Tania. Those rebels who were captured alive were interrogated, giving the troops and the CIA more valuable information about Che and his operation.

With only some twenty-three men at his side, Che continued to wander through northwest Bolivia during September 1967. The peasants who saw the men often thought they were seeing ghosts with guns or wild savages venturing out of the deep underbrush. Suffering from malnutrition, various diseases, and unbearable fatigue, the men must have looked like apparitions rising out of the jungles with their ragged clothes, overgrown beards, and overall hellish appearance. In a way they *were* ghosts. An asthma-racked Che and his men were functioning as spirits of a revolution that had been fought in a land faraway, now haunting a country, and as good as dead, caught in an ever-tightening net by the Bolivian army.

Che's group soon found itself boxed in a canyon. Despite the rebels' slim chance of escape and even slimmer chance of success, it still took an army to catch Che. By the end of September, more than fifteen hundred troops were reportedly looking for him, this "ghost" of revolution.

By early October, the rebels were on their last legs. On October 7 the remaining fifteen or so men (the others had deserted, been captured, or killed) found themselves at the bottom of the Churo Gorge, unfortunately located near the Andean Mountain towns of Vallegrande and La Higuera where the Bolivian army had set up strongholds. At the frontline of the troops were members of the U.S.-backed Second Ranger Battalion. The noose was tightening, and the next morning, October 8, now in a desperate situation, Che and his men were left with one chance to escape—to fight their way out of the hole that might as well have been their grave. In the ensuing gun battle, Che was shot in his left calf (another bullet piercing through his beret) while around him many of the other rebels fell or fled. His gun jammed and his leg injured, an armed soldier soon captured Che and a fellow rebel nicknamed Willy. Legend has it that Che told his captor, "Don't shoot. I am Che Guevara and worth more to you alive than dead."

The Death of a Rebel

Word spread quickly through the military ranks that the infamous Che Guevara was now a prisoner, and he was to be held under further orders. A memo sent to President Johnson (dated October 9, 1967) states that, "the Bolivians got Che Guevara" and that "The Bolivian unit engaged ... the one we have been training for some time ..." was involved. Taken to the village of La Higuera, Che was bound hand and foot and thrown onto the dirt floor of a schoolhouse. Next to him lay the dead bodies of two of his fellow rebels, a grim harbinger of what waited ahead. As Colonel Joaquín Zenteno Anaya questioned Che, CIA agent Felix Rodríguez recorded the encounter. He later recounted how Che "was a mess ... hair matted, clothes ragged and torn."

After rounds of interrogation by army officers in which he staunchly defended his belief in revolution and socialism, Che was left alone—a dirty ragged mess of blood and bone trussed up on a dirt floor—but still passionate.

By the afternoon of October 9, the order had been given: Che was to be eliminated. Accounts from those present suggest a desire on the part of United States to keep Che alive, fearing that he would be even more dangerous in death than in life ... a martyr for his cause. The action is even called "stupid" in one memo. However, for the Bolivian government, an imprisoned Che Guevara was too great a risk. The Bolivians feared an inevitable pressure to release Che, or the threat of armed attempts to do just that. But to hand him over to the United States seemed just as ill-advised. To do so would have meant the effort to quell the rebels had been what critics had been saying all along: that it was an exercise of U.S. imperialism.

Although the U.S. presence was invaluable in the capturing of Che, they were unable to influence his ultimate fate. Still, as outlined in a memo to President Johnson, the CIA wanted to try to use Che's death to their best advantage:

> *The death of Che Guevara carries three significant implications:*
>
> *It marks the passing of another of the aggressive, romantic revolutionaries ... and reinforces this trend.*
>
> *In the Latin American context, it will have a strong impact in discouraging would-be guerrillas.*
>
> *It shows the soundness of our "preventive medicine" assistance to countries facing incipient insurgency—it was the Bolivian 2nd Ranger Battalion, trained by our Green Berets from June–September of this year, that cornered him and got him.*
>
> *We have put these points across to several newsmen.*

As he heard gunfire silencing some of the captured rebels in a neighboring room, it is impossible to know what Che was thinking. It is the final mystery for all people, what the edge of death does to a person. It seems reasonable that Che would reflect on his family back in Cuba, the children he would never see grow up, and the wife he would never hold again. Perhaps Che's mind latched on to his prideful days of revolution and glory, fighting passionately alongside his friend Fidel Castro. His last moments may have been filled with thoughts about the people he had always fought for and with: his fellow rebels dying next door and the peasants forever toiling under the thumb of imperialism. Perhaps he thought about the sweeping roadtrips of his youth and how they had wound him through and into this continent he loved enough to die for. He may have even momentarily returned to his mother's side, reading his books and feeling her skirt rustle against his face as she soothed his asthma-racked body. Any such thoughts were Che's alone. When asked by Rodríguez if he had anything he wanted to say, Che simply asked that Castro be assured that revolution would soon triumph in America and that Aleida be told to remarry and try and be happy.

Che's executioner (a soldier named Mario Terán who had lost three friends to the rebels) was told not to shoot him in the face, but in the torso and legs, to make it look as if he had been killed in battle. Legend tells how, as the gun was raised and the trigger pulled, Che, defiant to the end, shouted out, "I know you've come to kill me! Shoot, coward, you are only going to kill a man!" After a hail of bullets and a cloud of dust, thirty-nine-year-old Che Guevara was no longer alive, but his story was not yet over.

Chapter 12

The Recovery, Return, and Rebirth of Che

Wherever death may surprise us, let it be welcome if our battle cry has reached even one receptive ear, if another hand has reached out to take up our arms, and other men come forward to join in our funeral dirge with the rattling of machine guns and with new cries of battle and victory.
—Che Guevara

Even though Che was dead, executed upon Bolivian military orders, the army was not through with him just yet. His body was strapped to a helicopter and flown to the village of Vallegrande, where photographs were taken as proof that he was really dead. Various military officers crowded around Che's corpse, his eyes wide open and staring straight ahead, almost as if he were still alive. Yet, the fire and intensity of Che Guevara was unquestionably gone, his eyes only a dim reminder of the passion that had blazed so fiercely within him. Death masks were made of his face and his hands amputated to prove the identity of the corpse. Initially his head was to be removed as well, but the idea was abandoned because of its obvious barbarity.

Much has been made about the Christ-like appearance of Che's corpse and, in truth, the similarity is impossible to miss: A martyr to the cause, his shaggy beard, emaciated face, and abused body all seem to echo the visage of the Christian savior. For some people, Che had come into this world to save them, only to be struck down by nonbelievers.

Scads of villagers, soldiers, and reporters came to view the corpse, all filing by to see firsthand that he was really dead. Many of the locals even took locks of his hair as souvenirs, proof that he had once been close enough to touch. In the coming years, many of those closely involved with Che's death would meet untimely ends of their own, leading some to believe in what is known as "Che's curse," as if Che himself were extracting revenge from beyond the grave.

Back in Cuba, Castro was slow to admit that Che was really gone. After all, reports of his death had circulated before. However, the photographs of both Che's body and his confiscated diaries were soon released and proved too powerful to ignore. On October 15, 1967, Castro took to Cuba's airwaves and broke the news: Che was indeed dead. Clearly upset, Castro told how Che had been killed in the Bolivian struggle and how his body had been laid out for public display. Three days of national mourning were declared as the news deeply moved the country. At a wake held on October 18, Castro eulogized his dead friend and fellow rebel at length, extolling his virtues:

> Che has become a model of man not only for our nation, but for any Latin American nation. Che raised revolutionary stoicism, the spirit of revolutionary sacrifice, the combativeness, the working spirit of the revolutionary to their highest expression. Che gave the ideas of Marxism-Leninism their freshest, purest, most revolutionary expression .... And when one speaks of proletarian nationalism and when one seeks an example of a proletarian nationalist, that example, above any other example, is the example of Che .... His blood was shed in Bolivia for the redemption of the exploited and the oppressed, the humble and the poor.

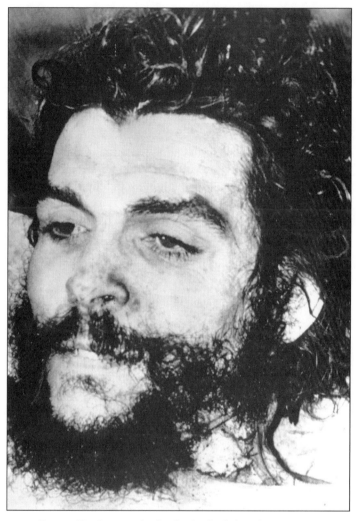

Ernesto Che Guevara shortly after his death (October 13, 1967).

(Central Press)

Castro called on Cuba's children to do their best to "be like Che." It is a pledge still heard throughout Cuban schools to this day.

However, not everyone was convinced of Castro's dedication to the ideals of Che. Daniel Alarcón, one of only three rebels to survive the Bolivian campaign (and a veteran of the Cuban Revolution and Che's mission to the Congo), broke with Castro and Cuba thirty years after the death of Che. In what was an embarrassing blow to Castro's image, this hero of the revolution came out publicly with his criticism. After declaring himself a political refugee, Alarcón said that Che, if were still alive, "would be indignant to see how Fidel Castro has converted the image of the flag to make the people work more every day to change nothing." Alarcón went on to assert that Che "would never have accepted or allowed a dictatorship like that under which the people now live." Castro quickly labeled Alarcón a traitor and a worm for his desertion and harsh words. But Alarcón was just one of many Cuba revolutionary veterans who had expressed deep misgivings about what Cuba had become.

In an October 1967 report filed by a Latin American specialist for the U.S. State Department's Bureau of Intelligence and Research titled *Guevara's Death: The Meaning for Latin America*, Che's legacy is foreshadowed:

> *News of Guevara's death will relieve most non-leftist*
> *Latin Americans who feared that sooner or later he might*
> *foment insurgencies in their countries. The demise of the*
> *most glamorous and reputedly effective revolutionary may*
> *even cause some Latin Americans to downgrade the seri-*
> *ousness of insurgency and the social factors which breed*
> *it. On the other hand, communists of whatever stripe*
> *and other leftists are likely to eulogize the revolutionary*
> *martyr—especially for his contribution to the Cuban*
> *Revolution—and to maintain that revolutions will*
> *continue until their causes are eradicated.*

Che's body remained a source of mystery and controversy for years to come. Initial Bolivian reports attributed Che's death to wounds received in battle. However, discrepancies in autopsy reports, eyewitness accounts, and conflicting government accounts discredited these claims, proving Che had been executed after his capture. Yet the body itself disappeared.

Despite all the evidence to the contrary (the photographs, eyewitness accounts, and Che's amputated hands), the absence of a tangible corpse gave rise to fantastic rumors that placed Che, alive, roaming the Bolivian jungles, having somehow outwitted his captors in the end. These types of stories are nothing new; human beings have always been prone to such fantasies when they have lost someone they were unwilling to part with. The idea of Che, still alive and patrolling the jungle, can be filed away with similar stories of a post-assassination John F. Kennedy sequestered on an island, of a shadowy Elvis Presley living out a secret life in some small Midwestern town, or of a badly disfigured Princess Diana kept hidden away from prying eyes at last. Moreover, believing that Che had eluded death (resurrected, so to speak) dovetailed nicely with the Christ analogy.

In another cloud of misinformation, the Bolivian government insisted that Che's corpse had been cremated. The claim was later be refuted by one of the government's own officers, which set off a chain of events that, almost thirty years after Che's death, uncovered the true whereabouts of his remains.

The Return of a Rebel

In 1995 Jon Lee Anderson (*Che Guevara: A Revolutionary Life*) interviewed Bolivian General Mario Vargas Salinas, a man present at the death of Che Guevara. Salinas revealed that Che, along with several of his fellow fighters, had not been cremated as Bolivian authorities had always claimed, but instead had been buried in a mass grave adjacent to a airstrip just outside the Central Bolivian town of Vallegrande. Anderson reported the exchange in *The New York Times*, and in response to considerable public pressure the Bolivian government launched a two-year search for the remains.

In the summer of 1997 the search came to an end. After months of digging, a team of Argentine, Bolivian, and Cuban forensic experts uncovered a mass grave near the Vallegrande site. One of the skeletons unearthed had no hands. A positive identification was soon made: Che was lost no more, and his remains were returned to Cuba in early July.

Che's remains were given a hero's burial in October 1997, thirty years after his death in the Bolivian jungle. The return of his bones must have been an emotional experience for the citizens of Cuba. To mark the occasion, a week of national mourning was enacted and more than two hundred fifty thousand people came to pay their respects to the memory of Che.

As fitting for a national hero, Che's remains came to rest in a specially built mausoleum in Santa Clara, the central Cuban city Che had so spectacularly taken during the revolution. To many Cubans the success in Santa Clara had not only been Che's most glorious moment, but the turning point in the revolution, the battle that clinched the rebels' victory. An emotional Castro took the opportunity to address the huge crowd gathered for the ceremony, including Che's widow and children. Castro stressed that Che's memory was eternal, always on display, and proving to Cuba and the world that the revolution is still alive: "His unerasable mark is now in history, and his luminous gaze of a prophet has become a symbol for all the poor of this world."

Che had been a powerful force for Castro and, even thirty years after his death, Che could still galvanize the country, reinforcing Castro's call for solidarity against imperialism. Addressing Che directly, Castro thanked him for "coming to reinforce us in the difficult struggle that we are undergoing today to preserve the ideas that you fought so hard for." Six fellow rebels whose remains had also been recovered were interred alongside Che, each man's bones resting inside a small coffin. As family members watched and thousands of Cubans stood in attention, Castro read from Che's farewell letter as the remains of his fallen comrade finally came to rest, a powerful reminder of the creed that drove Che all his life: "*Hasta la victoria siempre* [Ever onward to victory]!" The return of Che came at a time when Cuba truly needed a morale boost.

Three decades had done nothing but solidify Guevara's standing in Cuba; his image has endured as a powerful symbol of the revolution. (For an overview of Cuba in the years since Che's death, see "Post-Che Cuba," Appendix B, "Relevant Struggles and Histories.") In fact, any visitor to Cuba might think Che was still alive, running the country and enjoying the dedication of fervent Cubans across the island. His face, fifty feet tall, graces buildings, billboards, T-shirts, and posters like a quiet and powerful sentinel. Through hard times (especially in the wake of the collapse of the Soviet Union) Cubans have looked upon the face of Che Guevara to find not only hope but principled dedication as well. Those old enough to remember and appreciate Che have kept his memory alive.

The Rebirth of Che

In the decades since his death, Che Guevara has become an international symbol, both politically and culturally. His face can be found on everything from posters and T-shirts to watches and CD covers to skateboards and beer. Che even shows up on Broadway and movie screens, serving as a character in the musical *Evita*. The Korda photograph of Che became so ubiquitous and well known that it seemed to take on a life of its own, showing up in all sorts of unlikely places. It was not until Smirnoff used it without permission in a vodka advertisement (Chapter 7, "Growing Tensions and Emerging Ties") that use of the photo was curtailed.

Why has the image of Che endured? For those interested in politics and socialism, the reason is obvious: Che's "new man" remains an ideal, a construct to be emulated. His dedication to social causes and passion for the disenfranchised strikes a powerful chord among those who share similar views. But because of his passion, Che's name and image are often invoked regardless of the nature of the struggle, even if Che himself would have taken a very different stance. Because Che died striving for revolution, his image as an eternal fighter makes him all the more attractive. The details of his fight are often secondary to his image as rebel.

But what about the cultural Che? Had he known, Che would have been personally horrified by what he is now being used to sell and at the myriad places his face has appeared. His face has been expropriated from his life and assimilated as a marketing tool, a shorthand way to convey rebellion, to sell watches and vodka—that somehow his face alone makes a product more dangerous or desirable. When Hyde, a pot-smoking, smart-mouthed character on Fox television's *That '70s Show* wears a Che shirt, the audience "knows" he is a rebel. That Hyde and Che are very different kinds of rebels is overlooked, unless you happen know more about Che than just his face.

The great irony is that this mindset, that you can become what is suggested in an image by simply pulling on a T-shirt, is the very materialism Che spent his whole life fighting. Che was a rebel, but the truest kind. He was not a Marlon Brando type, fighting against "whatever you've got." Rebellion for Che was not simply for rebellion's sake; he had a goal, a purpose to his actions. He was a social rebel, fighting for what he believed was a common good, not simply what was best for himself.

Still, if Che's face on a T-shirt or coffee mug touches even one person, leads someone on a path of social awareness and involvement, or even simply inspires one to learn about Cuba, politics, or Che's life, perhaps there is some value in it. If not for Che's continued presence in realms other than the political, he might have faded into the background of history and international interest in him would most likely be faint. What an irony—to become a capitalist tool to further socialism. And with major motion pictures about Che's life in the works, his face is poised to become even more visible, but so will his story, in some form. The very fact that this book has made its way into your hands speaks to the power of Che's legacy: Something sparked an interest in Che for you, and that spark may very well have been a T-shirt, a CD cover, or even a vodka ad.

Che was a man who embodied the eradication of the individual, not the celebration of it. Even so, it was his unique individuality, his ability as one man to evoke so much change, that has granted him his fame and notoriety. His inability to look away from suffering, to step over the homeless in the street, or to ignore the submission of native populations makes him more of a champion than a rebel; a champion of social justice rather than a rebel against the status quo. While his politics may be questioned, his dedication and passion cannot. Che Guevara lived and died for his beliefs in a way that few others have matched. And, as we begin a new century, Che Guevara is still alive, his message as relevant as ever. He remains his own "new man," a vigilant warrior in the battle for what he saw as a better world. The question that remains is what the world will make of his example.

Fidel Castro

Fidel Castro, the son of a self-made man and one of nine children, began his education in the local public schools of Cuba. Soon recognized for his scholastic talents, he was enrolled in a school run by French priests, where he quickly gained a reputation for being unruly and a fighter, challenging the authority of the priests and jockeying for leadership among the students.

Hoping to break his young son's rebellious nature, Castro's father sent him to a Catholic private school known for its tough discipline and high academic standards. While at the school, Castro curbed his wild ways and learned the value of discipline and authority. After an early witnessing of U.S. soldiers' behavior toward Cuban citizens, whom the Americans treated as inferiors, Castro developed a strong aversion to U.S. influence in Cuban politics.

While in secondary school, Castro learned Cuban history and adopted José Martí, the father of Cuban independence from Spain, as his hero. Castro also developed his athletic and oratory skills during this time.

In 1945 Castro entered the University of Havana Law School, where he became involved in politics, often taking part in the violent confrontations among student political gangs.

As a young man Castro committed himself to the electoral removal of President Ramón Grau San Martín of the Auténtico Party. Grau allowed corruption to grow in business and politics, and Castro fought hard against his administration. Joining the Party of the Cuban People (the Ortodoxo Party, an offshoot of the Auténticos, formed as a result of the latter's corruption), Castro and the Ortodoxos publicly exposed government corruption and demanded reform. The party's founding principles included building a strong sense of national identity among Cubans, opposing the influence of powerful foreign nations in Cuba's affairs, supporting social justice, establishing economic independence for Cuba, and evenly distributing the nation's wealth through government control of natural and economic resources.

In 1947 Castro joined the Caribbean Legion, a group of political exiles from other Caribbean nations based in Cuba, in a failed effort to overthrow Rafael Trujillo, the dictator of the Dominican Republic, by launching an invasion from Cuba.

After the effort's failure, Castro focused on the electoral defeat of the candidates of the Auténtico Party. Campaign activities were often violent, and Castro quickly made himself known for his hotheaded speeches and valuable ability for political organization.

In April 1948 Castro attended the Ninth Pan American Union conference, a student conference held in Bogotá, Colombia. The conference was organized by Argentine president Juan Perón to protest U.S. domination of the Western Hemisphere. Upon arriving, Castro and a friend brought the conference to a halt and shocked delegates by showering them with pamphlets condemning U.S. influence in Latin America. The real shock came a few days later when Jorge Eliezer Gaitán, leader of the Colombian Liberal Party and mentor to the student rebels, was assassinated. Devastated at news of Gaitán's death, outraged students rioted in the streets. Later blamed for provoking the tumult, known as the Bogotazo, Castro was basically an observer.

The Bogotazo brought a new development to Castro's political thought. Believing Gaitán's commitment to reforming the political system through democratic channels only resulted in his own death, Castro began to believe that achieving change through the electoral process could not happen.

When Castro returned to Cuba, he became embroiled in the presidential campaign of 1948. Carlos Prío Socarrás, a seasoned politician and member of the Auténtico Party, was running against Eddy Chibás, the leader of the Ortodoxo Party. Castro was cynical about Cuban electoral politics, believing elections were often fixed and that Cuban politicians, be they elected officials or dictators, were owned by the United States. Castro formed a radical branch of the Ortodoxo Party called the Radical Action Orthodox wing. This organization supported Chibás in the 1948 election, but Prío Socarrás won despite Castro's efforts.

After Chibás committed suicide in 1951, Castro aspired to gain the leadership of the Ortodoxo Party and ran for a seat in the Cuban House of Representatives in the 1952 election. Before that election could occur, however, General Fulgencio Batista staged a bloodless coup d'etat and established a dictatorship that ended Castro's chance to attain office legally. Castro's cynicism morphed into rejection of electoral democracy, and he declared himself to be in favor of armed revolution.

Appendix B

Relevant Struggles and Histories

Throughout his life, Che Guevara would find himself embroiled in various conflicts: Argentina, Cuba, Bolivia, and the Congo would all factor heavily into Che's life and struggles. In attempting to understand the importance of Che, it is beneficial to know more about the places in which he lived and fought.

Argentine Shifts in Power

Argentine by birth, Che's first exposure to political struggle can be found within the twists of his own country. While not politically active in his younger years, both Che and his family were exposed to a climate of political unrest and revolution that foreshadowed Che's ultimate destiny.

- **Early 1900s.** In the first decade of the twentieth century, Argentina became one of the leading nations in South America. Its influence became more pronounced and influential, and in 1914 Argentina played a role in the mediation of a serious dispute between the United States and Mexico (when U.S. President Woodrow Wilson ordered the seizing of the port of Veracruz in eastern Mexico to prevent the delivery of weapons to a Mexican government run by Victoriano Huerta; the United States refused to recognize Huerta's government because he had seized power illegally). During World War I, Argentina remained neutral but played a major role in the supplying of food to the Allies.

- **1936.** General Augustín Justo was unseated in his presidency by Roberto M. Ortiz. Initially championed by members of a growing fascist movement, Ortiz did an about-face and took vigorous steps to strengthen democracy in Argentina. Countermeasures were adopted against the subversive activities of German agents, who had become extremely active after the victory of National Socialism in Germany. The corrupt electoral machinery of the country was overhauled. Ortiz proclaimed neutrality after the outbreak of World War II in 1939.

- **July 1940.** President Ortiz, unable to function because of illness, designated Vice President Ramón S. Castillo as acting president. Castillo's administration displayed pro-Axis tendencies, refused to sever ties with Germany and Japan, and looked to the rising Germany as a potential new market for exportation and supplier for Argentina's armed forces.

- **June 1943.** Castillo, who had officially succeeded to the presidency following the resignation of Ortiz in June 1942, was removed from office by a military group headed by General Arturo Rawson, who favored severance of relations with Germany and Japan. On the eve of his assumption of office as provisional president, however, Rawson's associates forced him to resign. The provisional presidency went to General Pedro Ramírez, one of the leaders of the revolt. Ramírez shortly abolished all political parties, suppressed opposition newspapers, and generally stifled the remnants of democracy in Argentina. In January 1944 in a complete reversal of foreign policy, his government broke diplomatic relations with Japan and Germany.

- **February 1944.** Fearful that war with Germany was imminent, a military junta, the so-called Colonels, forced Ramírez from office. The central figure in the junta was Colonel Juan Domingo Perón, chief of labor relations in the Ramírez regime. Despite declarations of sympathy with the Allied cause, the government continued the policy of suppression of democratic activity and of harboring German agents. In July the U.S. government accused Argentina of aiding the Axis powers. Finally, on March 27, 1945, when Allied victory in Europe was assured, the country declared war on Germany and Japan. In the following month the government signed the Act of Chapúltepec, a compact among American nations for mutual aid against aggressors. Argentina, with U.S. sponsorship, became a charter member of the United Nations in June. Shortly afterward, it was announced that elections would be held early in 1946.

Perónism

Juan Perón found his main support among the most depressed sections of the agricultural and industrial working class in Argentina. The Perónistas campaigned among these workers, popularly known as *descamisados* (Spanish for "shirtless ones" and of the working class), with promises of land, higher wages, and social security. The elections, held on February 24, 1946, resulted in a decisive victory for Perón.

As first lady of Argentina, Eva ("Evita") Perón (former actress Eva Duarte) managed labor relations and social services for her husband's government until her death in 1952. Adored by the masses, later immortalized on both stage and screen, and often characterized as a master manipulator, Evita was indispensable in securing the popularity of the Perónist movement.

In October 1946 President Perón enacted an ambitious five-year plan for the expansion of the economy. During 1947 he deported a number of German agents and expropriated about sixty German firms. These actions caused relations between Argentina and the United States to substantially improve. In March 1951 *La Prensa*, a leading independent daily newspaper, was suppressed. Severe restrictions were imposed on the anti-Perónista parties in the campaign preceding the national elections, which took place in November 1951.

President Perón was reelected by a large majority. Soon after the election, his beloved Evita died following a long bout with cancer.

Her death was a blow to Juan, both personally and politically. She had always been a key factor in his popularity and, without her, he lost some of his appeal. In an effort to keep the image of Evita alive, Juan soon announced plans for the construction of a monument to his late wife; it was to be a huge statue of her, the largest of its kind in the world. However, Perón would be overthrown before work on the project could even begin.

In January 1953 the government inaugurated a second five-year plan. The plan emphasized increased agricultural output instead of all-out industrialization, which had been the goal of the first five-year plan. During 1953 Argentina concluded important economic and trade agreements with several countries, notably Britain, the USSR, and Chile.

In November 1954 Perón claimed that a group of Roman Catholic clergymen was "fostering agitation" against the government. Despite Church opposition, the government passed legislation legalizing absolute divorce, granting all benefits of legitimacy to illegitimate children and legalized prostitution. The legislation furthered the division between Church and State.

On September 16, 1955, rebellious groupings in all three branches of the armed forces staged a concerted rebellion. After three days of civil war, approximately four thousand people were killed and Perón resigned. On September 20 the rebel leader Major General Eduardo Lonardi took office, promising to restore democratic government. Perón went into exile, first in Paraguay and later in Spain.

Throughout eighteen years of exile, however, Perón retained his labor support and influence in Argentine politics. He was finally allowed to return to Argentina in 1973 and was again elected president, with his third wife, Isabel de Perón, as vice president. He died in office on July 1, 1974.

The Congo

The Democratic Republic of the Congo, as it is now known, is a nation in central Africa with a total area of 905,365 square miles. Geographically the heart of Central Africa, the DRC is the third-largest country in Africa, after Sudan and Algeria. The Congo River runs through the densely forested region, hence the name.

The Congo region of Central Africa is a vast country rich in natural resources and marked by dense forests. Created by Belgian King Leopold I in the late nineteenth century, the region was first united as the Congo Free State. It was then called the Belgian Congo from 1908–60 when it gained independence as the Republic of the Congo. Its name was changed to the Democratic Republic of the Congo in 1964 and then to Zaire in 1971. In 1965 dictator Mobutu SeSe Seko seized control of the country, ruling for more than thirty years until his overthrow in 1997 by rebels led by Laurent Kabila. Kabila changed the country's name back to the Democratic Republic of the Congo (DRC).

The area continues to be a hotbed of political unrest with civil war breaking out again in August 1998. Rebel forces aligned with neighboring Rwanda, Burundi, and Uganda have been fighting the Congolese government, which is supported by Angola, Zimbabwe, and Namibia. The war has split the country roughly in two, with the rebels controlling the eastern half and the government controlling the west. Kisangani is the largest city held by the rebels. In early 2001 Kabila was assassinated and replaced by his son, Joseph Kabila. The Congolese conflict, which began with a rebellion against President Laurent Kabila, has drawn in the armies of some half a dozen nations, backing either the rebels or the government army. In the months following Kabila's assassination, it appeared as though the peace process was making headway with the implementation of a cease-fire and the deployment of UN peacekeeping troops into the region.

Bolivia

Bolivia, one of only two landlocked countries in South America (Paraguay being the other), features a largely indigenous Indian population that has preserved its native languages and much of its traditional way of life. Bolivia borders Peru and Chile in the west, Brazil in the east, and Paraguay and Argentina in the south.

The Andes Mountains run basically north to south in the western part of the country.

Bolivia, once a part of the ancient empire of the Incas, was conquered in 1538 by the Spanish conquistador Hernando Pizarro. Six years earlier, Pizarro's younger brother, Francisco, had claimed the neighboring country and core of the Inca Empire, Peru, as a Spanish possession. Within the next forty years, several Spanish settlements were formed in Bolivia as well as numerous silver mines in which the Native American population was forced to labor. During the period of Spanish rule, what is now Bolivia was called Alto Peru (Upper Peru).

After revolts in 1809 that led to the Wars of Independence, Alto Peru declared its independence from Spain on August 6, 1825, and took the name of Bolivia. The country was named after the South American revolutionary leader who drafted the region's constitution, Simón Bolívar. A long period of internal struggle (revolutionary and civil wars were commonplace) and instability followed as a long line of mostly military dictators ruled the country. In addition, Bolivia's borders were uncertain and often subject to conflict. Short wars and disputes with both Peru and Chile plagued the area.

Due to the expansion of mining, a boom in foreign investment soon led to the development of three large foreign mining corporations that dominated Bolivia's economic and political life. As in so many other South American countries, these mining corporations (along with large landowners and the military), effectively controlled Bolivia.

In 1952 a revolutionary party (*Movimiento Nacionalista Revolucionario*, or MNR) seized control of the government. The new regime embarked on a pro-labor (yet anti-communist) agenda that featured the nationalization of tin mines, the redistribution of land from expropriated estates, and the diversification of the economy. The army removed the MNR in 1964. Over the next two years the military government succeeded in instituting reforms in tin mining operations, including reopening the industry to private and foreign investment.

Post-Che Cuba

Despite the severe economic problems that plagued Cuba in the 1960s, Castro and his regime successfully redistributed wealth more equitably and improved the quality of life for most Cubans. The schools, medical facilities, retirement support, and public transportation that were provided made a tangible difference for many Cubans. Also, by reducing rents and utility charges, the cost of living in Cuba decreased and the poorest of the population saw their income rise, even in the face of a stumbling economy and the shortage of many goods.

It was clear by the end of the 1960s that the government had to make the stabilization of the economy its first priority. There would be no extensive social reform without a strong economy. In order to produce economic results, Castro relied heavily on Cuba's mainstay: sugar. He predicted that Cuba would produce ten million tons of sugar in the 1970 harvest. It was a risk that did not pay off. Despite a massive mobilization of efforts (many Cubans were forced to "volunteer" as unpaid labor in the sugar fields), Castro could not deliver, coming up one and a half million tons short of his avowed goal. As a result, all areas of the economy faltered because of the intensive labor and resources dedicated to the anticipated record harvest.

The agricultural disappointment brought political concerns to light for Castro as well. The USSR agreed to provide financial assistance to Cuba, but only in return for Castro enacting a Soviet-style bureaucracy that limited his personal influence on national policy. The Communist Party assumed more authority and pushed for efficient economic practices. In 1972 Cuba became a member of the trade association of communist nations, and by the mid-1980s the USSR accounted for more than half of Cuba's exports and imports.

The USSR-induced reforms did not reduce Castro's authority, however, even if that had been the intent. The new bureaucratic system left Castro free to deal with political issues and international affairs, and in 1976 Castro introduced a new constitution for Cuba. The legislation gave Cubans a greater voice in choosing their leaders and approving laws. Soon Castro was chosen president. More organizations were formed that allowed the people to interact with the central government at an even greater level. It would appear that the system has strived to achieve one goal of socialism: the factoring of the will of the people into their own governing.

By the early 1970s relations between the USSR and the United States improved. As a result, Cuba benefited from the lessening international tensions. The Organization of American States (OAS) voted to allow its members to determine their own relations with Cuba. For a short time, it appeared as if the United States, under President Gerald R. Ford, might actually make moves to normalize relations with Cuba, opening economic and diplomatic channels. But Cuba's commitment to supporting revolution threw a wrench in those works. In 1975 Cuba sent military forces into the African nation of Angola, newly independent from Portugal. The Cuban aid for the area's leftist forces only exacerbated the tension between Cuba and the United States.

Still, in 1977 (under the administration of President Jimmy Carter), Cuba and the United States each opened a diplomatic office in the other country, and Americans were allowed to visit Cuba as tourists. But a buildup of Soviet technicians and advisors in Cuba and Castro's continuing commitment to leftist rebels kept U.S.–Cuban relations tense. Castro continued to rise as an international leader, with Cuba often serving as the host country for global humanitarian conventions. He also served as the leader of the Non-Aligned Movement, a group of nations that strived to remain neutral during the Cold War.

Cuba was hardly a paradise, however. Although the political reforms had made significant differences in the lives of Cubans, criticism of the reforms was not tolerated. Any official or expert casting doubt on the government's programs was clamped down upon and censored, even punished. The ensuing frustration led to a watershed moment for Castro's Cuba in 1980 when a small group of Cubans broke into the Peruvian Embassy in Havana, asking for asylum. Soon the embassy was deluged with Cubans wanting the same. When President Jimmy Carter said that the United States would take them, Castro gave any Cuban who wanted to go the opportunity to do just that. The resulting flood of one hundred twenty thousand Cubans headed for the United States demonstrated to both presidents that all was not well in Cuba.

New reforms were established that allowed a somewhat limited open-market system in which farmers were allowed to provide food to urban areas where rations had been inadequate. However, in 1986 Castro reversed the market policy under what was known as the "Rectification of Errors and Negative Tendencies." In addition, Castro reinforced the importance of domestic goods over imported ones, downsized the bureaucracy of the Cuban government, and upped the hours of "voluntary labor" each Cuban was required to provide.

The collapse of the Soviet Union proved to be Cuba's greatest challenge, however. After the USSR broke apart (in 1991) into a number of smaller republics, Castro was told that the five-and-a-half-billion-dollar yearly aid previously provided by the USSR to Cuba would not be forthcoming. It was a shattering realization for the Cuban government: More than eighty-five percent of its foreign financial and economic relations were with the USSR and its allies.

The Cuban economy nearly bottomed out for good in 1993. Beginning in 1991 Cuba was forced to import sugar from Brazil and other Caribbean countries to ensure foreign trade commitments with eastern European countries. In what had to be a humbling move, Cuba borrowed money from capitalist countries and took on significant debt. As a result, extreme austerity measures were enacted on the Cuban people and crucial funds diverted from social programs to pay for the debt. The price of Cuba's imports rose dramatically while the price of its exports fell accordingly.

Despite diplomatic overtures floated by Castro to incoming President Bill Clinton, the United States passed the Cuba Democracy Act in 1992, a move that extended the trade embargo beyond U.S. companies. Foreign subsidiaries of U.S. companies trading with Cuba were penalized, as well as other nations that engaged in commerce with the island. In the aftermath, the economic situation in Cuba became even bleaker, resulting in skyrocketing inflation and the plummeting of the Cuban peso against foreign currency. The even distribution of wealth, a crucial plank in Cuban policy, was impacted when Castro allowed Cubans to spend American dollars in 1993. Suddenly Cubans were no longer equal. Any Cubans in the tourism industry or who received money from relatives living abroad found their buying power greatly increased, while those limited to Cuban pesos did not.

Social unrest began to grow in Cuba as recurring blackouts, constant shortages of food and other necessary goods, public transportation snafus, and the diminishing public health system made life on the island increasingly harder. More measures were enacted, and in 1993 the government broke up large state farms into workers' cooperatives. Soon the government again allowed free agricultural markets in an effort to supply food for a hungry populace. Foreign businesses, especially from Mexico, Canada, Britain, France, and Spain, were encouraged to set up partnerships with the Cuban government in the areas of tourism, medicine, and food exportation.

Still, the efforts by the government did little to quell growing discontent. In August 1994 a riot broke out in Havana with Castro personally having to convince the angry crowd to disperse. Following the fracas, Castro, as he had in 1980, again allowed any Cuban wishing to leave to do so. A record number of people began to leave Cuba by taking their chances in rafts. The United States found the sheer numbers of Cuban exiles overwhelming, and in 1994 pulled the plug on a twenty-eight-year-old policy of automatically granting asylum to Cubans. Soon Castro closed his borders, and the United States tightened the trade embargo even more. Even with stricter immigration policies in place, the United States agreed to continue to allow twenty thousand Cuban immigrants into the country each year. The plight of Cubans desperately hoping to make it to the United States reached its zenith in 1999 with the arrival of Elián Gonzalez, the six-year-old Cuban boy found floating at sea following his mother's death. For months the battle over the boy's future raged with Fidel Castro, Elián's Miami Cuban relatives, and virtually every U.S. politician locking horns over the issue. Eventually the well-documented case was resolved when armed federal agents took Elián from his Miami relatives and he was returned to his father in Cuba. The incident served as a powerful reminder of the deep divisions that remain between Cuba and the United States, with supporters from both sides taking the opportunity to distort the true image of the other.

In 2000 Congress took steps to relax the United States' trade embargo with Cuba, authorizing the sale of food and agricultural products to Cuba. Still, tight restrictions were placed on the transactions: They cannot be subsidized by the federal government or financed by U.S. banks. By April 2001 the first instances of regular shipping between the United States and Cuba in forty years was slated to begin. The Bush administration has stated its opposition to any further relaxation of the embargo.

As a new century begins, the future of Cuba remains uncertain. As Castro ages, so does the firsthand remembrance of the Cuban Revolution. With the eradication of the USSR and the ensuing diminished economic support, Cuba has turned to more traditional outlets for survival and slackened its once-ironclad rule. Will the trend continue, ultimately resulting in the casting off of any vestiges of socialism? Will the inevitable end of Castro's leadership also end Cuba as the world knows it? Whatever the future may hold for Cuba, its past has been firmly etched as one of revolution and reform, a history written largely through the impassioned efforts of Che Guevara.

Appendix C

Maps: Che on the Trail

Map of Argentina

- Rosario (birthplace)
- Misiones (early childhood)
- Buenos Aires (later childhood)
- Alta Gracia (near Córdoba, teenage years)

Map of South American Trip (*The Motorcycle Diaries*)

(*From Guevara, Ernesto "Che."* The Motorcycle Diaries: A Journey Around South America, *Verso: New York, 1995)*

Argentina:

- Córdoba, December 1951
- Leave Buenos Aires, January 4, 1952
- Villa Gesell, January 6
- Miramar, January 13
- Necochea, January 14
- Bahía Blanca, arrive January 16, leave January 21
- Choele Choel, January 25
- Piedra del Aguila, January 29
- San Martín de los Andes, January 31
- Nahuel Huapí, February 8
- Bariloche, February 11

Chile:

- Peulla, February 14
- Temuco, February 18
- Lautaro, February 21
- Los Angeles, February 27
- Santiago de Chile, March 1
- Vaparaíso, March 7
- Aboard the *San Antonio,* March 8 to 10
- Antofagasta, March 11
- Baquedano, March 12
- Chuquicamata, March 13 to 15
- Iquique, March 20
- Arica, March 22

Peru:

- Tacna, March 24
- Tarata, March 25
- Puno, March 26
- Sailing on Lake Titicaca, March 27

- Juliaca, March 28
- Sicuani, March 30
- Cuzco, March 31 to April 3
- Machu Picchu, April 4 to 5
- Cuzco, April 6 to 7
- Abancay, April 11
- Huancarama, April 13
- Huambo, April 14
- Huancarama, April 15
- Andahuaylas, April 16 to 19
- Huanta, April 20
- Ayacucho, April 22
- Huancayo, April 23
- La Merced, April 25 to 26
- San Ramón, April 28
- Tarma, April 30
- Lima, May 1 to 17
- Cerro de Pasco, May 19
- Pucallpa, May 24
- Aboard La Cenepa down the river Ucayali, off the Amazon, May 25 to 31
- Iquitos, June 1 to 5
- Aboard El Cisne, June 6 to 7
- San Pablo, leper colony, June 8 to 20
- By raft, the *Mambo-Tango*, on the Amazon, June 21

Colombia:

- Leticia, June 23 to July 1
- By plane to Bogotá, July 2 to 10
- Cúcuta, July 12 to 13

Venezuela:

- San Cristóbal, July 14
- Between Barquisimeto and Corona, July 16
- Caracas, July 17 to 26

Map of Cuba

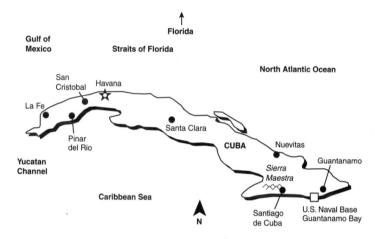

- Las Colorados (rebels' landing site)
- Sierra Maestra Mountains (rebel stronghold)
- Escambray Mountains (central Cuba—Che's second base of command)
- Santa Clara (central Cuban city, site of Che's most famous battle and his tomb)
- Havana (capital, site of the revolutionary shrine Plaza de la Revolución)
- Playa Gíron (site of Bay of Pigs)

Map of Congo

- Kisangani (formerly Stanleyville)
- Kigoma (initial base)

Map of Bolivia

Brazil

Peru

Brazil

BOLIVIA

Area of Che's
Bolivian Campaign

La Paz

Santa Cruz

Andes

Andes

Sucre

Chile

Paraguay

Argentina

- La Paz (Che's first stop in Bolivia)
- Nancahuazu (southeastern Bolivia—first command center)
- Churo Gorge (site of Che's capture—near La Higuera)
- La Higuera (site of Che's execution)
- Vallegrande (Che is brought here after his execution—site of the mass grave where Che was buried until 1997)

Appendix D

Che Guevara's "New Man"

by Ted Henken, M.A.

L ike many other aspects of the new socialist society to be built after the triumph of the Cuban Revolution, according to Che Guevara, the "new man" was already formed, incubated if you will, among the guerrilla fighters (the vanguard) during the clandestine struggle in the Sierra Maestra. The heroic self-sacrifice and moral motivation that was essential to the success of the armed struggle was to be applied to the day-to-day economic tasks of the new society. In the building of socialism in Cuba, the task was to spread or generalize this "new (socialist) man" throughout the "new (socialist) society." The idea was to try to apply the revolutionary passion and effervesce that was built during the revolutionary struggle to the challenges (economic, social, and political) that would inevitably arise in the building of socialism in Cuba on a day-to-day basis. As Guevara said in his March 1965 "Socialism and Man in Cuba" essay, the challenge was "to find the formula to perpetuate in day-to-day life the heroic attitude of the revolutionary struggle" because "in the attitude of our fighters, we could glimpse the man of the future."

Guevara wrote this important and widely influential essay during his three-month trip through Africa between December 1964 and March 1965 as he reflected upon the challenges of constructing an ethical and economically successful social system in Cuba.

The essay was originally a long letter written to the Uruguayan economist Carlos Quijano, the publisher of *Marcha*. It was first published in that journal and then published again in April 1965 in the Cuban magazine *Revolución*. The essay is both a philosophical and practical reflection upon the central problems to be encountered in the construction of socialism in Cuba.

According to Guevara, in the construction of the new economic base of socialism there is a great temptation of resorting to the same methods of individual economic stimulation used under capitalism. Guevara wrote, "We run the risk that we will not be able to see the forest for the trees. Pursuing the chimera of bringing into being socialism with the help of the very tools left to us by capitalism (the profit motive, individual material interest, etc.) we can arrive at a dead-end street. In this way, we will find that the economic base will have developed to the detriment of the development of individual consciousness. Instead, in order to construct communism, together with the material base we must construct the new man."

A key debate in the construction of the "new man" in Cuba has always been the use of moral over material incentives in socialist labor. Which were to be the central labor incentives favored and promoted by the new government? While moral incentives were favored by Guevara and seen as eventually becoming the singular mode of labor motivation, he realized that the road was long, and material incentives would continue to be important, if secondary, because they had been so central in the bourgeois capitalist society of the past. Guevara saw the problem of moral versus material incentives as a central strategic problem in the construction of the new (communist) society that he and Castro had in mind. Guevara argued that "we must gradually remove material incentives from the consciousness of our workers as the process of building socialism advances. Material stimulation will not be a part of the new society that is created, it will be extinguished along the road [to socialism]. We must prepare the conditions so that this type of mobilization that today is effective increasingly loses its importance and is gradually replaced by moral stimulation, a sense of duty, the new revolutionary consciousness."

Guevara felt that individual interest and material stimulation were fundamental motivational aspects under capitalism and as such were anachronistic and, in the long run, counterproductive in the construction of socialism. He argued:

> *Capitalist society employs economic coercion and individual material stimulation as its fundamental tools. The new society will create a distinct man, inserted in a collective that must satisfy his needs fully. This man will not be linked to this [new] society by raw economic coercion, but instead will assume labor as a social duty and necessity ... Key elements in the formation of the individual consciousness of the "new man" will include communist education, voluntary labor, education [in work as a] social duty, and the example of the Party and the directive cadres.*
>
> *We consider that material stimulation is an inheritance, a vestige, a residue of the previous society that reflects the mindset of the workers who saw it as an objective necessity in that era from an individual point of view. As such, material stimulation is a reality that we must take into consideration. Therefore, we can never [totally] oppose material stimulation and deny it, because it would be to deny reality.*

However, in the construction of a socialist society, Guevara saw it as playing a secondary and increasingly insignificant role.

Guevara first hinted at his ideas about moral incentives in a speech at Cuba's National Bank on January 29, 1960, where he said that in the destruction of the old society and the construction of the new, it was important not to neglect the transformation of "man himself." Specifically, he made the point that each individual must become the architect of a "new type of human being" (*nuevo tipo humano*). He understood this process as not simply one of the social and political structure forming the individual, but one of self-education, where the individual strived to transform him- or herself. In other words, for Guevara the formation of the "new man" is a simultaneous process of education (from outside) and self-education (from within), of interaction between the individual and society. He saw it as impossible to create the "new man" without simultaneously creating the "new society" and vice versa. Furthermore, Guevara argued that the "new man" must be formed with the active, willing, and conscientious participation of the individual, not through coercion as in capitalism.

This debate between moral and material incentives was paralleled by a debate between individual vs. social motivations in work. Guevara argued against the idea of work as a means to personal enrichment, professional advancement, and social prestige. Instead he advocated the idea that work was a means to the improvement of society as a whole. He argued that Cuba should prioritize and promote the idea of work as a social duty of the revolutionary. To this he added the policy of voluntary work after hours and on weekends (known in Cuba as "red Sunday"—*domingo rojo*). He wrote, "Voluntary work is not imposed but must develop spontaneously among the workers. It does not come into being through decree but through the initiative of the most advanced sectors of the mass of workers." Both in his different official positions in the new revolutionary government (between 1961–63—National Bank president and head of the industrialization ministry) and as a central theoretical writer on economic policy throughout the early 1960s, Guevara attempted to implement and promote these ideas. Unfortunately for the Cuban economy of the 1960s, in practice the ideals of moral incentives, work as a social duty, noncoercive voluntary labor (the three pillars of the consciousness of the "new man") often resulted in dramatic failures on the national scale.

Surprisingly, these debates are still very relevant in today's Cuba since Castro's government has openly, if reluctantly, employed capitalist methods (material incentives and individualistic motivations) in an attempt to save its socialist experiment. Ironically, capitalist strategies such as dollarization, self-employment, bonuses and incentive pay, foreign investment, farmers' markets and cooperatives, and hard-currency stores have all been implemented during the past decade in Cuba with the goal of preserving the ideals of socialism. It remains to be seen if this precarious and hotly debated balancing act will succeed.

Finally, it is important to recognize that Guevara's idea of the "new man" was never simply a theoretical doctrine or a policy prescription. It was also Guevara's own revolutionary journey writ large and made into a model for others to follow. It was a reflection of Guevara's own coming of age as a revolutionary—a kind of self-portrait of the revolutionary maturing of Guevara himself. In planning for the individual moral transformation of thousands of others, Guevara was really talking about the process of his own revolutionary transformation. Over a period of many years, he had reached the point where he could sacrifice himself for the ideals of an egalitarian socialist society. However, turning his exceptional personal experience into national policy has rarely met with success in economic terms. The glorious future inhabited by a society of selfless "new men" has proven in practice to always lie just beyond the next horizon.

Appendix E

Che Guevara Resources

Even now, in the twenty-first century, Che Guevara continues to be a popular subject of books and film, as well as on the Internet. So much so that the information out there can seem a bit staggering. The following are a few of the resources that proved useful in this project.

Che on the Page

Anderson, Jon Lee. *Che Guevara: A Revolutionary Life*. Grove Press: New York, 1997.

> One of the best, if not the best, English biography on Che; an indispensable book for the Che enthusiast.

Castaneda, Jorge G. *Compañero: The Life and Death of Che Guevara*. Knopf: New York, 1997.

> Another solid and exhaustive biography featuring extensive footnotes that leave no stone unturned.

Tabio, Paco Ignacio. *Guevara, Also Known as Che*. St. Martin's Press: New York, 1999.

> This biography makes effective use of Che's own words by inserting them into the narrative as if Che was telling you his story himself, making the book a pseudo-autobiography.

Guevara, Ernesto "Che." *The Motorcycle Diaries: A Journey Around South America.* Verso: New York, 1995.

Che's firsthand account of his formative journey through South America at age twenty-three: funny, tragic, political, and romantic.

Symmes, Patrick. *Chasing Che: A Motorcycle Journey in Search of the Guevara Legend.* Vintage Books: New York, 2000.

A revisiting of Che's route through South America: a terrific mix of South American history, Che's story, and evocative travel writing.

Guevara, Che. *Che Guevara Speaks.* Pathfinder Press: New York, 2000.

A compilation of Che's thoughts and writings, these concisely edited selections cover a wide range of Che's work from Cuba to Vietnam to his farewell letters. A good place to start for anyone interested in Che's political stance.

Deuthschmann, David, ed. *Che Guevara Reader: Writings by Ernesto Che Guevara on Guerrilla Strategy, Politics and Revolution.* Ocean Press: Melbourne, 1997.

Another great compilation of Che's writings with more content. A terrific place to hear from the man himself about his political beliefs.

Guevara, Che. *Guerrilla Warfare.* Lincoln and London: University of Nebraska Press, 1985.

Che's handbook of revolution: to some a bible, to others an obvious exercise in propaganda. Either way, this is an informative look at Che's guerrilla philosophy.

Loviny, Christopher. *Che: The Photobiography of Che Guevara.* Thunder's Mouth: New York, 1998.

A wonderful resource for any Che enthusiast, it's packed with rare photographs that bring Che to life in a way words simply cannot.

Castro, Fidel. *Che: A Memoir*. Ocean Press: Melbourne, 1994.

Castro's firsthand account of his relationship with Che. Although out-of-print, it's well worth a search.

Che on the Stage and Screen

Evita. Andrew Lloyd Weber and Tim Rice, stage (starring Patti Lupone and Mandy Patinkin: Original Broadway Cast Recording, MCA Records, 1979) and film (directed by Alan Parker, starring Madonna and Antonio Banderas: Hollywood Pictures, 1996).

This is a glamorized musical telling of the rise and fall of Evita Perón. Although Che is a featured player, little, if any, of his part is based on actions taken by the real Guevara. The character serves as the narrator and conscience of the film, representing the voice of the people. In fact, the character of Che is not given a last name; he's more of a device than a person (remember that "Che" is Argentine slang for "buddy"—the Everyman). Still, it's a fast-moving, tuneful, and eye-popping piece of work that can open the door to South American politics with little mental strain.

El Che: Investigating a Legend
Che Guevara: Restless Revolutionary
Ernesto "Che" Guevara: The Bolivian Diary (with English subtitles)

Three readily available VHS documentaries that cover Che's life. Much like the photobiography, these videos are indispensable when wanting to see Che in action.

13 Days. Directed by Ronald Donaldson, starring Kevin Costner: New Line Cinema, 2000.

The Cuban Missile Crisis comes to life in this taut, gripping, and well-acted film.

Company Man (Paramount Classics, 2001)
Bananas (MGM Home Video, 1971)

Slapstick and satirical comedy takes on Cuba and revolution: While *Company Man* is a direct spoof of the Bay of Pigs, Woody Allen's broad *Bananas* is far superior. Allen also has a cameo in *Company Man*.

Che on the Internet

www.cheguevara.com/

This well-designed and flashy site is packed with photos, writings, essays, and links to other Che sites.

www.el-comandante.com/

Another great site (in multiple languages) this is a treasure trove of photos, speeches, and articles.

www.che-lives.com/

This Che site features "Radio Rebelde," the che-lives.com radio station, as well as photos, links, and articles.

www.marxists.org/archive/guevara/

This site is a concise collection of writings with links to other Marxist sites.

krook.net/guevara.php

A great example of another individual greatly inspired by Che featuring links, sound files, photos, personal essays, and additional resources.

groups.yahoo.com/group/che-list

An informative and interesting e-mail discussion group for discussing Che and other revolutionary topics, both current and past.

encarta.msn.com

A solid resource for encyclopedic information.

Index

C

Ted Henken, M.A.

———————————◆————————————————————————◆———————————

Ted Henken, M.A., who is a doctoral candidate in Latin American Studies at Tulane University's Stone Center for Latin American Studies, has traveled to Cuba extensively to conduct research and attend academic seminars. His current research concerns the intersection between Cuba's second economy (*cuentapropistas*) and its emerging tourism economy. Currently Tulane's Cuban Studies Institute's in-country liaison and program coordinator in Cuba, Henken was born and raised in northwest Florida.

———————————◆————————————————————————◆———————————

Eric Luther

As a producer for CBS News in New York City, Eric J. Luther has covered disputed elections, entertainment, and crime and punishment. His work at CBS has enabled him to expand his knowledge and grasp of news and public affairs while honing his writing and reporting skills. Coupled with his undergraduate work (at SMU, in Dallas, Texas) in philosophy and political science, Eric's work experience enables him to turn a critical yet objective eye on Che Guevara.